GO MATH

Grade 6

Assessment Resources

ISBN   978-0-544-06691-5

6 7 8 9 10   0982   22 21 20 19 18 17 16 15 14

4500486618   B C D E F G

Contents

Introduction

Individual Student Profiles

Performance Tasks

Answer Sheets

Placement Test 1

Beginning-of-Year Diagnostic Test 5

Quizzes

Unit Tests and Performance Tasks

Benchmark Tests

Assessment Options

	Assessment Resources	Student Edition and Teacher's Edition	Online
			Personal Math Trainer Online Assessment and Intervention. Online homework assignment available. © my.hrw.com
Diagnostic/ Entry Level	• Placement Test • Beginning-of-Year Diagnostic Test	• *Are You Ready?*	• Diagnostic Test • *Are You Ready?* Intervention and Enrichment
Formative/ Progress Monitoring	• Module Quizzes (Levels B, D)	• Your Turn • Math Talk • Reflect • Questioning Strategies • Essential Questions • Lesson Quizzes • *Ready to Go On?* Quizzes • Module Assessment Readiness	• *Ready to Go On?* Intervention and Enrichment • Online Homework • Module Assessment Readiness • Online Quizzes and Tests
Summative	• Unit Tests (Levels A, B, C, D) • Unit Performance Tasks • Quarterly Benchmark Tests • Mid-Year Test • End-of-Year Test	• Unit Assessment Readiness • Unit Performance Tasks	• Unit Assessment Readiness • Online Quizzes and Tests

Using the Assessment Resources

The *Assessment Resources* provides the following tests to assess mastery.

Diagnostic/ Entry Level	**Placement Test** • Use to assess prerequisite skills mastery before beginning the school year. • For students who require intervention, use the online *Are You Ready?* Intervention.	**Beginning-of-Year Diagnostic Test** • Use to assess knowledge of the key objectives that will be taught in the current school year. • Use as a baseline for a student's mastery of math concepts and skills, and to evaluate growth during the school year.
Formative/ Progress Monitoring	**Module Quizzes** • Use to assess mastery of the concepts and skills taught in the Modules. • Use Level D for students who are considerably below level and require modified materials. For all other students use Level B.	
Summative	**Unit Tests** • Use to assess mastery of the concepts and skills taught in the Units. • Level A: for students who are slightly below level • Level B: for students who are on level • Level C: for advanced students • Level D: for students who are considerably below level and require modified materials	**Benchmark Tests** • Use for test prep. • There are four Benchmark Tests: two quarterly tests, the Mid-Year Test, and the End-of-Year Test.
	Performance Tasks • Use to provide alternate assessment at the end of each Unit. • These tasks are accessible to all students and suitable to be completed in a classroom. • Before starting the Performance Task, provide students with the *Scoring Rubric for Students* to establish the expectations and scoring rubrics for the task. Use the *Teacher's Guide Scoring Rubric* to assess students' work and their competency with applying the Mathematical Practices.	

Placement Test

Individual Student Profile

The Proficient? column provides a snapshot of a student's mastery of previous grade-level standards.

Each Student Edition Module begins with *Are You Ready?*, a tool to assess whether students have the prerequisite skills needed to be successful. *Are You Ready?* Intervention is also available online.

Name _____ Date _____ Class _____

COMMON CORE	Placement Test Items	Proficient? Yes/No	COMMON CORE	Placement Test Items	Proficient? Yes/No
5.G.1	23		5.NBT.5	5, 16	
5.G.2	28, 34		5.NBT.6	6, 8	
5.G.3	21		5.NBT.7	10, 11	
5.G.4	21		5.NF.1	9	
5.MD.1	18, 25		5.NF.2	35	
5.MD.2	31, 33		5.NF.3	36	
5.MD.3a	22		5.NF.4a	13	
5.MD.3b	22		5.NF.4b	19	
5.MD.4	22, 24		5.NF.5a	27	
5.MD.5a	24		5.NF.5b	30	
5.MD.5b	26		5.NF.6	32	
5.MD.5c	24		5.NF.7	36	
5.NBT.1	1, 7		5.NF.7b	20	
5.NBT.2	14		5.NF.7c	12	
5.NBT.3a	1		5.OA.1	17	
5.NBT.3b	2		5.OA.2	15	
5.NBT.4	3, 4		5.OA.3	28, 29	

Beginning-of-Year Diagnostic Test

Individual Student Profile

The Proficient? column provides a snapshot of a student's knowledge of key objectives that will be taught in this grade. The Diagnostic Test can be used as a baseline for a student's mastery of objectives and to evaluate growth.

Name _____ Date _____ Class _____

COMMON CORE	Student Edition Modules	Diagnostic Test Items	Proficient? Yes/No
6.EE.1	9	30, 31, 32, 76, 77	
6.EE.2	15	85	
6.EE.2a	10	37	
6.EE.2a	10	37	
6.EE.2c	10	38, 78	
6.EE.3	10	33, 39	
6.EE.4	10	33, 39	
6.EE.5	11	34, 35, 36, 40, 41, 42	
6.EE.6	11	34, 35, 36, 40, 41, 42, 79	
6.EE.7	11, 13	34, 35, 36, 40, 41, 42, 54, 79, 84, 85	
6.EE.9	12	43, 44, 46, 47, 72, 73	
6.G.1	13	48, 50, 51, 52, 53, 54, 55, 69, 80, 81, 82, 83, 84	
6.G.2	15	58	
6.G.3	14	64	
6.G.4	15	57	
6.NS.1	4	13, 14, 15, 66	
6.NS.2	5	16	
6.NS.3	5	17, 18, 19, 67, 68	
6.NS.4	2, 4, 14	5, 6, 12, 65	
6.NS.5	1	1, 3	
6.NS.6	3	8	
6.NS.6a	1, 3	1, 3, 9, 10	
6.NS.6b	14	56	
6.NS.6c	1, 3, 12	1, 3, 9, 10, 45	

Beginning-of-Year Diagnostic Test

Individual Student Profile (continued)

Name _____ Date _____ Class _____

COMMON CORE	Student Edition Modules	Diagnostic Test Items	Proficient? Yes/No
6.NS.7a	1, 3	2, 7, 11	
6.NS.7b	1, 3	2, 7, 11	
6.NS.7c	1, 3	4, 9, 10	
6.NS.7d	1	4	
6.NS.8	12, 14	45, 56	
6.RP.1	6	21	
6.RP.2	6	22, 71	
6.RP.3	6, 7	22, 23, 26, 28, 71, 74, 75	
6.RP.3a	6, 7	21, 23, 27, 74	
6.RP.3b	6, 7	22, 27, 28, 71, 75	
6.RP.3c	8	20, 29, 70	
6.RP.3d	7	24, 25	
6.SP.2	16	59, 60	
6.SP.3	16	59, 60	
6.SP.5a	16	62	
6.SP.5b	16	62	
6.SP.5c	16	59, 60, 61, 63	
6.SP.5d	16	59, 60	

Mathematical Practices

Performance Tasks

Teacher's Guide

Performance Tasks provide an alternate way for teachers to assess students' mastery of concepts. This method of assessment requires the student to create answers by using critical thinking skills.

Through observation or analysis of students' responses, teachers can determine what the students know, do not know, and whether the students have any misconceptions.

Assigning Performance Tasks

Discuss with students what is expected before they start the Performance Task. Provide the *Scoring Rubric for Students* to help them understand the scoring criteria.

- Encourage discussion of new ideas and viability of other students' reasoning and work.

- Encourage multiple approaches, and emphasize that not just one answer is correct.

- Encourage students to initiate a plan.

- Encourage students to manage, analyze, and synthesize information.

- Encourage students to use appropriate tools and math models to solve the problems, and remind students to attend to precision.

Use the *Teacher's Guide Scoring Rubric* to help assess the complex learning outcomes.

Performance Tasks

Scoring Rubric for Students

What you are expected to do:

- ☐ Make a plan. If the plan does not work, change it until it does work.
- ☐ Use accurate reasoning to represent the problem.
- ☐ Fully explain the steps that you used to find the solution.
- ☐ Use different methods and models to help you find the solution.
- ☐ Use appropriate tools such as rulers, geometry tools, and calculators.
- ☐ Use clear language to explain your answers. Check that your answers are accurate.
- ☐ Look for patterns and explain your reasoning using different representations such as symbols, words, or graphs.
- ☐ Find efficient ways to solve the problems, and explain general rules clearly.

Your teacher will need to see all your work. Be sure to include the following:

- ☐ Drawings, tables, and graphs to support your answers.
- ☐ Clearly written sentences to explain your reasoning.
- ☐ All the steps in your solution.
- ☐ The answer; check that it is reasonable and answers the question.

Performance Tasks
Teacher's Guide Scoring Rubric

Mathematical Practices	Level 4	Level 3	Level 2	Level 1
Make sense of problems and persevere in solving them.	Student makes a plan and follows it, or adjusts it to obtain a solution.	Student makes a viable plan but implementation has minor flaws.	Student makes a plan, but it has major flaws that the student is unable to address.	Student shows no evidence of making a plan.
Reason abstractly and quantitatively.	Student uses accurate reasoning to represent the problem.	Student reasoning shows a minor flaw.	Student reasoning is missing a critical step.	Student shows little evidence of mathematical reasoning.
Construct viable arguments and critique the reasoning of others.	Student fully explains the steps that lead to the conclusion.	Student skips a step in the explanation.	Student has missing or out-of-sequence steps in the explanation.	Student makes no attempt to explain the steps used.
Model mathematics [using graphs, diagrams, tables, formulas].	Student uses appropriate models and implements them correctly.	Student chooses an appropriate model, but makes minor error(s) in implementation.	Student chooses a model but is unable to relate it effectively to the problem.	Student is unable to model the relationship.
Use appropriate tools [e.g., ruler, paper/pencil, technology] strategically.	Student chooses appropriate tools and uses them effectively.	Student chooses an appropriate tool, but makes minor error(s) in its use.	Student chooses an appropriate tool, but cannot apply it properly to the problem.	Student chooses an inappropriate tool or none at all.
Attend to precision.	Student uses clear language and accurate calculations.	Student uses some vocabulary incorrectly and/or makes minor error(s) in calculations.	Student use of language is confusing and/or makes errors in calculations.	Student does not provide an explanation; calculations are inaccurate.
Look for and make use of structure.	Student finds and uses patterns and processes, and expresses them accurately.	Student finds and uses patterns and processes, but makes minor error(s) in expressing them.	Student finds patterns and processes, but cannot apply them successfully.	Student is unable to find patterns and processes that are appropriate.
Look for and express regularity in repeated reasoning.	Student finds shortcuts and/or generalizations and expresses them clearly.	Student finds shortcuts and/or generalizations, but makes minor errors.	Student finds a shortcut or generalization, but does not represent it effectively.	Student is unable to find shortcuts and/or generalizations.

Multiple-Choice Answer Sheet

Test Title _____

1. Ⓐ Ⓑ Ⓒ Ⓓ	26. Ⓐ Ⓑ Ⓒ Ⓓ
2. Ⓐ Ⓑ Ⓒ Ⓓ	27. Ⓐ Ⓑ Ⓒ Ⓓ
3. Ⓐ Ⓑ Ⓒ Ⓓ	28. Ⓐ Ⓑ Ⓒ Ⓓ
4. Ⓐ Ⓑ Ⓒ Ⓓ	29. Ⓐ Ⓑ Ⓒ Ⓓ
5. Ⓐ Ⓑ Ⓒ Ⓓ	30. Ⓐ Ⓑ Ⓒ Ⓓ
6. Ⓐ Ⓑ Ⓒ Ⓓ	31. Ⓐ Ⓑ Ⓒ Ⓓ
7. Ⓐ Ⓑ Ⓒ Ⓓ	32. Ⓐ Ⓑ Ⓒ Ⓓ
8. Ⓐ Ⓑ Ⓒ Ⓓ	33. Ⓐ Ⓑ Ⓒ Ⓓ
9. Ⓐ Ⓑ Ⓒ Ⓓ	34. Ⓐ Ⓑ Ⓒ Ⓓ
10. Ⓐ Ⓑ Ⓒ Ⓓ	35. Ⓐ Ⓑ Ⓒ Ⓓ
11. Ⓐ Ⓑ Ⓒ Ⓓ	36. Ⓐ Ⓑ Ⓒ Ⓓ
12. Ⓐ Ⓑ Ⓒ Ⓓ	37. Ⓐ Ⓑ Ⓒ Ⓓ
13. Ⓐ Ⓑ Ⓒ Ⓓ	38. Ⓐ Ⓑ Ⓒ Ⓓ
14. Ⓐ Ⓑ Ⓒ Ⓓ	39. Ⓐ Ⓑ Ⓒ Ⓓ
15. Ⓐ Ⓑ Ⓒ Ⓓ	40. Ⓐ Ⓑ Ⓒ Ⓓ
16. Ⓐ Ⓑ Ⓒ Ⓓ	41. Ⓐ Ⓑ Ⓒ Ⓓ
17. Ⓐ Ⓑ Ⓒ Ⓓ	42. Ⓐ Ⓑ Ⓒ Ⓓ
18. Ⓐ Ⓑ Ⓒ Ⓓ	43. Ⓐ Ⓑ Ⓒ Ⓓ
19. Ⓐ Ⓑ Ⓒ Ⓓ	44. Ⓐ Ⓑ Ⓒ Ⓓ
20. Ⓐ Ⓑ Ⓒ Ⓓ	45. Ⓐ Ⓑ Ⓒ Ⓓ
21. Ⓐ Ⓑ Ⓒ Ⓓ	46. Ⓐ Ⓑ Ⓒ Ⓓ
22. Ⓐ Ⓑ Ⓒ Ⓓ	47. Ⓐ Ⓑ Ⓒ Ⓓ
23. Ⓐ Ⓑ Ⓒ Ⓓ	48. Ⓐ Ⓑ Ⓒ Ⓓ
24. Ⓐ Ⓑ Ⓒ Ⓓ	49. Ⓐ Ⓑ Ⓒ Ⓓ
25. Ⓐ Ⓑ Ⓒ Ⓓ	50. Ⓐ Ⓑ Ⓒ Ⓓ

Multiple-Choice Answer Sheet

Test Title _____

51. (A) (B) (C) (D)
52. (A) (B) (C) (D)
53. (A) (B) (C) (D)
54. (A) (B) (C) (D)
55. (A) (B) (C) (D)

56. (A) (B) (C) (D)
57. (A) (B) (C) (D)
58. (A) (B) (C) (D)
59. (A) (B) (C) (D)
60. (A) (B) (C) (D)

61. (A) (B) (C) (D)
62. (A) (B) (C) (D)
63. (A) (B) (C) (D)
64. (A) (B) (C) (D)
65. (A) (B) (C) (D)

66. (A) (B) (C) (D)
67. (A) (B) (C) (D)
68. (A) (B) (C) (D)
69. (A) (B) (C) (D)
70. (A) (B) (C) (D)

71. (A) (B) (C) (D)
72. (A) (B) (C) (D)
73. (A) (B) (C) (D)
74. (A) (B) (C) (D)
75. (A) (B) (C) (D)

76. (A) (B) (C) (D)
77. (A) (B) (C) (D)
78. (A) (B) (C) (D)
79. (A) (B) (C) (D)
80. (A) (B) (C) (D)

81. (A) (B) (C) (D)
82. (A) (B) (C) (D)
83. (A) (B) (C) (D)
84. (A) (B) (C) (D)
85. (A) (B) (C) (D)

86. (A) (B) (C) (D)
87. (A) (B) (C) (D)
88. (A) (B) (C) (D)
89. (A) (B) (C) (D)
90. (A) (B) (C) (D)

91. (A) (B) (C) (D)
92. (A) (B) (C) (D)
93. (A) (B) (C) (D)
94. (A) (B) (C) (D)
95. (A) (B) (C) (D)

96. (A) (B) (C) (D)
97. (A) (B) (C) (D)
98. (A) (B) (C) (D)
99. (A) (B) (C) (D)
100. (A) (B) (C) (D)

Name _____ Date _____ Class_____

Placement Test

1. What is the value of 7 in 1.207?
   A 7×0.1 C 7×0.001
   B 7×0.01 D 7×0.0001

2. Which symbol makes the statement true?

   $$0.025 \bigcirc 0.052$$

   A =   C >
   B <   D ≈

3. Which of the following shows 2.1851 rounded to the nearest tenth?
   A 2.1   C 2.19
   B 2.185   D 2.2

4. William bought 6 CDs for $8.97 each. About how much did he spend?
   A $9   C $54
   B $48   D $60

5. There were 630 concert tickets sold. Each ticket cost $21. How much money was raised from selling the tickets?
   A $1,890   C $12,600
   B $12,230   D $13,230

6. What is the value of the expression below?

   $$2,686 \div 34$$

   A 77   C 88
   B 79   D 97

7. Candace knows that $4 \times 36 = 144$. Given that, what is the value of 4×0.36?
   A 0.0144   C 1.44
   B 0.144   D 14.4

8. What is the value of the expression below?

   $$12.96 \div 27$$

   A 0.48   C 48
   B 4.8   D 480

9. What is the value of the expression below?

   $$\frac{2}{3} + \frac{1}{6}$$

   A $\frac{1}{2}$ C $\frac{3}{12}$
   B $\frac{3}{9}$ D $\frac{5}{6}$

10. The grid below shows the product of 0.3 and 0.4. What is that product?

    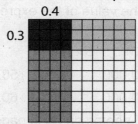

    A 0.012   C 1.2
    B 0.12   D 12

11. The grid below shows the quotient of $0.42 \div 0.6$. What is that quotient?

    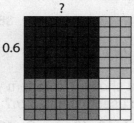

    A 0.06   C 0.6
    B 0.07   D 0.7

12. Pat needs boards that are $\frac{1}{2}$ foot long. Which equation shows how many $\frac{1}{2}$-foot pieces he can get from a 4-foot long board?

    A $4 + \frac{1}{2} = 4\frac{1}{2}$ C $4 \div \frac{1}{2} = 8$
    B $4 \times \frac{1}{2} = 2$ D $\frac{1}{2} \div 4 = \frac{1}{8}$

Name _____ Date _____ Class_____

Placement Test

13. Jake drew the diagram below. Which number sentence does the picture show?

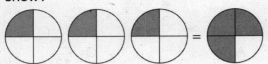

A $\frac{1}{4}\times 3=\frac{3}{4}$ C $\frac{1}{3}\times 4=\frac{3}{4}$

B $\frac{1}{4}\div 3=\frac{3}{4}$ D $3\div\frac{1}{4}=\frac{3}{4}$

14. What is the value of the expression below?

$$5\times 10^6$$

A 5,000,000   C 50,000,000

B 6,000,000   D 60,000,000

15. Joy put 6 photos on each page of her album. When she was done, she had 2 pictures left over. She put 38 pictures in the album. Which equation can be used to find how many pages Joy filled?

A $38\div x=6+2$ C $38=6x+2$

B $38=2x+6$ D $38=\frac{x}{6}+2$

16. Which list shows the pattern you would get if you used the rule 12*n*?

A 12, 14, 16, 18   C 12, 13, 14, 15

B 12, 24, 36, 48   D 12, 22, 42, 52

17. Find the value of the expression below.

$$[(10+26)\div 6]\div 3$$

A 2   C 18

B 6   D 36

18. Al has a roll of 4 feet of ribbon. How many 8-inch pieces can he cut from the roll?

A 2 pieces   C 6 pieces

B 5 pieces   D 8 pieces

19. Ayisha is painting a picture on the canvas shown below.

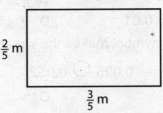

What is the area of the canvas?

A $\frac{2}{5}$ m²   C $\frac{6}{5}$ m²

B $\frac{3}{5}$ m²   D $\frac{6}{25}$ m²

20. Vinh solved the equation below.

$$7\div\frac{1}{6}=42$$

Which of the following can Vinh use to check his work?

A $42\times\frac{1}{3}=14$ C $42\times\frac{6}{7}=6$

B $42\times\frac{1}{6}=7$ D $42\times\frac{6}{7}=36$

21. Which list of terms describes the figure below in as many ways as possible?

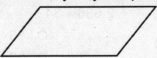

A square, parallelogram

B rectangle, quadrilateral

C trapezoid, parallelogram, quadrilateral

D parallelogram, quadrilateral

22. Jalyn built a large cube out of smaller cubes. Each small cube is 1 cubic unit. What is the volume of the large cube?

A 9 cubic units   C 18 cubic units

B 12 cubic units   D 27 cubic units

Placement Test

23. Lu is graphing the ordered pair (3, 5). Starting at the origin, what does she need to do?

    A Move 3 units up and 5 units to the right, and draw a dot at that point.

    B Move 3 units up and 3 units to the right, and draw a dot at that point.

    C Move 3 units to the right and 5 units up, and draw a dot at that point.

    D Move 5 units to the right and 3 units up, and draw a dot at that point.

24. Emily built a rectangular prism out of cubes. The first layer has 5 rows of 4 cubes each. There are 3 layers. What is the volume of the prism?

    A 12 cubic units   C 20 cubic units

    B 15 cubic units   D 60 cubic units

25. Rosemary is wrapping gifts. Each gift is decorated with a bow that is made of 60 centimeters of ribbon. Rosemary has 3 meters of ribbon. How many gifts can she put bows on?

    A 5 gifts   C 50 gifts

    B 6 gifts   D 60 gifts

26. Which of these is **not** a formula that can be used to find the volume of a cube?

    A $\ell \times w \times h$

    B $2(\ell + w)$

    C $s \times s \times s$

    D Bh

27. Without calculating the answer, is $\frac{1}{3} \times \frac{7}{15}$ greater than or less than $\frac{1}{3}$?

    A the same

    B less than

    C greater than

    D impossible to tell

28. The table below shows the number of books read by Beth. Which graph shows this relationship?

Number of Weeks	1	2	3
Number of Books	2	4	6

A
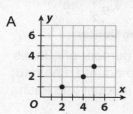
C
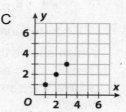
B
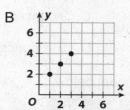
D
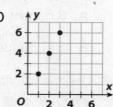

29. Use the two patterns below.

    Add 4: 0, 4, 8, …
    Add 2: 0, 2, 4, …

    What are the first four ordered pairs formed from corresponding terms of the two patterns?

    A (0, 1), (2, 2), (4, 3), (6, 4)

    B (1, 4), (2, 8), (3, 12), (4, 16)

    C (0, 2), (4, 4), (8, 6), (10, 8)

    D (0, 0), (4, 2), (8, 4), (12, 6)

30. Without calculating the answer, will $6\frac{1}{4} \times \frac{3}{4}$ be greater than or less than $6\frac{1}{4}$?

    A the same

    B less than

    C greater than

    D impossible to tell

Placement Test

31. The line plot below shows the number of ounces of juice Daniel poured into glasses.

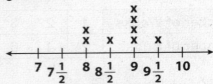

Juice Served in Ounces

Which shows the number of ounces Daniel would have poured if he had poured the same amount into each glass?

A 8 ounces

C 9 ounces

B $8\frac{3}{4}$ ounces

D $9\frac{1}{2}$ ounces

32. Use the fraction model below.

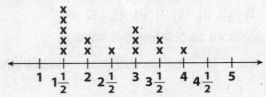

Pia sewed 7 skirts. Each skirt used $\frac{2}{5}$ yard of fabric. How much fabric did Pia use altogether?

A $1\frac{1}{5}$ yards

C $2\frac{4}{5}$ yards

B $2\frac{1}{5}$ yards

D $7\frac{1}{5}$ yards

33. The line plot below shows the hours of soccer practice that Bianca had.

Hours of Soccer Practice

How many hours of soccer practice did Bianca have altogether?

A 16.5 hours

C 34 hours

B 28 hours

D 49.5 hours

34. The table below shows data for 6 softball players. It shows the number of hours each player practiced last week. It also shows the number of hits each player got in yesterday's game. Which graph shows this relationship?

Practice Hours	1	2	3	1	2	3
Number of Hits	2	4	5	1	6	4

A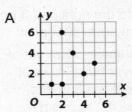

C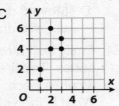

B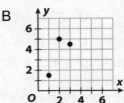

D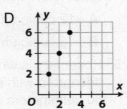

35. Phil ate $\frac{2}{5}$ of a pizza. Caroline ate $\frac{1}{4}$ of a pizza. How much did they eat in all?

A $\frac{1}{3}$ pizza

C $\frac{13}{20}$ pizza

B $\frac{2}{9}$ pizza

D $1\frac{1}{3}$ pizza

36. Look at the pattern below. How should the third shape be labeled?

1          $1 \div 2$, or $\frac{1}{2}$?

A $\frac{1}{2} \div \frac{1}{2}$, or $\frac{1}{4}$

C $\frac{1}{2} \div \frac{1}{2}$, or 4

B $\frac{1}{2} \div 2$, or $\frac{1}{4}$

D $\frac{1}{2} \div 2$, or 4

Beginning-of-Year Diagnostic Test

1. Which lettered point is graphed at the opposite of 2 on the number line below?

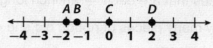

   A *A*

   B *B*

   C *C*

   D *D*

2. Candice recorded outdoor temperatures as –5°C, 2°C and 1°C. Which of the following correctly compares the three temperatures?

   A $-5 < 1 < 2$

   B $1 < 2 < -5$

   C $2 < 1 < -5$

   D $-5 < 2 < 1$

3. Which pair of numbers shows an integer and its opposite?

   A $7, -7$

   B $7, \frac{1}{7}$

   C $-7, -\frac{1}{7}$

   D $-\frac{1}{7}, \frac{1}{7}$

4. What is the absolute value of –5?

   A $-\frac{1}{5}$ C 0

   B $\frac{1}{5}$ D 5

5. What is the greatest common factor of 4 and 8?

   A 1

   B 2

   C 4

   D 8

6. What is the least common multiple of 10 and 20?

   A 1   C 10

   B 5   D 20

7. Jason plotted points on a number line at the four values below.

   $$0.75, \frac{2}{3}, 0.25, \text{ and } \frac{7}{8}$$

   Which of these values is farthest from zero?

   A 0.75

   B $\frac{2}{3}$

   C 0.25

   D $\frac{7}{8}$

8. To which set or sets below does the number $\frac{1}{2}$ belong?

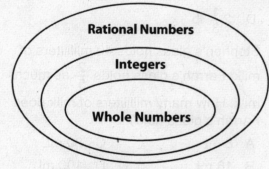

   A whole numbers only

   B rational numbers only

   C integers and rational numbers only

   D whole numbers, integers, and rational numbers

9. Which pair of points graphed below have values that are opposites?

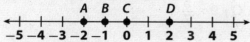

   A *A* and *B*

   B *B* and *D*

   C *C* and *E*

   D *A* and *D*

10. Which number line shows the values of |1|, |−3| and |5|?

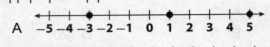

A

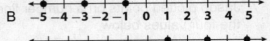

B

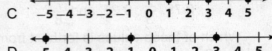

C

D

11. Susie divided a 3-pound bag of apples into 2 equal piles. How many pounds of apples are in each pile?

A $\frac{1}{2}$ lb

B $\frac{2}{3}$ lb

C $1\frac{1}{2}$ lb

D $2\frac{1}{3}$ lb

12. Stephen's glass holds 40 milliliters of milk. Farrah's glass holds $\frac{2}{5}$ as much milk. How many milliliters of milk does Farrah's glass hold?

A 8 mL   C 80 mL

B 16 mL   D 100 mL

13. Which of the following is equal to $7 \div \frac{9}{5}$?

A $9 \times \frac{7}{5}$

B $7 \times \frac{9}{5}$

C $9 \times \frac{5}{7}$

D $7 \times \frac{5}{9}$

14. Leah cut a 7-inch piece of ribbon into pieces that are each $\frac{1}{2}$ an inch long. How many pieces of ribbon did she cut?

A 1 piece

B 7 pieces

C 14 pieces

D 21 pieces

15. Jonas is making a trail mix recipe that calls for 3 cups of nuts and 1 cup of raisins. Jonas mixes the nuts and raisins together. He will then divide the mixture into plastic bags containing $\frac{1}{2}$ cup of trail mix in each bag. How many plastic bags does Jonas need?

A 1 plastic bag

B 2 plastic bags

C 8 plastic bags

D 10 plastic bags

16. Serena has 6,000 seeds to plant in her vegetable garden. She will plant 100 seeds per row. How many rows of vegetables will she have?

A 6 rows

B 60 rows

C 600 rows

D 6,000 rows

17. Jessica hit a golf ball 150.75 yards. Kayla hit a golf ball 130.25 yards. How much farther did Jessica hit a golf ball?

A 10.25 yards

B 20.5 yards

C 30.5 yards

D 281 yards

Beginning-of-Year Diagnostic Test

18. Gabriel drives 80 kilometers in one hour. How many kilometers does he drive in 1.5 hours?

    A   24.75 km

    B   30 km

    C   120 km

    D   300 km

19. A pitcher can hold 5.2 liters of water. How many 0.4-liter glasses of water can be poured from the pitcher?

    A   2.08 glasses

    B   5.8 glasses

    C   13 glasses

    D   52 glasses

20. Alissa's budget is shown in the circle graph below. Her total monthly budget is $1,000. How much does Alissa spend on rent?

    A $30   C $250

    B $150   D $300

21. In Evan's math class, there are 7 boys and 10 girls. Which of the following is the ratio of boys to girls in Evan's math class?

    A $\frac{10}{7}$ C $\frac{10}{17}$

    B $\frac{7}{10}$ D $\frac{7}{17}$

22. Sara bought a 20-ounce jar of strawberry jam for $4. What is the unit price?

    A $0.20/oz   C $2.00/oz

    B $0.40/oz   D $5.00/oz

23. Zach is making a recipe that requires 1 cup of vinegar and 2 cups of water. Which of the following combinations shows the same ratio of vinegar to water?

    A   2 cups of vinegar to 1 cup of water

    B   2 cups of vinegar to 4 cups of water

    C   4 cups of vinegar to 3 cup of water

    D   4 cups of vinegar to 5 cups of water

24. Liam bought 1 gallon of juice at the grocery. How many quarts of juice did he buy?

    A   1 qt   C   3 qt

    B   2 qt   D   4 qt

25. Delia measured a doorway to be 1 meter wide. Which of these is a nearly equivalent measurement?

    A   15 miles

    B   10.5 yards

    C   3.3 feet

    D   98.7 inches

26. Nora bikes 30 miles per hour. Jiro bikes 45 miles per hour. If Nora and Jiro each bike for 2 hours, how many more miles does Jiro bike?

    A   15 mi   C   75 mi

    B   30 mi   D   150 mi

27. The table below shows the number of books on shelves at a library. Which of the following represents the number of books?

Books	21	42	105	147
Shelves	1	2	5	7

    A   shelves × 3

    B   shelves × 21

    C   shelves + 15

    D   shelves + 20

Beginning-of-Year Diagnostic Test

28. On a certain map, 2 inches represents 20 miles. Longwood and Milltown are 4 inches apart on the map. What is the actual distance between Longwood and Milltown?

 A 20 mi   C 80 mi

 B 40 mi   D 100 mi

29. What percent of the rectangle below is shaded?

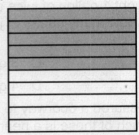

 A 20%   C 40%

 B 30%   D 50%

30. What is the value of the power below?

$$4^2$$

 A 1   C 8

 B 4   D 16

31. What are all the factors of 9?

 A 1, 2, 3

 B 2, 3, 6, 9

 C 1, 3, 9

 D 1, 2, 3, 6, 9

32. Use the order of operations to simplify the expression below.

$$10 + (8 - 2)^2 \div 2$$

 A 8   C 23

 B 16   D 28

33. Which of the following expressions is equivalent to the expression below?

$$2(7x + 3)$$

 A $9x + 3$

 B $14x + 6$

 C $9x - 6$

 D $14x - 3$

34. Which is a solution of the equation below?

$$x - 9 = 4$$

 A $x = -5$

 B $x = -13$

 C $x = 5$

 D $x = 13$

35. A 45° angle is complementary to angle x. Which of the following equations represents this situation?

 A $45 + x = 90$

 B $45 = x - 90$

 C $45 + x = 180$

 D $45 = x + 180$

36. Which inequality is shown on the number line below?

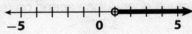

 A $p < 1$

 B $p \le 1$

 C $p > 1$

 D $p \ge 1$

37. Write an algebraic expression for the phrase below.

   2 less than twice a number n

 A $2 - n - n$

 B $n - 2$

 C $6 - 2n$

 D $2n - 2$

38. Evaluate the expression below for $x = 4$.

$$6(x + 8)$$

 A 6

 B 8

 C 60

 D 72

Beginning-of-Year Diagnostic Test

39. Combine like terms to simplify the expression below.

$$14x - (2x + y)$$

   A $12x$

   B $12x - y$

   C $14x - y$

   D $12x + 2$

40. The school band has d drummers and 5 violinists. There are 2 more violinists than drummers. Which of the following equations represents the situation?

   A $d = 5 + 2$

   B $d = 5 - 2$

   C $d = 2 - 5$

   D $d = 2 \times 5$

41. A student bought a book for $7 and a pen. The total cost was $9. Which of the following equations can be used to find the cost of the pen?

   A $p = 7b$

   B $p = 9b$

   C $9 + p = 7$

   D $7 + p = 9$

42. Solve the equation below.

$$\frac{m}{2} = 5$$

   A $m = \dfrac{1}{5}$

   B $m = 5$

   C $m = \dfrac{1}{10}$

   D $m = 10$

Use the table for 43 and 44.

Auto Repair Charges

Hours, x	1	2	5
Charge, y ($)	90	180	450

43. Which equation expresses y in terms of x?

   A $y = 90x$

   B $y = 180x$

   C $x = 90y$

   D $x = 2y$

44. What is the charge for a repair that takes 3 hours?

   A $360   C $150

   B $270   D $135

Use the graph for 45–47.

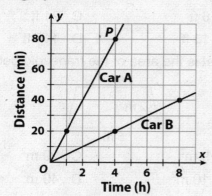

45. What are the coordinates of point P?

   A $(2, 8)$ C $(6, 4)$

   B $(4, 80)$ D $(80, 4)$

46. What is the dependent variable?

   A Car A

   B Car B

   C time

   D distance

Beginning-of-Year Diagnostic Test

47. Which equation represents Car B?

    A $y = 6x$

    B $y = 5x$

    C $y = 60x$

    D $y = 50x$

48. A parallelogram has a base of 10 centimeters and a height of 4 centimeters. What is the area of the parallelogram?

    A 4 cm^2

    B 10 cm^2

    C 40 cm^2

    D 100 cm^2

49. A rectangular prism has a volume of 210 cubic feet. The prism is 5 feet long and 7 feet wide. What is the height of the prism?

    A 6 ft   C 21 ft

    B 13 ft   D 111 ft

50. What is the area of the trapezoid below?

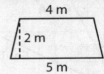

    A 9 m^2 C 20 m^2

    B 10 m^2 D 40 m^2

51. A right triangle has a height of 20 centimeters and a base of 10 centimeters. What is the area of the triangle?

    A 100 cm^2

    B 200 cm^2

    C 300 cm^2

    D 400 cm^2

52. What is the area of the rhombus shown below?

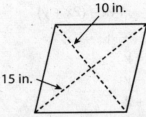

    A 25 in^2 C 150 in^2

    B 75 in^2 D 225 in^2

53. A triangle has an area of 240 square inches. The height of the triangle is 15 inches. What is the length of the base of the triangle?

    A 12 in.   C 32 in.

    B 15 in.   D 45 in.

54. A lawn in the shape of a trapezoid has an area of 1,800 square meters. The length of one base is 50 meters, and the length of the other base is 40 meters. What is the width of the lawn?

    A 25 m   C 35 m

    B 30 m   D 40 m

55. What is the area of the polygon shown below?

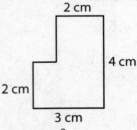

    A 2 cm^2 C 10 cm^2

    B 8 cm^2 D 12 cm^2

Beginning-of-Year Diagnostic Test

56. What is the distance between points *A* and *B* on the grid?

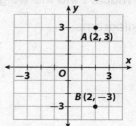

A 3 units

B 4 units

C 6 units

D 7 units

57. Charlene is wrapping the box below. How much wrapping paper will she need?

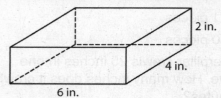

A 24 in.²

B 44 in.²

C 48 in.²

D 88 in.²

58. A swimming pool in the shape of a rectangular prism is 10 feet long, 20 feet wide, and 5 feet deep. How much water could the swimming pool hold?

A 500 ft³

B 1,000 ft³

C 1,500 ft³

D 2,500 ft³

59. What is the median of the data represented in the box plot below?

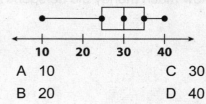

A 10

B 20

C 30

D 40

60. Which data value has the greatest frequency in the dot plot below?

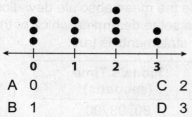

A 0

B 1

C 2

D 3

61. Sandra worked 6 hours on Wednesday, 5 hours on Thursday, and 4 hours on Friday. What is the mean number of hours she worked over the three-day period?

A 2 h

B 3 h

C 4 h

D 5 h

62. The histogram below shows the number of hours per month students in Mr. Carter's class watch television. How many students watch television between 1 and 10 hours per month?

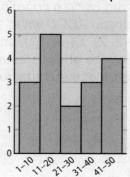

A 3 students

B 4 students

C 5 students

D 6 students

Beginning-of-Year Diagnostic Test

63. For 3 days in a row, Fiona and Gary timed how long they took to brush their teeth. Use the mean absolute deviation of each data set to determine which of the following statements is true.

Fiona's Time (seconds)
90, 93, 90

Gary's Time (seconds)
70, 67, 115

A Fiona's teeth-brushing time is more variable than Gary's.

B Gary's teeth-brushing time is more variable than Fiona's.

C Fiona and Gary are equally variable in their teeth-brushing time.

D Gary spends more time brushing his teeth than Fiona, on average.

64. Toni is designing a rug using a coordinate plane. She uses polygon *ABCD* with vertices $A(2, 2)$, $B(-2, 2)$, $C(-2, -2)$, and $D(2, -2)$. Each unit on the grid represents 1 foot. What is the area of the actual rug?

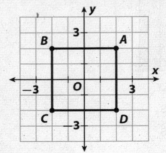

A 2 ft^2

B 4 ft^2

C 8 ft^2

D 16 ft^2

65. Ava's dog weighs 52 kilograms. Marty's dog weighs $\frac{3}{4}$ as much. Find the weight of Marty's dog in kilograms.

A 13 kg

B 26 kg

C 39 kg

D 65 kg

66. Hayley cut a $10\frac{1}{2}$-foot rope into pieces that are each $\frac{1}{2}$ foot long. How many pieces of rope did she cut?

A 2 pieces

B 10 pieces

C 21 pieces

D 40 pieces

67. A caterpillar crawls 25 inches in one minute. How many inches does it crawl in 5 minutes?

A 5 in.

B 50 in.

C 70 in.

D 125 in.

68. Jungwon has $15. Notepads cost $2.50 each. How many notepads can Jungwon buy?

A 6   C 37

B 17   D 60

69. Noah bought 5 pounds of onions at $2 per pound and a bag of salad greens for $4. How much money did he spend?

A $10

B $14

C $20

D $22

Beginning-of-Year Diagnostic Test

70. Oliver's total monthly budget is shown in the circle graph below.

Oliver's monthly budget is $2,000. How much money does he save each month?

A $200

B $500

C $600

D $700

71. Sara bought a 24-ounce can of tomato sauce for $6. What is the unit price per ounce?

A $0.25

B $0.60

C $2.50

D $4.00

72. Conrad bought 1 gallon of bottled water at the supermarket. How many cups of water did he buy?

A 4   C 16

B 8   D 24

73. The table below shows the fees David charges for yard work.

David's Yard Work Fees

Hours	1	2	5
Fee (dollars)	35	70	175

How much money does David charge for yard work that takes 4 hours?

A $35   C $140

B $70   D $175

74. A falcon flies 300 kilometers per hour. A goose flies 140 kilometers per hour. If a falcon and a goose each fly for 2 hours, how many more kilometers will a falcon fly?

A 160 km

B 240 km

C 320 km

D 440 km

75. On a city map, 2 inches represents 10 miles. The library and the bank are 5 inches apart on the map. What is the actual distance in miles between the library and the bank?

A 1 mile

B 10 miles

C 20 miles

D 25 miles

76. What is the value of the expression below?
$$(7)^3$$

A 1

B 7

C 49

D 343

77. Use the order of operations to simplify the expression below.
$$990 \div (12 - 9)^2$$

A 35

B 110

C 325

D 5,402

78. Evaluate the expression below for $x = 5$.
$$5(x + 7)$$

A 12

B 15

C 50

D 60

Beginning-of-Year Diagnostic Test

79. Last year, the tree in Pedro's front yard was 5 feet tall. This year, the tree is 2 feet less than the height of Pedro's house. Pedro's house is 17 feet tall. How tall is the tree?

   A   12 ft

   B   15 ft

   C   19 ft

   D   22 ft

80. A parallelogram has a base of 7 meters and a height of 10 meters. What is the area of the parallelogram in square meters?

   A   7 m^2 C   35 m^2

   B   14 m^2 D   70 m^2

81. What is the area of the triangle shown below?

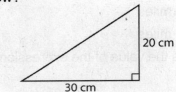

   A   30 cm^2

   B   60 cm^2

   C   300 cm^2

   D   600 cm^2

82. What is the area of the rhombus shown below?

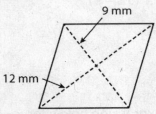

   A   36 mm^2

   B   54 mm^2

   C   108 mm^2

   D   216 mm^2

83. A triangle has an area of 400 square inches. The length of the base of the triangle is 10 inches. What is the height of the triangle?

   A   10 in.

   B   20 in.

   C   40 in.

   D   80 in.

84. A trapezoid has an area of 342 square yards. The length of one base is 17 yards, and the length of the other base is 21 yards. What is the height of the trapezoid?

   A   18 yd

   B   19 yd

   C   38 yd

   D   40 yd

85. A rectangular prism has a volume of 572 cubic inches. The prism is 4 inches long and 13 inches wide. What is the height of the prism?

   A   5 in.

   B   11 in.

   C   42 in.

   D   58 in.

MODULE 1

Integers

Module Quiz: B

1. Which names the opposite and absolute value of –9?

   A –9, 0   C 9, 9

   B 9, 0   D –9, –9

2. Which names the opposite and absolute value of 12?

   A –12, 0   C 12, +12

   B –12, 12   D –12, –12

3. 3 and –3 are _____.

   A absolute values   C opposites

   B positive   D negative

4. Numbers with the same absolute value

   are _____.

   A equal to zero

   B always positive

   C always negative

   D equally distant from zero

5. How would you use a number line to order integers from least to greatest?

   A Graph the integers, then read them from right to left.

   B Graph the integers, then read them from left to right.

   C Graph the absolute values, then read them from left to right.

   D Graph the absolute values, then read them from right to left.

6. Four workers are repairing a bridge at these distances from the roadway.

   Worker 1: 7 feet below the roadway
   Worker 2: 13 feet above the roadway
   Worker 3: 13 feet below the roadway
   Worker 4: at the roadway

   Which shows the distances in order from highest to lowest?

   A 0, –7, 13, –13   C 13, 0, –13, –7

   B 13, –13, –7, 0   D 13, 0, –7, –13

7. The farther an integer is from zero, the

   _____ its absolute value.

   A less   C greater

   B more negative   D opposite

8. To represent the opposite of a loss of 5 points on the stock market, you could use

   A –5   C $\frac{1}{5}$

   B 0   D 5

9. Five chemistry students observed the following mixture temperatures.

Student	Mixture Temperature (°C)
Alex	–5
Casey	3
Gabriella	–4
Ernie	5
Morgan	–1

   Which shows the temperatures in order from greatest to least?

   A –5, –4, –1, 3, 5

   B 5, –5, –4, 3, 1

   C 5, 3, –1, –4, –5

   D 5, 3, –5, –4, –1

10. Roger's dog Ty lost and gained weight over a six-week period.

Week	1	2	3	4	5	6
Loss/Gain	–3	2	–4	1	–2	0

   Which shows Ty's weight changes in order from greatest loss to greatest gain?

   A 2, 1, 0, –2, –3, –4

   B 0, 1, 2, –2, –3, –4

   C –4, –3, –2, 2, 1, 0,

   D –4 –3, –2, 0, 1, 2

MODULE 1 **Integers**

11. Over a business week, the lost-and-found department at a train station received and returned several items. The table shows the items received (+) and returned (−).

Items Received and Returned				
Mon.	Tues.	Wed.	Thurs.	Fri.
4	−3	5	0	−5

Graph and label the changes on the number line.

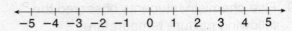

12. Katia and Thomasina play a computer game and record these scores.

   Katia: 8, 6, −4, −7, 2, 0, 3
   Thomasina: −11, 0, 8, 7, 5, −7, 11

   Compare Katia's and Thomasina's least

   scores. _____

13. Complete. To find the absolute value of a

   number, find the _____

   from zero and write the distance as a

   _____ integer.

14. Complete. The set of integers is made up

   of positive integers, _____

   integers, and _____.

15. Complete. You can use the symbol _____

   to show a number is greater than another

   and the symbol _____ to show a number is

   less than another.

16. Complete. The _____ of

   −7 and _____ is 7.

17. The opposite of the absolute value of

   −8 is _____. Explain.

   _____

   _____

For 18–20, use the table.

In an athletic event, competitors both climb and dive. The table below shows some of their climbs and dives.

Student	Climb (ft)	Dive (ft)
Al	25	−9
Beth	13	−12
Chaz	15	−7
Dora	24	−11
Earl	20	−13

18. Which competitor makes the shortest

   climb? _____

19. Which competitor makes the deepest

   dive? _____

20. Which competitor covers the greatest distance in climbs and dives?
   (Hint: Use absolute values.)

   _____

21. A submarine is at 756 feet. How many feet will it need to rise to be at the

   surface? _____

MODULE 1 **Integers**

Module Quiz: D

1. Which describes 9 and –9?

   A positive integers

   B opposites

   C absolute values

2. Which is the absolute value of 9 and –9?

   A –9   C 9

   B 0

3. Numbers with the same absolute value

   are _____

   A equal

   B equally distant from zero

   C always positive

4. Which numbers are in order from greatest to least?

   A 6, 4, 0, –1, –5   C –5, –1, 0, 4, 6

   B 6, –5, 4, –1, 0

5. How would you use a number line to order integers from greatest to least?

   A Graph the absolute values, then read them from left to right.

   B Graph the integers, then read them from left to right.

   C Graph the integers, then read them from right to left.

6. Three workers are building a house at these distances from the surface.

   Worker 1: 3 feet below the surface
   Worker 2: 5 feet above the surface
   Worker 3: at the surface

   Which shows the distances in order from lowest to highest?

   A 0, 3, 5   C 0, –3, 5

   B –3, 0, 5

7. The farther an integer is from 0, the

   _____ its absolute value.

   A greater   C negative

   B less

8. Which represents a $3 loss?

   A –3   C $\frac{1}{3}$

   B 0

9. The average height of an American woman is almost 5 feet 5 inches. The table shows how much taller or shorter than the average four women are.

Woman	Inches
Lucy	–3
Maria	1
Opal	–1
Patti	2

   Which woman is tallest?

   A Lucy   C Maria

   B Patti

10. The average height of an American man is almost 5 feet 10 inches. The table shows how much taller or shorter than the average four men are.

Men	Inches
Rob	3
Steve	–2
Umberto	–7
Vincent	1

    How tall is the shortest man?

    A 5 feet 10 inches

    B 5 feet

    C 5 feet 3 inches

11. The smaller the absolute value of a

    negative number, the _____ the number is.

    A larger

    B smaller

    C farther from zero

MODULE 1

Integers

12. The table shows the weight losses and gains (in lbs.) for a dog over 6 months.

J	A	S	O	N	D
−3	−2	4	0	3	−4

Graph the losses and gains on the number line.

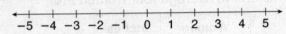

13. Paula's scores for a computer game were −7, 5, −3, −6, 1, −1, and 2.

Put them in order from least to greatest.

_____

14. The absolute value of a number is its

_____ from zero.

15. Absolute value is always

_____ or zero.

16. The symbol ____ means "less than."

17. The absolute value of −6 and 6 is ____ .

For 18–21, use the table.

The average score on a test was 82. The table shows how far above or below this number five students' scores were.

Student	Difference
A	−3
B	4
C	−2
D	−5
E	7

18. Which student had the highest score?

_____

19. What was that score? ____

20. Which student's score was closest to

average? _____

21. Whose score was 86?

_____

22. A kite descends to the ground from a height of 32 feet. Use an integer to describe the descent.

_____

For 23–25, use the table.

In Rhonda's school, the average amount of time spent on homework on weeknights was 56 minutes. The table shows how far above and below average five students' times were.

Student	Difference
Fred	−5
Gina	0
Hanna	3
Ilsa	−3
Jon	5

23. Which students' differences were

opposite? _____

24. Who spent the least amount of time on

homework? _____

25. Which student spent the average amount of time on homework?

_____

26. Which integers are greater than −3 and

less than 0? _____

MODULE 2

Factors and Multiples

Module Quiz: B

1. Which of these is a factor of 15?

    A 2   C 10

    B 3   D 30

2. Which is **not** a factor of 36?

    A 3   C 36

    B 6   D 72

3. Which is the GCF of 8 and 12?

    A 2   C 24

    B 4   D 96

4. Rose picked 18 tulips and 20 daffodils. She divided the flowers into groups so that the same number of tulips and daffodils were in each bouquet. What is the greatest number of bouquets she could have made?

    A 2   C 90

    B 5   D 180

5. Which of the following is a multiple of 8?

    A 4   C 20

    B 8   D 100

6. Which of the following is **not** a multiple of 12?

    A 12   C 100

    B 24   D 144

7. Every fourth visitor to a museum gets a free bumper sticker. Every tenth visitor to that museum gets a free key chain. Which visitor each day will be the first one to get both the bumper sticker and the key chain?

    A tenth   C fortieth

    B twentieth   D hundredth

8. Julie has two email accounts. She checks one of them every two hours. The other one she uses less often. She only checks it every 24 hours. She checked each account on Monday at 2 p.m. When will she again check each account at the same time?

    A next Monday at 2 A.M.

    B next Monday at 2 P.M.

    C Tuesday at 2 A.M.

    D Tuesday at 2 P.M.

9. Which pair of numbers has a GCF of 3?

    A 3 and 18   C 8 and 24

    B 12 and 18   D 1 and 3

10. Which pair of numbers has a LCM of 12?

    A 1 and 6   C 2 and 6

    B 2 and 3   D 3 and 4

11. Which is the way to express 18 + 24 as the product of the GCF and another sum?

    A $2 \times (9 + 12)$

    B $3 \times (6 + 8)$

    C $4 \times (4 + 6)$

    D $6 \times (3 + 4)$

12. Jesse kept track of how far above or below par her golf scores for 9 holes were. She wrote them in the order they happened: −1, 0, 3, 2, 2, −2, 0, 1, 4. Which list shows her scores in order from below par to above par?

    A 0, 0, −1, 1, −2, 2, 2, 3, 4

    B −2, −1, 0, 0, 1, 2, 2, 3, 4

    C −1, −2, 0, 0, 1, 2, 2, 3, 4

    D 4, 3, 2, 2, −2, 1, −1, 0, 0

MODULE 2 **Factors and Multiples**

13. James says that 12 is a common factor of 3 and 4. June says that 12 is a common multiple of 3 and 4. Who is correct?

    _____

14. What is the GCF of 21 and 30?

    _____

15. What is the LCM of 21 and 30?

    _____

16. Kevin solved a problem by making these lists:

    12: 24, 36, 48, (60)

    15: 15, 30, 45, (60)

    What problem was Kevin solving?

    _____

    _____

17. Every sixth visitor to an animal shelter gets a free animal calendar. Every twentieth visitor gets a free animal toy. Which visitor each day will be the first one to get both the calendar and the animal toy?

    _____

18. Marta took 48 pictures of flowers and 36 pictures of beautiful scenery. She wants to display the pictures so there is the same number of each kind of picture in each display. What is the greatest number of displays she can make?

    _____

19. Make a list of possible pairs of numbers that have a LCM of 48.

    _____

20. Make a list of possible pairs of numbers that have a GCF of 7.

    _____

21. Mel has to put the greatest number of bolts and nuts in each box so each box has the same number of bolts and the same number of nuts. Should Mel use the greatest common factor or the least common multiple to solve the problem?

    _____

22. A student expressed a sum of two whole numbers as $5 \times (8 + 3)$. What were the two whole numbers?

    _____

23. A park district has 25 elm trees and 20 oak trees to be planted. They are separating the trees for different areas. They want each area to have the same number of elm trees and the same number of oak trees. What is the greatest number of areas that can be created?

    _____

24. What is the absolute value of −8 and 8?

    _____

MODULE 2

Factors and Multiples

Module Quiz: D

1. Which of these is a factor of 10?

   A 2

   B 4

   C 20

2. Which is **not** a factor of 12?

   A 3

   B 6

   C 24

3. Which is the GCF of 4 and 12?

   A 2

   B 4

   C 12

4. Bill cut out 6 squares and 8 circles. He divided the cutouts into groups so that the same number of squares and circles were in each group. What is the greatest number of groups he could have made?

   A 2   B 3

   C 4

5. Which of the following is a multiple of 7?

   A 14   B 17

   C 22

6. Which of the following is **not** a multiple of 9?

   A 9   B 19

   C 90

7. Every third visitor to a museum gets a free bumper sticker. Every fifth visitor to that museum gets a free key chain. Which visitor each day will be the first one to get both the bumper sticker and the key chain?

   A 3rd

   B 5th

   C 15th

8. Gabriella volunteers at the hospital every 4th day. She volunteers at the food pantry every 6th day. She volunteered at the hospital and the food pantry both on March 31. On what date will she next volunteer at both?

   A April 12

   B April 16

   C May 1

9. Which pair of numbers has a GCF of 6?

   A 3 and 18

   B 6 and 12

   C 12 and 24

10. Which pair of numbers has a LCM of 20?

    A 4 and 5

    B 2 and 10

    B 5 and 10

11. Which is the way to express $10 + 12$ as the product of the GCF and another sum?

    A $2 \times (5 + 6)$

    B $2 \times (8 + 10)$

    C $4 \times (2 + 3)$

12. Jason listed his game scores: −1, 0, 3, 2, 6, −5. Which list shows his scores in order least to greatest?

    A 0, −1, 2, 3, −5, 6

    B −1, −5, 0, 2, 3, 6

    C −5, −1, 0, 2, 3, 6

MODULE 2 — Factors and Multiples

13. Karen says that 6 is a common factor of 2 and 3. Ken says that 6 is a common multiple of 2 and 3. Who is correct?

_____

14. What is the GCF of 12 and 16?

_____

15. What is the LCM of 6 and 7?

_____

16. Wilhelm solved a problem by making these lists:

    10: 20, (30), 40, 50, 60

    15: 15, (30), 45, 60

    What problem was he solving?

_____

17. Every fourth customer gets a free calendar. Every sixth customer gets a coupon for $1 off their meal. Which customer will be the first one to get both the calendar and the coupon?

_____

18. Carole has 18 red beads and 24 blue beads. She is making bracelets. Each bracelet is to have the same number of red beads and blue beads. What is the greatest number of bracelets she can make?

_____

19. List a pair of numbers that has a LCM of 12.

_____

20. Make a list of two possible pairs of numbers that have a GCF of 5.

_____

21. Phil has to put the greatest number of apples and oranges in each box so each box has the same number of apples and oranges. Should Phil use the greatest common factor or the least common multiple to solve the problem?

_____

22. A student expressed a sum of two whole numbers as $3 \times (2 + 5)$. What were the two whole numbers?

_____

23. There are 12 girls and 15 boys in a class. The teacher wants to make reading groups with the same number of girls and the same number of boys in each group. What is the greatest number of reading groups that can be made?

_____

24. What is the absolute value of −2?

_____

MODULE 3 — Rational Numbers
Module Quiz: B

1. Dale has a special deck of cards. Each card has a different rational number on it. The cards are 0.25, $\frac{4}{5}$, $\frac{2}{9}$, 0.48, and $\frac{8}{11}$. How many cards have a value that is greater than $\frac{1}{2}$?

   A none of these   C two

   B one   D three

2. Which set of rational numbers is correctly ordered from least to greatest?

   A −0.48, −0.47, −0.46, −0.45

   B −0.48, −0.46, −0.47, −0.45

   C −0.45, −0.47, −0.48, −0.46

   D −0.45, −0.46, −0.47, −0.48

3.

Point	Coordinate
A	−0.31
B	−0.33
C	−0.38
D	−0.29

   Which number line shows the correct placement of the points in the table above?

4. Kendra placed the numbers $-\frac{3}{8}$, 0.27, −0.3, and $\frac{4}{7}$ on the number line. Which of the numbers is furthest from zero?

   A $-\frac{3}{8}$ C 0.27

   B −0.3   D $\frac{4}{7}$

5. Mandy divided a 12-pound bag of oranges into 5 equal piles. Which rational number represents the weight of the oranges in each pile?

   A $\frac{1}{5}$ C $2\frac{1}{6}$

   B $\frac{5}{12}$ D $2\frac{2}{5}$

6. Which statement about rational numbers is **not** correct?

   A All rational numbers are also integers.

   B Zero is a rational number.

   C All integers also rational numbers.

   D All rational numbers can be written in the form $\frac{a}{b}$.

7. Philip wrote the numbers $3\frac{1}{5}$, $3\frac{1}{7}$, $5\frac{1}{8}$, and $1\frac{5}{6}$ in the form $\frac{a}{b}$. What is the greatest numerator that Philip wrote?

   A 11   C 22

   B 16   D 41

MODULE 3

Rational Numbers

8. Dori claims that 3.52 is not a rational number because it is not written as a ratio of integers. Is she correct? Explain why or why not.

_____

_____

12. If x is a rational number and y is the opposite of x, why do x and y have the same absolute value?

_____

_____

9. **Times in 100-meter Dash**

Runner	Time (s)
Rebekah	12.45
Kori	12.54
Lin	12.48
Shelly	12.44

Four runners ran the 100-meter dash. The times are shown in the table above. Which runner had the fastest time?

_____

13. **Daily Temperatures in Chicago**

Day	Temperature
Monday	−1.2°C
Tuesday	−2.0°C
Wednesday	−1.8°C
Thursday	−1.4°C

The table shows the daily temperatures for a four-day period in Chicago.

On which day or days was the temperature lower than −1.5°C?

_____

10. Write the numbers -2.1, $-1\frac{5}{6}$, $-1\frac{2}{3}$, and -2.2 in the form $\frac{a}{b}$, from greatest to least.

_____

14. Explain how to write the rational number 3.21 in the form $\frac{a}{b}$.

_____

_____

11.

Which lettered points in the number line above have absolute value less than 3?

_____

15. Kevin compared the absolute values of $-2\frac{1}{8}$, -2.25, $2\frac{3}{8}$, -2.29, and $2\frac{4}{11}$. Which number has the greatest absolute value?

_____

_____

MODULE 3

Rational Numbers

Module Quiz: D

1. What is the absolute value of –10.5?

   A –10.5

   B 0

   C 10.5

2. Which statement is correct?

   A $-1.5 < -2$

   B $-2.5 < -3$

   C $-3.5 < -2.5$

3. Trina guessed a rational number between 2 and 4 that is **not** an integer. Which is a possible number that she guessed?

   A –2.8

   B 3

   C 3.2

4. Which number line shows $\frac{1}{3}$ graphed?

   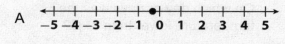

   A ⟨─┼─┼─┼─┼─┼─●─┼─┼─┼─┼─┼─⟩
       –5 –4 –3 –2 –1 0 1 2 3 4 5

   B ⟨─┼─┼─┼─┼─┼─┼─●─┼─┼─┼─┼─⟩
       –5 –4 –3 –2 –1 0 1 2 3 4 5

   C ⟨─┼─┼─┼─┼─┼─┼─┼─┼─●─┼─┼─⟩
       –5 –4 –3 –2 –1 0 1 2 3 4 5

5. Which of the following sets of rational numbers is correctly ordered from greatest to least?

   A –0.2, –0.8, –1.1

   B –0.2, –1.1, –0.8

   C –1.1, –0.8, –0.2

6. What is the opposite of –0.8?

   A –8

   B 0

   C 0.8

7. George placed the numbers $-\frac{1}{2}$, 0.2 and $\frac{8}{9}$ on the number line. Which of the numbers is furthest from zero?

   A $-\frac{1}{2}$

   B 0.2

   C $\frac{8}{9}$

8. Kim poured a 24-ounce container of orange juice into 5 cups. She poured the same amount of juice into each cup. Which rational number represents the amount of juice in each cup?

   A $\frac{5}{24}$

   B 5

   C $\frac{24}{5}$

9. ⟨─┼─┼─●─┼●●┼─●─┼─●─┼─┼─┼─⟩
        A B C D E
      –5 –4 –3 –2 –1 0 1 2 3 4 5

   What is the location of the point labeled *B* in the number line above?

   A –1.2

   B –0.8

   C 1.2

10. Which of the following is an example of a rational number that is not an integer?

   A –3

   B 1

   C $\frac{1}{3}$

MODULE 3

Rational Numbers

11. Benjamin plotted −1.5 and 1.6 on a number line. Which point is further from zero?

_____

12.   **Times in 50-meter Dash**

Runner	Time (s)
Steve	7.41
Mike	7.38
Daniel	7.43
Mauricio	7.25

Four runners ran the 50-meter dash. The times are shown in the table above. Which runner had the fastest time?

_____

13. Write the numbers −2.1, −1.8, −2.5 and −2.7 from greatest to least.

_____

14. What is the absolute value of −65.6?

_____

15. What number is the opposite of $-2\frac{1}{8}$?

_____

16. Hannah claims that −3 is not a rational number because it is not written as a ratio of integers. Is she correct? Explain why or why not.

_____

17.   **Daily Temperature in Detroit**

Day	Temperature
Monday	2.2°C
Tuesday	2.5°C
Wednesday	3.1°C
Thursday	3.6°C

The table shows the daily temperatures for a four-day period in Detroit.

On which day or days was the temperature lower than 3° C?

_____

18. Write the number 10.5 in the form $\frac{a}{b}$.

_____

19. Kevin compared the absolute values of $-10\frac{1}{8}$, −9.25, $8\frac{3}{8}$ and −12.4. Which number has the greatest absolute value?

_____

Name _____ Date _____ Class_____

| MODULE 4 | **Operations with Fractions** |

Module Quiz: B

1. Which of the following is equivalent to $\frac{2}{5} \times \frac{3}{8}$?

   A $\frac{3}{8} \div \frac{2}{5}$ C $\frac{2}{5} \div \frac{8}{3}$

   B $\frac{2}{5} \div \frac{3}{8}$ D $\frac{5}{2} \div \frac{8}{3}$

2. Linda's container of cranberry juice holds 200 milliliters. Harry's container holds $\frac{7}{8}$ as much juice. How many milliliters of cranberry juice do the two containers hold?

   A 100   C 300
   B 175   D 375

3. In the number line shown below, which lettered point represents the quotient of $1\frac{7}{8}$ divided by $\frac{1}{2}$?

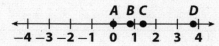

   A A   C C
   B B   D D

4. Melania walked her dog $2\frac{1}{5}$ miles. Cathy walked her dog $1\frac{3}{4}$ times as far as Melania did. How many more miles did Cathy walk her dog?

   A $1\frac{13}{20}$ C $3\frac{17}{20}$

   B $2\frac{1}{10}$ D $3\frac{19}{20}$

5. What is the reciprocal of $2\frac{3}{8}$?

   A $-\frac{19}{8}$ C $\frac{8}{19}$

   B $-\frac{8}{19}$ D $\frac{19}{8}$

6. Dairon needs 20 pieces of string $\frac{3}{8}$ inch in length. He cut a $4\frac{7}{8}$-inch piece of string into pieces that are $\frac{3}{8}$ of an inch long each. How many more pieces of string does he need?

   A 6   C 13
   B 7   D 15

7. James has a piece of construction paper with an area of $65\frac{1}{4}$ inches. It is $9\frac{2}{3}$ inches long. What is the width of the piece of construction paper in inches?

   A 6   C 7

   B $6\frac{3}{4}$ D $67\frac{1}{2}$

8. Alexis divided a $1\frac{3}{4}$ pound bag of apples among her three friends. How many pounds of apples did each friend receive?

   A $\frac{7}{12}$ C $\frac{3}{4}$

   B $\frac{2}{3}$ D $\frac{5}{6}$

9. What is the GCF of 8 and 24?

   A 4   C 12
   B 8   D 16

Original content Copyright © by Houghton Mifflin Harcourt. Additions and changes to the original content are the responsibility of the instructor.

27

MODULE 4

Operations with Fractions

10. Alexander reads $\frac{1}{8}$ of a book each night. How long will it take him to read $\frac{3}{4}$ of the book?

_____

11. Carmen measured a room to be $10\frac{1}{2}$ feet by $12\frac{5}{8}$ feet. What is the area of the room written as a decimal?

_____

12. Tom is making meatloaf with $\frac{3}{4}$ pound of turkey and $\frac{5}{6}$ pound of ground beef. What is the LCM he should use to find the total number of pounds of meat?

_____

13. Multiplying a number by $\frac{4}{5}$ then dividing by $\frac{2}{5}$ is the same as multiplying by what number?

_____

14. Rajendra has $14\frac{4}{5}$ pounds of trail mix. He is putting them into bags that hold $1\frac{1}{2}$ pounds each. Does he have enough trail mix to completely fill 8 bags? Explain why or why not.

_____

15. Seven people decide to share $\frac{3}{8}$ of a bag of marbles equally. What fraction of the bag of marbles does each person receive?

_____

16. Dustin completed $\frac{3}{8}$ of a homework assignment that has 24 problems. Kelsey completed $\frac{4}{15}$ of a homework assignment that has 30 problems. Who completed more problems?

_____

17. Brent divided $3\frac{1}{5}$ by a number and got $4\frac{1}{2}$. What number did he divide by?

_____

18. Alyssa claims that dividing by $\frac{4}{5}$ is the same thing as multiplying by 5 then dividing by 4. Is she correct? Explain why or why not.

_____

19. Juanita is measuring a table for her dining room. The area of the table is $46\frac{7}{8}$ square feet. The length of the table is $7\frac{1}{2}$ feet. Juanita does not want to purchase a table that is greater than 6 feet wide. Should she purchase the table? Explain why or why not.

_____

MODULE 4

Operations with Fractions

Module Quiz: D

1. What is the quotient of $\frac{2}{5} \div \frac{8}{5}$?

   A $\frac{1}{4}$

   B $\frac{7}{13}$

   C $\frac{16}{25}$

2. Avery's water bottle holds 300 milliliters. Dashawn's container holds $\frac{3}{4}$ as much water. How many milliliters of water do both containers hold?

   A 225

   B 425

   C 525

3. What is the value of $\frac{3}{4} \div \frac{3}{8}$?

   A $\frac{1}{2}$

   B $\frac{8}{3}$

   C 2

4. Last Saturday, Flavia walked her dog $1\frac{2}{5}$ miles. Shazell walked her dog 5 times as far. How many miles total did both girls walk their dogs?

   A $6\frac{2}{5}$

   B 7

   C $8\frac{2}{5}$

5. What is the reciprocal of $\frac{3}{5}$?

   A $-\frac{3}{5}$

   B 0

   C $\frac{5}{3}$

6. Li needs 15 pieces of string each $\frac{1}{2}$ of a inch long. She cut a 6-inch piece of string into pieces that are each $\frac{1}{2}$ of an inch long. How many more pieces of string does she need?

   A 3

   B 6

   C 12

7. Jenna has a piece of paper that is 84 square inches in area. It is $10\frac{1}{2}$ inches long. What is the length of the piece of paper in square inches?

   A $\frac{21}{2}$

   B 8

   C 42

8. Dillon divided a $3\frac{1}{3}$ pound bag of pears among his five friends. How many pounds of pears did each friend receive?

   A $\frac{2}{3}$

   B 1

   C 5

9. What is the GCF of 3 and 12?

   A 3

   B 6

   C 12

| **MODULE 4** | **Operations with Fractions** |

10. Ming reads $\frac{1}{4}$ of a book each night. How long will it take her to read $\frac{3}{4}$ of the book?

_____

11. Roberto measured his garden to be 10 feet by $12\frac{1}{2}$ feet. He plants vegetables in one-half of the garden. What is the area of his vegetable garden?

_____

12. What is the product of $\frac{1}{2}$ and $\frac{5}{6}$?

_____

13. Multiplying a number by 2 and then dividing by 3 is the same as multiplying by what number?

_____

14. Cora put 16 cups of flour into bags that hold $\frac{1}{2}$ cup each. How many bags did she fill?

_____

15. What is 36 divided by $\frac{1}{4}$?

_____

16. What is the reciprocal of $\frac{1}{3}$?

_____

17. What is the difference of 5 and $\frac{2}{5}$? Show your work.

_____

18. What is the reciprocal of $3\frac{1}{5}$?

_____

19. What number is the greatest common factor of 12 and 15?

_____

20. Brent divided $3\frac{1}{2}$ by 7. What number did he get?

_____

21. Kathy claims that dividing by $\frac{1}{5}$ is the same thing as multiplying by 5. Is she correct? Explain why or why not.

_____

_____

22. What is the greatest common factor of 15 and 20?

_____

23. Brian bought a 15-pound bag of concrete. He split the bag into smaller bags that each hold $2\frac{1}{2}$ pounds. How many smaller bags did he fill?

_____

Name _____ Date _____ Class_____

Operations with Decimals
Module Quiz: B

1. Adam spent $3.42 on orange juice. Orange juice costs $0.12 per ounce. How many ounces of orange juice did Adam buy?

   A 25.5   C 27.5

   B 26.5   D 28.5

2. Alexis rode her bike 4.5 miles. Johnny rode his bike 8.1 miles. How many more miles did Johnny ride his bike?

   A 3.6   C 4.6

   B 2.7   D 12.6

3. Fran reads 54 pages per hour. If she reads a total of 257 pages one weekend, how many hours to the nearest hundredth does she read?

   A 4.76   C 5

   B 4   D 47.59

4. How many 0.2-liter glasses of water are contained in a 3.6-liter pitcher?

   A 18   C 30

   B 20   D 36

5. Tomasso's family used 24.5 gallons of gas to drive 548.8 miles. How many miles did they drive for each gallon of gas?

   A 20.1   C 22.8

   B 22.4   D 24.5

6. Phillip bought apples from the grocery for $2.20 per pound. If he bought 2.5 pounds of apples on Monday and 1.2 pounds of apples on Tuesday, how much did he spend on apples in total?

   A $2.64   C $8.14

   B $5.50   D $8.80

7. Amery drives 50 miles in one hour. How many miles does he drive in 2.25 hours?

   A 100   C 120

   B 112.5   D 125

8. Maura cut a 5.25-inch piece of string into pieces that are each 0.75 inches long. How many pieces of string did she cut?

   A 6   C 8

   B 7   D 9

9. Shafiq measured a piece of construction paper to be 6.75 inches wide by 8.25 inches long. What is the area of the piece of construction paper in square inches?

   A 48.1875   C 55.5125

   B 49.01   D 55.6875

10. Connor bought 40 pencils for $0.35 each. Mara bought 70 pencils at the same price. How much more money did Mara spend?

    A $3.50   C $14.00

    B $10.50   D $24.50

11. Clayton biked $\frac{3}{8}$ of the 14.5 miles between his house and the beach. How many miles does he still need to bike before he reaches the beach?

    A 5.4375   C 9.0625

    B 7.25   D 9.125

12. Veri made $25 babysitting. If she makes $8 an hour, how many hours did she babysit?

    A 3   C $3\frac{1}{12}$

    B $3\frac{1}{8}$ D 4

MODULE 5 **Operations with Decimals**

13. Joshua earns $8.20 per hour when he works at the college library. How much money does he earn by working at the library for 4.5 hours?

_____

14. **Indira's Clothing Shop Orders**

Item	Quantity	Price
T-shirt	50	$392.50
Sweater	25	$440.25

Indira can order T-shirts and sweaters at the prices and quantities shown in the table. By how much does the price of one sweater exceed the price of one T-shirt?

_____

15. Karl rode his bicycle $\frac{3}{8}$ of the distance from Lakeview to Bay Cove, which is 24.1 miles. How many more miles does he need to ride to complete his trip?

_____

16. Jordan saved $\frac{4}{5}$ of the amount he needs to buy a $80 video game. If he earns $7.75 per hour by working at a pizza shop, how many hours does he need to work to save the rest of the money for the video game? (Round to the nearest hour.)

_____

17. Emma is saving to buy a video game console that costs $249. She already saved $60 and plans to save $22 per week. After how many weeks will she have saved enough money for the video game console?

_____

18. Colin earned $46 raking leaves. If he worked 1.5 hours yesterday and 4.25 hours today, how much did he earn per hour?

_____

19. At the market, 2.4 pounds of carrots cost $1.68 and 1.8 pounds of broccoli cost $1.53. How much more does 1 pound of broccoli cost than 1 pound of carrots?

_____

20. **Food Prices**

Item	Price (per pound)
Beef	$11.99
Chicken	$6.49

The prices of different items at a food market are shown in the table above. Kevin wants to purchase 2.5 pounds of beef and 1.8 pounds of chicken. How much does he spend?

_____

21. Naomi drank $\frac{3}{4}$ of a 20.8-ounce container of apple juice. How many ounces of apple juice did Naomi drink?

_____

MODULE 5

Operations with Decimals

Module Quiz: D

1. Elena spent $2.50 on pineapple juice. Pineapple juice costs $0.10 per ounce. How many ounces of pineapple juice did Elena buy?

   A 0.25

   B 2.5

   C 25

2. What is the product of 0.5 and 3.5?

   A 0.14

   B 1.75

   C 7

3. Shaniqua can read at a speed of 50 pages per hour. She reads 275 pages one weekend. How many hours does she read?

   A 5

   B 5.5

   C 6

4. How many 0.5-liter glasses of water can be poured from a full 6-liter pitcher?

   A 3

   B 6

   C 12

5. Alvin's family used 20.5 gallons of gas to drive 492 miles. How many miles did they drive on each gallon of gas?

   A 20

   B 22

   C 24

6. What is 3.5 divided by 0.7?

   A 5

   B 10

   C 20

7. David drives 40 miles in one hour. How many miles does he drive in 1.5 hours?

   A 50

   B 60

   C 70

8. Kyle cut a 4-foot piece of rope into pieces that are each 0.25 feet long. How many pieces of rope did he cut?

   A 1

   B 4

   C 16

9. Talia measured a piece of construction paper to be 6.1 inches wide by 8.2 inches long. What is the area of the piece of construction paper in square inches?

   A 14.3

   B 48.3

   C 50.02

10. Calvin bought 20 pencils at $0.45 each. How much change did he get from a $10 bill?

    A $1.00

    B $9.00

    C $10.00

11. Billy drove $\frac{1}{2}$ of the 7.5 miles between his house and the mall. How many miles did he drive?

    A 3.25

    B 3.75

    C 4.25

12. What is the value of 0.4×0.25?

    A 0.1

    B 1

    C 1.6

MODULE 5   **Operations with Decimals**

13. Tommy earns $7.50 per hour when he works at his neighborhood pet store. How much money does Tommy earn by working 4 hours?

    _____

14. **Kelly's Clothing Shop Orders**

Item	Quantity	Price
T-shirt	100	$659.00
Sweater	50	$600.00

Kelly orders T-shirts and sweaters from a clothing company. She buys them at the prices and quantities that are shown in the table above. How much more does one sweater cost than one T-shirt?

    _____

15. What is $\frac{4}{5}$ of 20.5?

    _____

16. At a track meet, a four-person relay team completed their race in 84.4 seconds. What was the average time for each runner?

    _____

17. What is the product of 0.4 and 2.5?

    _____

18. What is the value of 40.4 divided by 4?

    _____

19. What is the product of 0.3 and 0.6?

    _____

20. Ellie earned $18.40 by babysitting. She worked 2.3 hours. How much money was Ellie paid per hour?

    _____

21. At the market, 2.4 pounds of peas cost $1.68. How much does one pound of peas cost?

    _____

22. **Food Prices**

Item	Price (lb)
Tuna Salad	$9.99
Chicken Salad	$7.99

The prices of different items at a food market are shown in the table above. Ryan wants to buy 0.75 pounds of tuna salad and 0.5 pounds of chicken salad. How much does he spend to the nearest cent?

    _____

23. Bria drank an 8-ounce glass of water from a 32-ounce container of water. How many more 8-ounce glasses were left?

    _____

24. What is the value of 0.15 divided by 0.05?

    _____

MODULE 6

Representing Ratios and Rates

Module Quiz: B

1. Which of the following ratios is **not** equivalent to the other three?

   A $\frac{2}{3}$ C 4 to 6

   B $\frac{4}{5}$ D 8 to 12

2. In Timra's math class, there are 12 boys and 15 girls. Which of the following is the ratio of boys to girls in Timra's math class?

   A $\frac{12}{27}$ C $\frac{15}{12}$

   B $\frac{12}{15}$ D $\frac{27}{12}$

3. Kimmy bought a 5-kilogram can of peanuts for $4.50. What is the unit price?

   A $0.05/kg   C $0.50/kg

   B $0.45/kg   D $0.90/kg

4. There are 250 bricks used to build a wall that is 20 feet high. How many bricks will be used to build a wall that is 30 feet high?

   A 260   C 375

   B 330   D 400

5. Johanna can jog 3,000 feet in 5 minutes. If she jogs at the same rate, how many feet can she jog in 8 minutes?

   A 4,000 ft   C 5,600 ft

   B 4,800 ft   D 6,400 ft

6. Andrea deposits $350 dollars in her checking account on Tuesday. On Wednesday she withdraws $100. On Thursday she deposits $75. Which of the following shows the change in Andrea's account from Tuesday to Thursday?

   A 350 − 100 − 75

   B 350 − 100 + 75

   C 350 + 100 − 75

   D 350 + 100 + 75

7. Alexa is making a recipe that requires 1 cup of water and 4 cups of flour. Which of the following combinations shows the same ratio of water to flour?

   A 2 cups of water to 3 cups of flour

   B 2 cups of water to 4 cups of flour

   C 2 cups of water to 8 cups of flour

   D 3 cups of water to 6 cups of flour

8. Misti bought a package of three T-shirts for $18.75. What is the unit price per T-shirt?

   A $6.25   C $12.50

   B $6.50   D $15.75

9. Which of the following ratios is equivalent to 2:3?

   A $\frac{1}{2}$ C $\frac{12}{13}$

   B $\frac{4}{6}$ D $\frac{20}{25}$

10. Which of the following is equal to the absolute value of 5 + 7 − 15?

    A −3   C 3

    B 0   D 27

11. Arjun can type 40 words per minute. Dalia can type 55 words per minute. If Arjun and Dalia each type for 30 minutes, about how many more words will Dalia type?

    A 45   C 900

    B 450   D 1,200

12. The local farmer's market sells a 4-pound basket of apples for $5.60. Each apple weighs about 4 ounces. What is the price per apple?

    A $0.35   C $0.45

    B $0.40   D $0.50

MODULE 6 | # Representing Ratios and Rates

13. The ratio of white marbles to blue marbles in Connie's bag of marbles is equal to 2:3. There are more than 20 marbles in the bag. What is a possible number of white marbles and blue marbles in the bag?

_____

14. Javier bought a 20-ounce smoothie that contains 450 total calories. How many calories does the smoothie contain per ounce?

_____

15.

Gemma's Soup Recipe

Ingredient	Quantity (c)
Water	4
Chicken Stock	3.5
Mixed Vegetables	8
Spices	1

Gemma's soup recipe is shown in the table above. What is the ratio of chicken stock to mixed vegetables? Express the ratio as a fraction in simplest form and as a decimal.

_____

16. The ratio of elephants to tigers at the local zoo is 1:4. There are 16 elephants at the zoo. How many tigers are there?

_____

17. One afternoon, Kassim's sandwich shop sells 15 sandwiches in 45 minutes. If the shop continues to sell sandwiches at the same rate, about how many sandwiches will the shop sell in 3 hours?

_____

18. Barry's deck of cards contains 40 blue cards and 70 red cards. Max's deck of cards contains the same number of blue cards, but the ratio of blue cards to red cards is 8:9. How many total cards does Max's deck of cards contain?

_____

19. Anabel uses 5 gallons of gas to drive 140 miles on the highway. If she travels at the same rate, how many miles can she drive on 7 gallons of gas?

_____

20. Kellan's lemonade recipe uses 4 scoops of lemonade powder for every 2.5 cups of water. Kellan uses 10 scoops of lemonade powder to make a batch of lemonade. How much water should he use?

_____

21. The ratio of forks to knives in Mabel's kitchen drawer is 4 to 5. There are 16 forks in the drawer. How many knives are there?

_____

22. On Monday, Janelle earned $16 for 2 hours of babysitting. Getting paid the same rate, she earned $40 for babysitting on Saturday. How many hours did Janelle babysit on Saturday?

_____

23. Karen read 20 pages of her book in a half hour. If she reads for 3 hours at that same rate, about how many pages of her book can Karen read?

_____

MODULE 6

Representing Ratios and Rates
Module Quiz: D

1. Which of the following ratios is **not** equivalent to the other two?

   A $\frac{1}{2}$

   B 1 : 2

   C 2 to 1

2. In Alana's math class, there are 12 boys and 13 girls. What is the ratio of boys to girls?

   A $\frac{12}{13}$

   B $\frac{13}{12}$

   C $\frac{12}{25}$

3. Fernando bought 5 pencils for $1.00. What is the unit price per pencil?

   A $0.20

   B $0.50

   C $0.95

4. Which of the following numbers is an integer?

   A 0.5

   B 1

   C $\frac{3}{2}$

5. Davita can jog 2,000 feet in 4 minutes. If she jogs at the same rate, how many feet can she jog in 8 minutes?

   A 2,000 ft

   B 3,000 ft

   C 4,000 ft

6. What is the opposite of –2?

   A $-\frac{1}{2}$

   B 0

   C 2

7. The ratio of red marbles to blue marbles in a bag is 2 to 3. Which of the following could be the number of red and blue marbles in the bag?

   A 4 red marbles and 5 blue marbles

   B 4 red marbles and 6 blue marbles

   C 6 red marbles and 8 blue marbles

8. Ana bought a package of two DVDs for $12.00. What is the unit price per DVD?

   A $2.00

   B $6.00

   C $10.00

9. Which of the following ratios is equivalent to 3 : 4?

   A $\frac{2}{3}$

   B $\frac{3}{4}$

   C $\frac{4}{3}$

10. Which of the following is equal to the absolute value of –15?

    A –15

    B 0

    C 15

11. Preston can type 40 words per minute. If he types at that same rate, about how many words can Preston type in 30 minutes?

    A 70

    B 120

    C 1,200

12. The local farmer's market sells a 4-pound basket of pears for $6.00. What is the price per pound?

    A $1.50/lb

    B $2.00/lb

    C $4.00/lb

MODULE 6

Representing Ratios and Rates

13. The ratio of catfish to trout in the local pond is 1 to 3. If there are 200 catfish in the pond, how many trout are there?

_____

14. A 10-ounce container of milk contains 200 calories. How many calories does each ounce of milk contain?

_____

15. **Cole's Soup Recipe**

Ingredient	Quantity (c)
Water	4
Chicken Stock	6
Mixed Vegetables	10
Spices	2

Cole's soup recipe is shown in the table above. What is the ratio of water to chicken stock? Express the ratio as a fraction in simplest form.

_____

16. The ratio of dogs to cats at the pet store is 1 : 2. There are 15 dogs. How many cats are there?

_____

17. The ratio of blue tacks to red tacks on the bulletin board is 3 to 5. There are 50 red tacks. How many blue tacks are on the board?

_____

18. Rya uses 4 gallons of gas to drive 120 miles on the highway. If she gets that same gas mileage, how many miles can she drive on 1 gallon of gas?

_____

19. Zak bought a board game that includes 30 blue game pieces and 40 green game pieces. What is the ratio of blue game pieces to green game pieces?

_____

20. In Ms. Henrick's class, there are 10 boys and 12 girls. What is the ratio of boys to girls? Express your answer as a fraction in simplest form.

_____

21. Kori earns $9 per hour working at the local library. If she works 5 hours on Saturday, how much money will she earn?

_____

22. Marcus can read about 40 pages of a book in one hour. If he reads at that same rate for 2 hours, about how many pages will Marcus read?

_____

23. Michael bought a box of 20 pretzel rods for $4.40. What is the price per pretzel rod?

_____

MODULE 7

Applying Ratios and Rates
Module Quiz: B

1.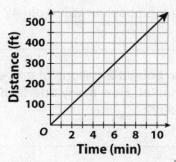

   The graph above shows Marnie's rate while walking. Which of the following is an ordered pair on the graph?

   A (2, 100)   C (4, 250)

   B (3, 200)   D (8, 500)

2. What is the relationship between a centimeter and a meter?

   A They are the same.

   B A meter is 10 times longer than a centimeter.

   C A meter is 100 times longer than a centimeter.

   D A centimeter is 100 times longer than a meter.

3. On a certain map, 2.5 inches represents 15 miles. Bay City and Greenwood are 4 inches apart on the map. What is the actual distance between Bay City and Greenwood?

   A 24 mi   C 36 mi

   B 30 mi   D 40 mi

4. It takes Benjamin 28 minutes to mow 2 lawns. Assuming the lawns are the same size and Benjamin works at the same speed, about how long will it take him to mow 5 lawns?

   A 14 min   C 70 min

   B 60 min   D 84 min

5. A can of soup has a volume of 12 fluid ounces. About how many milliliters is this?

   A 12 mL

   C 120 mL

   B 29.6 mL

   D 355 mL

6. Which of the following is equal to the product of $3\frac{1}{2}$ and $\frac{4}{7}$?

   A $\frac{1}{4}$ C 2

   B $\frac{1}{2}$ D $3\frac{1}{2}$

7. Salvatore charges $9 per hour for babysitting. Kendra charges $8.50 per hour. If they both work for 6 hours, how much more money would Salvatore earn?

   A $3.00   C $4.00

   B $3.50   D $4.50

8. Anna can buy 3 sweatshirts for a total of $45. How much would it cost if she were to buy 5 sweatshirts at the same price?

   A $15   C $60

   B $45   D $75

9. The ratio of blue chairs to red chairs in Ms. Vickers' class is 2 to 5. Which of the following **cannot** represent the total number of chairs in Ms. Vickers' class?

   A 14   C 28

   B 20   D 35

10. The ratio of red marbles to blue marbles in a bag is 3:4. Which of the following is a possible total number of marbles?

   A 21   C 32

   B 30   D 40

MODULE 7

Applying Ratios and Rates

11. Morganville and Newton are 24 miles apart. On a map, the two cities are 3 inches apart. What is the map scale?

_____

12. L'Shanda rode her bike 2.5 miles. Shanay rode her bike 3 miles. How many more **feet** did Shanay ride her bike than L'Shanda?

_____

13. Factory A can produce 45 machines in 20 minutes. Factory B can produce 30 machines in 15 minutes. If both factories produce machines for 2 hours, which factory will produce more machines? How many more machines will be produced?

_____

_____

14. A sailboat travels 3 miles in 1.5 hours. The table below shows the distance traveled by the boat at various times. Complete the table.

Time (h)	Distance (mi)
0	0
0.5	
1	
1.5	3
2	
2.5	
3	

15. Stefano paid $7 per hour to rent a bicycle. Jordana paid $9 per hour to rent a bicycle. If they both rent bicycles for 3 hours, how much more will Jordana pay?

_____

16. What is the absolute value of –4?

_____

17. Trayvon bought 2 gallons of milk at the supermarket. How many quarts of milk did he buy?

_____

18. The ratio of Rock songs to Dance songs on Jonathan's MP3 player is 5:6. The total number of Rock and Dance songs Jonathan has is between 100 and 120. How many Rock songs does he have?

_____

19. How do you convert gallons to liters? Explain.

_____

_____

20. Flavia plotted the distance-time graph of a car traveling 40 miles per hour. Jenya plotted the distance-time graph of a car traveling 50 miles per hour. How are the graphs similar? How are they different?

_____

_____

_____

_____

21. Brian wants to purchase a piece of fabric that is between 49 and 53 inches long. He can choose between three pieces of fabric. Choice A is $4\frac{3}{4}$ feet long. Choice B is $4\frac{1}{2}$ feet long. Choice C is $4\frac{1}{4}$ feet long. Which piece of fabric should Brian purchase?

_____

_____

Name _____ Date _____ Class_____

1. The ratio of boys to girls in Anya's class is 10 to 15. There are 20 boys. How many girls are there?

   A 25   C 40

   B 30

2.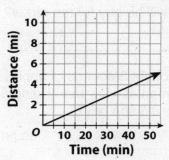

   The graph above shows Tomasso's rate while jogging. Which of the following is an ordered pair on the graph?

   A (10, 1)

   B (15, 3)

   C (30, 5)

3. Connor bought a pack of 4 notebooks for $8.20. What was the unit price?

   A $2.00

   B $2.05

   C $4.20

4. On a certain road map, the scale is 1 inch = 10 miles. Aurora Springs and Glendale are 3 inches apart on the map. What is the actual distance between Aurora Springs and Glendale?

   A 3 mi

   B 13 mi

   C 30 mi

5. The distance from the post office to the supermarket is 0.5 km. What is the distance in meters?

   A 5 m   C 500 m

   B 50 m

6. Which of the following is equal to the product of 2 and $\frac{1}{4}$?

   A $\frac{1}{2}$

   B $\frac{9}{4}$

   C 8

7. Gretchen earns $7 per hour at the local pizza shop. If she works 3 hours in an afternoon, how much money does she earn?

   A $10

   B $21

   C $73

8. Delia can buy 3 sweatshirts for a total of $30. How much would it cost if she were to buy 4 sweatshirts at the same price?

   A $40

   B $120

   C $50

9. A foot is 12 inches long. If an inch is about 2.54 centimeters long, how many centimeters are in a foot?

   A 2.54 cm

   B 14.54 cm

   C 30.48 cm

MODULE 7

Applying Ratios and Rates

10. Nandeville and Henningsburg are 10 miles apart. On a map, the two cities are 2 inches apart. How many miles does 1 inch represent on the map?

_____

11. Latisha's water bottle can hold 0.3 liters. How many milliliters can it hold?

_____

12. A factory can produce 20 machines in 1 hour. On weekdays, the factory operates for 8 hours per day. How many machines can the factory produce in 1 weekday?

_____

13. Briana took a train that travels at a speed of 30 miles per hour. The table below shows the distance the train has traveled at different times since beginning its trip.

Time (h)	Distance (mi)
0	0
1	30
2	
	90

Fill in the missing values to complete the table.

14. Paulina rode her bike 1.5 km. How many meters did she ride her bike?

_____

15. What is the absolute value of –5?

_____

16. Kevin pays $7 per hour to rent a bicycle. If he rents the bicycle for 5 hours, how much will he pay for the rental?

_____

17. Erin bought 2 pounds of apples at the supermarket. How many kilograms of apples did she buy?

_____

18. There are 10 red marbles and 20 green marbles in a bag. Colleen says the ratio of red marbles to green marbles is 10 to 20. Fritz disagrees and says the ratio is 1:2. Which student is correct? Explain your answer.

_____

_____

_____

_____

19. Dora cut a piece of string that is 33 centimeters long. What is the length of the piece of string in meters?

_____

20. What is the sum of $\frac{1}{7}$ and $\frac{2}{7}$?

_____

21. Fiona's laptop computer weighs 2.5 kilograms. What is the weight of the computer in grams?

MODULE 8

Percents

Module Quiz: B

1.

   What percent of the rectangle above is shaded?

   A 20%   C 40%

   B 30%   D 80%

2. What percent of 20 is 40?

   A 50%   C 100%

   B 75%   D 200%

3. Which of the following is a rational number that is **not** an integer?

   A −2   C 0

   B −0.5   D 4

4. Annabelle picked 65 apples at a local orchard. 40% of the apples were green apples. How many green apples did Annabelle pick?

   A 20   C 25

   B 24   D 26

5. Dalia saved $3,000 last year. She saved $600 in the month of January. What percent of the total amount of money she saved last year did Dalia save in the month of January?

   A 20%   C 40%

   B 30%   D 60%

6. Ana completed 40% of her homework assignment. Her assignment contains 30 math problems. How many problems does Ana still need to complete?

   A 12   C 16

   B 14   D 18

7.

   The percent of Tom's budget he spends on different types of expenses is shown in the circle graph above. Tom's total monthly budget is $2,500. How much does he spend on Groceries?

   A $375   C $625

   B $500   D $750

8. Which of the following is the reciprocal of $1\frac{2}{3}$?

   A $-\frac{5}{3}$ C $\frac{5}{3}$

   B $\frac{3}{5}$ D $\frac{3}{2}$

9. Javier drove 45 miles. This represents 60% of his entire trip. What is the total number of miles in Javier's trip?

   A 27 mi   C 75 mi

   B 45 mi   D 105 mi

10. Marjani's garden contains roses, daffodils, and tulips. About $\frac{3}{5}$ of the flowers are tulips. What percent of the flowers in Marjani's garden are **not** tulips?

    A 40%   C 60%

    B 50%   D 70%

MODULE 8

Percents

11. Dave found that about $\frac{8}{9}$ of the students in his class have a cell phone. What percent of the students in his class do **not** have a cell phone?

_____

12. What number is 40% of 720?

_____

13. **Lorenzo's Survey Results**

Food	Number of Students
Pizza	8
Hamburger	12
Pasta	14
Steak	6

Lorenzo recorded the favorite food of students in his class. According to the results of the survey, what percent of the students chose Hamburger?

_____

14. What percent of 50 is 10?

_____

15. Reniel saves 30% of every paycheck. His paycheck last week was $560. How much did Reniel save last week?

_____

16. Alexander correctly answered 44 out of 50 questions on his geography test. What percent of the questions did he answer incorrectly? Express your answer as a percent and as a decimal.

_____

17. The ratio of pens to pencils in Carlo's case is 4:5. He has 16 pens. How many pencils does Carlos have?

_____

18. **Cathy's Clothing**

Color	Percent
Red	10%
Yellow	20%
Blue	50%
Orange	20%

Cathy recorded the percent of her clothing that is Red, Yellow, Blue, or Orange. The results are shown in the table. If Cathy has 145 pieces of clothing, how many pieces of Yellow clothing does she own?

_____

19. Darnell's team scored 40 points at the game. Darnell scored 15% of the team's points. How many points did Darnell score?

_____

20. What number is 25 percent of 400?

_____

21. Kylie drank 35% of a 400-mL container of water. Eugenia drank 45% of a 350-mL container of water. Who drank more water? Explain how you know.

_____

_____

22. What number is 40% of 200?

_____

MODULE 8

Percents

Module Quiz: D

1. What percent of the circle below is shaded?

   A 25%

   B 50%

   C 75%

2. What is 10% of 50?

   A 5

   B 15

   C 60

3. Syeda has finished 20% of her math assignment. The assignment includes 50 problems. How many problems has Syeda completed?

   A 2

   B 10

   C 20

4. Guillermo saved 25% of his paycheck last week. His paycheck was $1,000. How much money did Guillermo save?

   A $25

   B $250

   C $500

5. Raul drove 80 miles. This represents 50% of his entire trip. What is the total number of miles in Raul's trip?

   A 40 mi

   B 130 mi

   C 160 mi

6. Tom spends 30% of his monthly budget on rent. His total monthly budget is $3,000. How much does Tom spend on rent?

   A $90

   B $300

   C $900

7. Which of the following numbers is the reciprocal of $\frac{2}{3}$?

   A $-\frac{2}{3}$

   B 1

   C $\frac{3}{2}$

8. Of the flowers in Bella's garden, $\frac{1}{5}$ are tulips. What percent of the flowers in the garden are tulips?

   A 20%

   B 30%

   C 50%

9. What percent of the square below is shaded?

   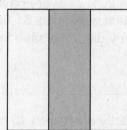

   A $33\frac{1}{3}$%

   B 50%

   C $66\frac{2}{3}$%

MODULE 8

Percents

10. Maria found that about $\frac{3}{4}$ of the students in her class take the bus to school. What percent of the students in her class take the bus to school?

_____

11. What number is 30% of 200?

_____

12. Larissa asked 40 students to name their favorite food. 10 students said their favorite food was pizza. What percent of the students Larissa surveyed said their favorite food was pizza?

_____

13. In Mr. Diaz's class, 20% of the students received a grade of "A" on their report cards. There are 25 students in Mr. Diaz's class. How many students received a grade of "A" on their report cards?

_____

14. Mike saves 20% of every paycheck. His paycheck last week was $1,500. How much money did Mike save from that paycheck?

_____

15. Theo correctly answered 40 out of 50 questions on his spelling quiz. What percent of the questions did Theo answer correctly? Express your answer as a percent and as a decimal.

_____

16. What is the decimal equivalent of 40%?

_____

17. Edison has a bag of 300 marbles. 25% of the marbles are blue. How many marbles in the bag are blue?

_____

18. In Alessandro's class, 5 students live in Oakdale. There are 20 students in Alessandro's class. What percent of the students live in Oakdale?

_____

19. Adam has saved 35% of the $400 he needs to save to buy a bike. How much money has Adam saved so far?

_____

20. Luisa hiked 7 miles of a 21-mile trail. What percent of the trail did she hike?

_____

21. What number is 15% of 50?

_____

22. Lindsay ate $\frac{7}{8}$ of an apple. What percent of the apple did he eat?

_____

23. Barak spent $20 at the arcade. This represents 10% of the money he earned by working at the pizza parlor last week. How much money did Barak earn at the pizza parlor last week?

_____

Name _____ Date _____ Class _____

Generating Equivalent Numerical Expressions
Module Quiz: B

1. Which expression shows the prime factorization of 48?

   A $2^4 \times 3$ C 4×12

   B $2^3 \times 3^2$ D 24^2

2. A yearbook page will show 20 photos displayed in rows. Each row must contain the same number of photos. How many different ways can the photos be arranged?

   A 3 ways   C 5 ways

   B 4 ways   D 6 ways

3. Which power does **not** have a value of 64?

   A 2^6 C 8^2

   B 4^3 D 32^2

4. Which powers are listed in order from least value to greatest value?

   A $\left(\dfrac{1}{4}\right)^0, 8.8^1, (-5)^2, -1^3$

   B $(-5)^2, -1^3, \left(\dfrac{1}{4}\right)^0, 8.8^1$

   C $-1^3, \left(\dfrac{1}{4}\right)^0, 8.8^1, (-5)^2$

   D $(-5)^2, 8.8^1, \left(\dfrac{1}{4}\right)^0, -1^3$

5. Which step should be performed first when simplifying $18 - 3 + 11 \times 2 + 5$?

   A $-3 + 11$ C $18 - 3$

   B $2 + 5$ D 11×2

6. Derek uses a $50 gift card to purchase 3 books for $12 each and a calendar for $9. Which expression represents the amount of money left on the gift card?

   A $50 - 12^3 - 9$

   B $50 - 3(12 + 9)$

   C $3 \times 12 + 9$

   D $50 - 3 \times 12 - 9$

7. Which expression is equivalent to $7.2 \times 7.2 \times 7.2$?

   A $3(7.2)$ C 7.3^2

   B 7.2^3 D $7^3 \times 2^3$

8. A recipe for pancake batter uses 2 cups of flour and makes 10 small pancakes. How many cups of flour are needed to make batter for 25 small pancakes?

   A 3 cups   C 5 cups

   B 4 cups   D 6 cups

9. What is the value of the expression

   $2 \times \dfrac{3^3 + 1}{7} + 5 \times 8$?

   A 48   C 104

   B 98   D 144

10. Prisha buys 2.5 pounds of tomatoes that cost $0.54 per pound. How much does Prisha pay for the tomatoes?

    A $1.08   C $3.04

    B $1.35   D $4.63

11. What is the sum of the prime factors of 105, not including 1?

    A 6   C 15

    B 12   D 26

12. A phone tree is used to let committee members know a meeting is cancelled. The committee chair calls 5 people. Those 5 people each call 5 people, and those additional people each call 5 people. How many members have been called?

    A 25   C 155

    B 125   D 625

13. Which expression has a value of 39?

    A $24 \times 2 - 8 + 4^2 \div 8 - 6$

    C $24 \times 2 - 8 + 4^2 \div (8 - 6)$

    B $24 \times (2 + 8) + 4^2 \div 8 - 6$

    D $24 \times 2 - (8 + 4^2) \div 8 - 6$

MODULE 9

Generating Equivalent Numerical Expressions

14. Which power has a greater value?

    $(-3)^2$ or -2^3

    _____

15. Wooden blocks are stacked to form a cube 3 blocks wide, 3 blocks long, and 3 blocks high. How many blocks are used?

    _____

16. Three different rectangles have an area of 28 square units. What are the possible whole-number dimensions of the rectangles?

    _____

    _____

17. Use parentheses to rewrite the expression below so that it has a value of 33.

    $15 \div 3 + 2 \times 11$

    _____

18. Write $5.3 \times 5.3 \times 5.3 \times 5.3$ as a power.

    _____

19. Adrian purchases 6 tubes of paint and 3 paintbrushes at a craft store. Each tube of paint costs $2.50 and each paintbrush costs $0.50. He has a coupon for $2.00 off his purchase. How much does he pay?

    _____

20. Complete the following statement.

    As the value of n in the expression $\left(\dfrac{1}{4}\right)^n$ increases, the value of the expression

    _____

21. What is the prime factorization of 88?

    _____

22. A teacher tells 6 students the title of the next school play. Those 6 students each tell the title to 6 students. Then those additional students each tell the title to 6 students. How many students have been told the title of the next play?

    _____

23. Write 16 as a power two different ways.

    _____

24. A suit costs $95. Barry has a discount coupon for 10% off and the city has a 4.5% sales tax. What is the final cost of the suit?

    _____

25. What is the value of the expression below?

    $$36 \div \dfrac{2^5}{8} + 7 \times (3 + 11)$$

    _____

26. A website developer is designing a website for a clothing company. Clothing items will be arranged on a web page in a rectangular display showing 32 clothing items, with the same number of items in each row. How many ways can the display be arranged?

    _____

MODULE 9 Generating Equivalent Numerical Expressions
Module Quiz: D

1. Which expression represents "15 to the sixth power"?

   A 15^6

   B $6(15)$

   C 6^{15}

2. A restaurant bill for $47.50 is divided equally among 5 people. How much does each person pay?

   A $7.50

   B $8.50

   C $9.50

3. Which expression shows the prime factorization of 66?

   A $3^2 \times 11$

   B $2 \times 3 \times 11$

   C 6×11

4. What is the value of the expression $\dfrac{35}{2^3 - 1}$?

   A 5

   B 7

   C 12

5. The table shows the number of words a person types for different amounts of time. What is the rate of words typed per minute?

Minutes	3	5	9
Words Typed	105	175	315

   A 29 words per minute

   B 35 words per minute

   C 70 words per minute

6. Which power has a value of 27?

   A 3^2

   B 3^3

   C 3^9

7. A tutor invited 2 students to a study group. Those 2 students each invited 2 students to the study group. Then those additional students each invited 2 students to the study group. How many total students are invited to the study group?

   A 6

   B 8

   C 16

8. Which number is a prime factor of 210?

   A 7

   B 9

   C 11

9. Which power has a base of 2 and an exponent of 6?

   A 2^6

   B 6^2

   C 12^6

10. A sporting goods store wants to display 64 sneakers in rows. Each row must contain the same number of sneakers. Which of the arrangements is **not** a possible arrangement?

    A 4 rows of 16 sneakers

    B 8 rows of 8 sneakers

    C 3 rows of 21 sneakers

11. Which expression is equivalent to $9 \times 9 \times 9 \times 9$?

    A $4(9)$

    B 4^9

    C 9^4

12. Which step should be performed first when simplifying $25 - (14 - 8) + 3 \times 2$?

    A 3×2

    B $25 - 14$

    C $14 - 8$

MODULE 9

Generating Equivalent Numerical Expressions

13. What is the prime factorization of 42?

_____

14. What is the value of any nonzero number raised to the power of 0?

_____

15. What is the value of the expression below?

$$9 + 4^2 \div 2$$

_____

16. Which operation should be performed first when simplifying the expression below?

$$4 + 12 - 5 \times 7$$

_____

17. On Monday, Ethan sends an email to 3 friends. The next day, each of the friends forwards the email to 3 friends, and so on, as shown in the table. How many people received the email by Thursday?

Day	People Who Received Email
Monday	3
Tuesday	3×3
Wednesday	$3 \times 3 \times 3$

_____

18. Paul has a given number of square floor tiles to be arranged so that each row has the same number of tiles. Two possible arrangements are listed below.

   • 8 rows of 12 tiles

   • 16 rows of 6 tiles

How many tiles does Paul have?

_____

19. What is the base of the power 6^7?

_____

20. Anna is designing a rectangular garden that has an area of 182 square feet, and the length is longer than the width. The table lists the possible whole-number dimensions for the garden. Which dimensions are missing?

Length (ft)	182	26	14	
Width (ft)	1	7	13	

Length: _____

Width: _____

21. What is the value of the expression below?

$$18 - 3(1 + 5)$$

_____

22. Rewrite $(-17) \times (-17) \times (-17)$ as a power.

_____

23. At an online bookstore, Alicia downloads 3 books for $9 each and 2 magazines for $4 each. Write an expression that represents the total amount of money she spends.

_____

24. Which power has a greater value?

$$1^6 \text{ or } 5^2$$

_____

25. Wooden blocks are stacked to form a cube 4 blocks wide, 4 blocks long, and 4 blocks high. Write the number of blocks used as a power.

_____

MODULE 10

Generating Equivalent Algebraic Expressions
Module Quiz: B

1. What do two equivalent expressions **always** have in common?

   A the same value

   B the same variables

   C the same constants

   D Both have an equal sign.

2. What **must** be included in an algebraic expression?

   A an equals sign

   B at least one variable

   C one or more numbers

   D an operation such as addition

3. Which algebraic expression could represent the phrase below?

   a number n decreased by 5

   A $5 - n$

   B $n - 5$

   C $\dfrac{n}{5}$

   D $n - \dfrac{1}{5}$

4. Which phrase does **not** have the same meaning as $\dfrac{-3}{w}$?

   A negative 3 times a number w

   B negative 3 divided by a number w

   C a number w divided into negative 3

   D the quotient of negative 3 and a number w

5. What is the value of the expression $h - 20$ when $h = 60$?

   A 30

   B 40

   C 80

   D 120

6. Which value for the variable w makes the value of this expression 10?

   $$\dfrac{50}{w}$$

   A $w = \dfrac{1}{5}$ C $w = 60$

   B $w = 5$ D $w = 500$

7. Find the value of the expression below for $x = 10$.

   $$x^2 - 2(x + 5)$$

   A 10   C 85

   B 70   D 90

8. Which property justifies the fact that $5(x - 2)$ is equivalent to $5x - 10$?

   A commutative

   B associative

   C distributive

   D identity

9. Which of the following is equivalent to the expression below?

   $$4x + 3(2x - 1) - 4x$$

   A $6x - 3$ C $14x - 3$

   B $6x + 3$ D $14x + 3$

10. What are the like terms in the expression below?

    $$3x + 8 + 3y + 8x$$

    A 8 and $8x$ C $3x$ and $8x$

    B $3x$ and $3y$ D $3x$, $3y$, and $8x$

11. At 6 P.M. the temperature was –2°F. By midnight, the temperature had dropped 5 degrees. What was the temperature at midnight?

    A –7°F   C 3°F

    B –3°F   D 7°F

MODULE 10 **Generating Equivalent Algebraic Expressions**

12. Identify the variable and the constant in the expression below.

$$18 + t$$

variable: _____

constant: _____

13. Write an algebraic expression for the phrase below. Use k for the variable.

the product of a number and six

_____

14. Translate the algebraic expression below into words.

$$g - 12$$

_____

15. Change the question marks to make a bar model that represents $6 + x$.

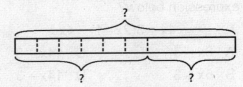

16. Anna, Vickie, and Luanna are sisters. Anna is 3 years older than Vickie, and Luanna is 2 years younger than Vickie. Use v for Vickie's age. Write expressions to show the ages of the other two sisters.

Anna's age: _____

Luanna's age: _____

17. Evaluate the expression below for $m = 350$.

$$3.5m$$

_____

18. Chang is 6 inches taller than Nancy. Use n for Nancy's height. Write an expression for Chang's height.

_____

Evaluate the expression for $n = 60$. What does your answer represent?

_____

_____

19. A student is evaluating the expression below for $n = 3.7$.

$$12.8 + 6(n - 0.5)$$

In what order should the student do the steps?

Step 1: Substitute _____ for n.

Step 2: _____

Step 3: _____

Step 4: _____

20. Use the distributive property to simplify the expression below.

$$5x(x - 4)$$

_____

21. Combine like terms to simplify the expression below.

$$5y - 8x - y + 12x$$

_____

22. There are 40 boys in a computer club. The ratio of girls to boys is 2 to 5. How many girls are in the club?

_____

MODULE 10

Generating Equivalent Algebraic Expressions
Module Quiz: D

1. Which expression is equivalent to 8 − 3?

   A 1×5

   B $3 - 8$

   C $8 - 5$

2. Which of these is an algebraic expression?

   A $3 - 1.4$

   B $1.4 - 3$

   C $1.4 - n$

3. Which expression shows 10 less than a number n?

   A $n + 10$

   B $n - 10$

   C $10 - n$

4. Which phrase has the same meaning as the expression below?

   $$\frac{3}{w}$$

   A 3 minus w

   B 3 divided by w

   C w divided by 3

5. Find the value of the expression below for $h = 6$.

   $$h - 2$$

   A 4

   B 8

   C 12

6. When does the expression below equal 10?

   $$n + 3$$

   A when $n = 7$

   B when $n = 10$

   C when $n = 13$

7. Find the value of the expression below for $x = 3$.

   $$x^2 + 5$$

   A 8

   B 11

   C 14

8. Which shows the distributive property?

   A $5x + 2 = 2 + 5x$

   B $5(x + 2) = 5x + 10$

   C $5(x + 2) = 5(2 + x)$

9. Choose the expression that is equivalent to the expression below.

   $$3(2x - 1)$$

   A $6x - 3$

   B $6x - 1$

   C $32x - 1$

10. What are the like terms in the expression below?

    $$3x + 8 + 8x$$

    A 8 and $3x$

    B $8x$ and 8

    C $3x$ and $8x$

11. Use the temperature data shown in the table below.

Time	Temperature
6 P.M.	−2°F
midnight	−7°F

    How did the temperature change from 6 P.M. to midnight?

    A decrease of 5 degrees

    B increase of 5 degrees

    C increase of 9 degrees

Generating Equivalent Algebraic Expressions

12. Identify the variable and the constant in the expression below.

    $n + 3$

    variable: _____

    constant: _____

13. Complete the expression for the phrase below.

    a number h multiplied by six

    _____ × _____

14. Fill in the blanks to rewrite the expression below in words.

    $g - 12$

    a number _____ decreased by _____

15. The bar model below is one way to show an algebraic expression.

    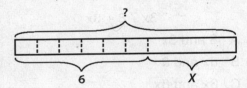

    What expression does the model show?

    _____

16. Anna is 3 years older than Vickie. Luanna is 2 years younger than Vickie. Complete the two expressions below to show the ages. The variable v stands for Vickie's age.

    Anna's age: $v +$ _____

    Luanna's age: $v -$ _____

17. Use 10 for m. Then find the value of the expression $3.5m$.

    _____

18. Chang is 6 inches taller than Nancy. Use n for Nancy's height. Complete the expression below.

    Chang's height: $n +$ _____

    Evaluate the expression for $n = 60$.

    $n + 6 =$ _____ + _____ = _____ in.

    What does this tell you about Chang's height?

    _____

    _____

19. A student is evaluating the expression below for $n = 3.7$.

    $$12.8 + 6(n - 0.5)$$

    The student substitutes 3.7 for n. Write the new expression.

    _____

    What step should the student do next?

    _____

20. Use the distributive property. Simplify the expression below.

    $5(x - 2) =$ _____ − _____

21. Combine like terms.

    $5y - 8 - y =$ _____ − _____

22. There are 40 girls in a computer club. The ratio of girls to boys is 2 to 5. How many boys are in the club? Complete this table to find out.

Girls	2	10	20	40
Boys	5	25	50	

    There are _____ boys in the club.

MODULE 11

Equations and Relationships
Module Quiz: B

1. For which equation is $x = 5$ a solution?

   A $2 + x = 3$ C $\dfrac{x}{2} = 10$

   B $3x = 15$ D $x - 7 = 12$

2. Which of the following is an equation?

   A $\dfrac{y}{9} - 3$ C $\dfrac{y}{9} = 3$

   B $9 - 2$ D $7 + y$

3. Which of the equations below shows the relationship in the table?

x	15	5	3	1
y	1	3	5	15

   A $y = 15x$ C $y = x + 2$

   B $y = x - 14$ D $y = \dfrac{15}{x}$

4. Sahil got 28 questions right on the math test. Angelina got 7 more wrong answers than Sahil. There were 40 questions on the test. How many answers did Angelina get right on the math test? Which equation represents this situation?

   A $a + 7 = 12$ C $7 + 12 = a$

   B $a + 7 = 28$ D $7 = 40 - a$

5. Which is the solution to the equation below?

   $$9 = n + 3$$

   A 3   C 12

   B 6   D 27

6. Which equation has a solution of 12?

   A $x - 6 = 6$ C $4 = x - 16$

   B $x + 6 = 6$ D $4 = 8 + x$

7. Which is the solution to the equation below?

   $$-3 = t - 12$$

   A −9   C 9

   B 4   D 15

8. Gavin wants to buy a skateboard that sells for $49.99. An advertisement says that next week that skateboard will be on sale for $42.50. How much will Gavin save if he waits until next week to buy the skateboard?

   A $3.51   C $17.49

   B $7.49   D $92.49

9. Which equation has a solution of 8?

   A $\dfrac{r}{2} = 16$ C $8 = \dfrac{r}{8}$

   B $4r = 16$ D $-2r = -16$

10. Which is the solution to the equation below?

    $$32 = \dfrac{q}{2}$$

    A 16   C 46

    B 30   D 64

11. Luis walked for 16 minutes. Natalie walked for w minutes. Luis walked twice as long as Natalie. How long did Natalie walk?

    A 4 minutes   C 14 minutes

    B 8 minutes   D 32 minutes

12. Jesse uses 19 beads to decorate each picture frame. In all, Jesse used 133 beads. How many picture frames did Jesse make?

    A 2,527 frames   C 114 frames

    B 152 frames   D 7 frames

13. Which number line below represents the inequality $x \le -4$?

    A

    B

    C

    D

Equations and Relationships

14. Decide whether $n = 9$ is a solution to the equation $2 + n = 7$. Write *yes* or *no*.

_____

15. The weight of a goat increased by 12 pounds is 38 pounds. Write an equation to represent the situation.

_____

16. Twelve inches is cut from a board. The remaining board is 18 inches long. Write an equation to represent the situation.

_____

17. Decide whether $n = 3.5$ is a solution to the equation $2n = 70$. Write *yes* or *no*.

_____

18. Solve the equation below.
$$m - 3 = 13.8.$$

_____

19. Solve the equation below.
$$2.3 = p + 0.6$$

_____

20. Denise scored 3 fewer points than Carter scored. Denise scored 18 points. How many points did Carter score?

Write an equation to represent the situation. Then solve the equation to answer the problem.

_____

_____

21. The sales tax on a $250 computer is $17.50. Find the sales tax rate.

_____

22. Last year, Mark was 46 inches tall. This year, Mark's height is 3 inches less than Peter's height. Peter is 51 inches tall. How tall is Mark?

Write an equation to represent the situation. Then solve the equation to answer the problem.

_____

_____

23. Graph the inequality $x \le 8$.

_____

24. Solve the equation below.
$$\frac{d}{1.2} = 6$$

_____

25. There are 144 pencils in a box. If each member of the class gets 8 pencils, there will be no pencils left over. How many members of the class are there?

Write an equation to represent the situation. Then solve the equation to answer the problem.

_____

_____

26. Jeff found 3 times as many seashells as his sister. Jeff found 39 seashells. How many seashells did his sister find?

Write an equation to represent the situation. Then solve the equation to answer the problem.

_____

_____

MODULE 11

Equations and Relationships

Module Quiz: D

1. For which of the equations below is $x = 2$ a solution?

   A $2 + x = 2$

   B $x - 7 = 5$

   C $3x = 6$

2. Which of the following is an equation?

   A $\dfrac{y}{9} - 3$

   B $\dfrac{y}{9} = 3$

   C $9 - 3$

3. On the math test, Beth got 7 fewer correct answers than Bill. Bill got 28 questions right. How many answers did Beth get right on the math test? Which of the equations below represents this situation?

   A $b + 7 = 28$

   B $7 + 28 = b$

   C $b - 7 = 28$

4. Which is the solution to the equation below?

   $$9 = n + 3$$

   A 3

   B 6

   C 12

5. Sean wants to buy a DVD that sells for $12. An advertisement says that next week that DVD will be on sale for $9. How much money will Gavin save if he waits until next week to buy the DVD?

   A $3

   B $9

   C $21

6. Which of the equations below has a solution of 12?

   A $x - 6 = 6$

   B $4 = x - 16$

   C $x + 6 = 6$

7. Which of the following number lines represents the inequality below?

   $$x < 4$$

   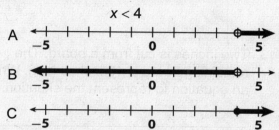

8. Which of the following is the solution to the equation below?

   $$15 = \dfrac{q}{3}$$

   A 3

   B 5

   C 45

9. Jesse uses 10 beads to decorate each picture frame. In all, Jesse used 40 beads. How many picture frames did Jesse make?

   A 4 frames

   B 50 frames

   C 400 frames

10. The outdoor temperature was 0° at midnight. The temperature went down 3° each hour for the next 4 hours. What was the temperature at 4 A.M.?

    A 7°

    B −3°

    C −12°

Equations and Relationships

11. Decide whether $s = 9$ is a solution to the equation $2 + s = 7$. Write *yes* or *no*.

_____

12. The weight of a package increases by 2 pounds. The new weight of the package is 8 pounds. Write an equation to represent the situation.

_____

13. Two inches is cut from a board. The remaining board is 10 inches long. Write an equation to represent the situation.

_____

14. Decide whether $n = 3$ is a solution to the equation $2n = 6$. Write *yes* or *no*.

_____

15. Solve the equation below.
$$m - 3 = 12$$

_____

16. Solve the equation below.
$$15 = p + 6$$

_____

17. Denise scored 3 fewer points than Carter scored. Denise scored 8 points. How many points did Carter score?

Write an equation to represent the situation. Then solve the equation to answer the question.

_____

_____

18. The sales tax on a $100 camera is $8.00. Find the sales tax rate.

_____

19. Sue's height is 3 inches less than Ed's height. Ed is 56 inches tall. How tall is Sue?

Write an equation to represent the situation. Then solve the equation to answer the question.

_____

20. Graph the inequality $x \leq 2$.

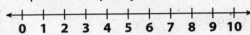

21. Solve the equation below.
$$\frac{d}{2} = 6$$

_____

22. There are 24 pencils in a box. Each student in a class gets 6 pencils. There are no pencils left over. How many students are in the class?

Write an equation to represent the situation. Then solve the equation to answer the question.

_____

_____

23. Hector found twice as many seashells as his sister. Hector found 20 seashells. How many seashells did his sister find?

Write an equation to represent the situation. Then solve the equation to answer the question.

_____

_____

| MODULE 12 | **Relationships in Two Variables** |

Module Quiz: B

Use the grid for 1–3.

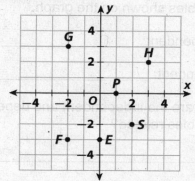

1. Which point is located at (−2, 3)?

   A point S   C point G

   B point F   D point H

2. What are the coordinates of point S?

   A (−2, 2)   C (2, 0)

   B (2, −2)   D (2, 2)

3. Which points are on the axes?

   A E and S

   B E and F

   C P and H

   D P and E

4. The table shows a bicycle rider moving at a constant rate of speed.

Time, x (h)	1	2	3
Distance, y (mi)	12	24	36

   What is the dependent variable in this situation?

   A rate

   B time

   C speed

   D distance

5. Use the ordered pairs shown in the table below.

x	20	30	40	50
y	30	45	60	75

   Which equation represents the data in the table?

   A $x = 1.5y$ C $y = 1.5x$

   B $x = \frac{1}{3}y$ D $y = \frac{2}{3}x$

6. Use the relationship shown on this graph.

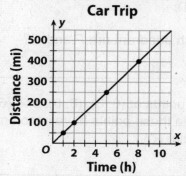

   Which equation shows the distance y in terms of the number of hours x?

   A $y = 2x$ C $y = x + 98$

   B $y = 50x$ D $y = 400 + 8x$

7. How many centimeters are there in 5 meters?

   A 0.5   C 500

   B 50   D 5,000

8. What is the solution to the inequality below?

$$-8m \geq 40$$

   A $m \geq 5$ C $m \leq -5$

   B $m \leq 32$ D $m \leq 5$

MODULE 12

Relationships in Two Variables

Use the grid for 9–11.

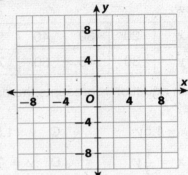

9. Graph P(–6, –4), Q(–4, –6), and R(6, –4).

10. In which quadrant are P and Q?

_____

11. Graph points at (6, 6), (6, 0), and (6, 2). What do these points have in common with point R?

_____

Use the graph for 12–14.

12. What quantities are shown on the graph?

_____

13. Identity the independent and dependent variables shown on the graph.

independent: _____

dependent: _____

14. How are the independent and dependent variables related?

_____

Use the table for 15–17.

Lakeside Canoe Rentals

Hours, x	2	5	7
Charge, y ($)	20	50	70

15. Write an equation that expresses y in terms of x.

_____

16. How much does it cost to rent a canoe for 3.5 hours?

_____

17. Graph the relationship shown in the table on the grid below.

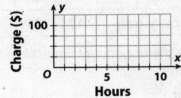

18. Complete the sentence below.

24 is _____ % of 60.

Name _____ Date _____ Class_____

Relationships in Two Variables
Module Quiz: D

Use the grid for 1–3.

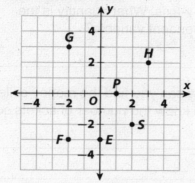

1. Which point has the ordered pair (2, –2)?

   A point *H*

   B point *P*

   C point *S*

2. Which ordered pair shows the location of point *H*?

   A (2, 2)

   B (3, 0)

   C (3, 2)

3. Points *G* and *F* have the same *x*-coordinate. What is it?

   A –4

   B –2

   C 3

4. The table below shows the number of miles a bicycle rider goes in 1, 2, and 3 hours.

Time, *x* (h)	1	2	3
Distance, *y* (mi)	12	24	36

   What are the two variables in the situation shown by the table?

   A speed and time

   B time and distance

   C distance and speed

5. Use the ordered pairs in the table below.

x	20	30	40	50
y	40	60	80	100

   Which equation shows how to get *y* if you are given *x*?

   A $x = 2y$

   B $y = 2x$

   C $y = \frac{1}{2}x$

6. This graph shows a car moving at a constant speed. For example, in 8 hours the car travels 400 miles.

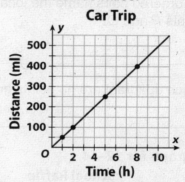

   Car Trip

   Which equation shows the line on the graph?

   A $y = 2x$

   B $y = 50x$

   C $y = 400x$

7. How many centimeters are there in 2 meters?

   A 2   B 20   C 200

8. What is the solution to this inequality?

   $-m > 5$

   A $m < -5$

   B $m > -5$

   C $m > 5$

MODULE 12

Relationships in Two Variables

Use the grid for 9–11.

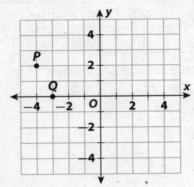

9. Graph point A at (−2, 4).
   Graph point B at (2, −3).

10. What ordered pairs name the locations of points P and Q?

_____

11. In which quadrant are no points graphed?

_____

Use the graph for 12–14.

12. The independent variable is shown on the x-axis. What quantity is the independent variable?

_____

13. The dependent variable is shown on the y-axis. What quantity is the dependent variable?

_____

14. How can you find the money collected if you know the number of tickets sold?

_____

_____

Use the table for 15–17.

Lakeside Canoe Rentals

Hours, x	0	5	10
Charge, y ($)	0	50	100

15. The equation $y = 10x$ shows how the cost relates to the number of hours. How much does it cost to rent a canoe for 8 hours?

_____

16. If you have $60, for how many hours can you rent a canoe?

_____

17. Graph the three ordered pairs from the table. Connect them with a line.

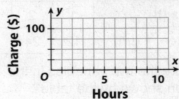

18. Complete this sentence

   10 is _____ % of 50.

MODULE 13

Area and Polygons

Module Quiz: B

1. A parallelogram has a base of 12 centimeters and a height of 8 centimeters. What is the area of the parallelogram?

   A 96 cm²   C 36 cm²

   B 48 cm²   D 192 cm²

2. What is the area of the trapezoid below?

   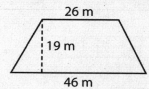

   A 342 m²   C 684 m²

   B 598 m²   D 1,368 m²

3. A right triangle has a height of 13 centimeters and a base of 16.4 centimeters. What is the area of the triangle?

   A 106.6 cm²   C 1,013.2 cm²

   B 453.3 cm²   D 3,626.4 cm²

4. What is the area of the rhombus shown below?

   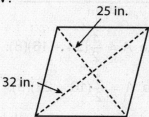

   A 57 in²   C 400 in²

   B 386 in²   D 800 in²

5. What is the area of polygon *ABCDE*?

   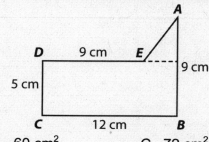

   A 60 cm²   C 72 cm²

   B 66 cm²   D 75 cm²

6. A triangle has an area of 230.86 square inches. The height of the triangle is 23.8 inches. What is the length of the base of the triangle?

   A 23.8 in.

   B 10.1 in.

   C 19.4 in.

   D 2,747.234 in.

7. Which equation is shown by the information in the table?

x	2	4	6	8	10
y	5	9	13	17	21

   A $y = 2x + 1$

   B $y = x + 2$

   C $y = 3x - 1$

   D $y = 2x + 2$

8. A parking lot in the shape of a trapezoid has an area of 12,052.1 square meters. The length of one base is 82.4 meters, and the length of the other base is 108.6 meters. What is the width of the parking lot?

   A 126.2 m   C 252.4 m

   B 63.1 m   D 189.3 m

9. A point is located in Quadrant IV of the coordinate plane. Which of the following could be the ordered pair of this point?

   A (3, 5)   C (−3, −5)

   B (3, −5)   D (−3, 5)

10. A scalene triangle has an area of 20.335 square centimeters. The height of the triangle is 8.3 centimeters. What is the length of its base?

    A 2.45 cm   C 4.9 cm

    B 2.5 cm   D 9.8 cm

MODULE 13 **Area and Polygons**

11. Find the area of the unfolded box bottom. Show your work.

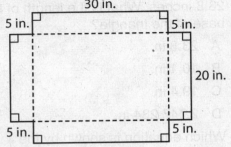

30 in.

5 in.   5 in.

20 in.

5 in.   5 in.

12. You are given a formula and told that it is a formula for the area of a quadrilateral. Can you tell whether it is the formula for the area of a rectangle, parallelogram, trapezoid, or rhombus? Explain your reasoning.

_____

_____

_____

_____

13. Find the area of the unshaded portion of this figure. The figures shown below are a trapezoid and a rhombus.

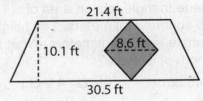

21.4 ft

10.1 ft   8.6 ft

30.5 ft

_____

_____

14. Write the equation shown by the table and graph the equation on the coordinate plane below.

x	2	3	4	5	6
y	5	6	7	8	9

_____

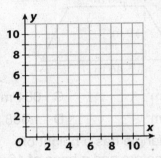

15. Scott and Tara were asked to find the area of this trapezoid:

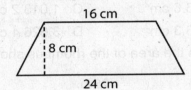

16 cm

8 cm

24 cm

Scott wrote $A = \frac{1}{2}(24 + 16)(8)$.

Tara wrote $A = \frac{1}{2}(16 + 24)(8)$.

Which student is correct? Explain.

_____

_____

_____

Name _____ Date _____ Class_____

MODULE 13

Area and Polygons

Module Quiz: D

1. What is the area of the parallelogram below? Use the formula $A = bh$.

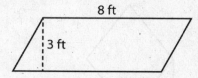

8 ft

3 ft

   A   24 ft^2

   B   11.5 ft^2

   C   12 ft^2

2. What is the area of the trapezoid below? Use the formula $A = \frac{1}{2}(b_1 + b_2)h$.

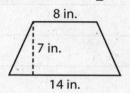

8 in.

7 in.

14 in.

   A   29 in^2

   B   77 in^2

   C   154 in^2

3. What is the unknown angle measure in the triangle below?

60°

60°

   A   75°   C   120°

   B   60°

4. The point $(-3, -2)$ is located in which quadrant of the coordinate plane?

   A   Quadrant III

   B   Quadrant IV

   C   Quadrant I

Use the figure for 5 and 6.

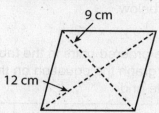

9 cm

12 cm

5. Which of the following equations could be used to find the area of the rhombus?

   A $A = \frac{1}{2}(9 + 12)$

   B $A = \frac{1}{2}(9)(12)$

   C $A = (9)(12)$

6. What is the area of the rhombus?

   A   54 cm^2

   B   21 cm^2

   C   108 cm^2

7. What is the area of the figure shown below?

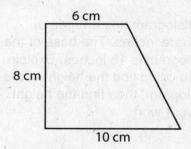

6 cm

8 cm

10 cm

   A   48 cm^2

   B   64 cm^2

   C   80 cm^2

8. A triangle has a base of 15 inches and a height of 11 inches. What is the area of the triangle? Use the formula $A = \frac{1}{2}bh$.

   A   165 in^2

   B   160 in^2

   C   82.5 in^2

Area and Polygons

9. Complete the table of values for the equation below.

$$y = x + 2$$

Name the ordered pairs in the table, and then graph the equation on the coordinate grid.

x	1	2	3	4	5
y	3				

Ordered pairs:

(1, 3), _____, _____,

_____, _____

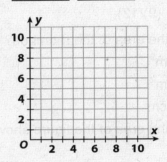

10. A parallelogram has an area of 108 square inches. The base of the parallelogram is 18 inches. Explain how you could find the height of the parallelogram, then find the height. Show your work.

_____

_____

_____

_____

_____

11. Explain how you could find the area of the figure below.

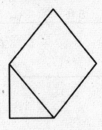

_____

_____

_____

_____

_____

_____

12. What is the area of the figure shown below? Explain your reasoning.

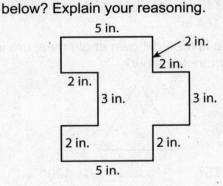

_____

_____

_____

MODULE 14

Distance and Area in the Coordinate Plane
Module Quiz: B

1. Which point on the coordinate plane is a reflection of point *A* across the *y*-axis?

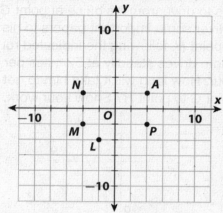

   A point *L*   C point *N*

   B point *M*   D point *P*

2. Which of the following is a reflection of (2, 4) across the *x*-axis?

   A (2, −4)   C (−2, 4)

   B (−2, −4)   D (4, 2)

3. What is the area of the figure below?

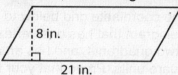

8 in.

21 in.

   A 84 in^2 C 168 in^2

   B 160 in^2 D 336 in^2

4. On a coordinate plane, what is the distance between the point at (4, 7) and the point at (−4, 7)?

   A 8 units   C 12 units

   B 11 units   D 14 units

5. Which of the following completes the table below?

Point	Reflected across *y*-axis	Reflected across *x*-axis
(2, 7)	(−2, 7)	

   A (2, 7)   C (2, −7)

   B (−2, 7)   D (−2, −7)

6. On a coordinate plane, what is the distance between the point at (7, 6) and the point at (7, −9)?

   A 2 units   C 14 units

   B 13 units   D 15 units

7. A polygon plotted on the coordinate plane has 6 vertices. What is the shape of the polygon?

   A quadrilateral   C octagon

   B hexagon   D pentagon

8. What is the perimeter of the figure on the coordinate plane below?

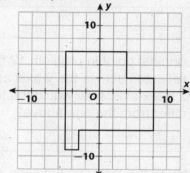

   A 53 units   C 55 units

   B 54 units   D 56 units

9. What is the area of the figure on the coordinate plane below?

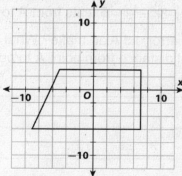

   A 144 units^2 C 126 units^2

   B 128 units^2 D 252 units

10. Which point is a reflection of (−4, −3) across the *y*-axis?

   A (−3, −4)   C (3, 4)

   B (4, −3)   D (4, 3)

MODULE 14 Distance and Area in the Coordinate Plane

11. A point that is 7 units from the *y*-axis is reflected across the *y*-axis. What is the distance of this new point from the *y*-axis? Explain how you know.

_____

_____

12. A point at (−5, 7) is reflected across the *x*-axis. The new point is then reflected across the *y*-axis. What ordered pair names the third point? Explain.

_____

_____

13. If the original point in problem 12 first had been reflected across the *y*-axis and then across the *x*-axis, how would the third point differ from the one above?

_____

14. Alan found the distance between point *A*(−8, −4) and point *B*(3, −4). His work is shown below.

    −8 to the *y*-axis = 8 units

    3 to the *y*-axis = 3 units

    |−8| − |3| = 5 units from *A* to *B*

    What error did Alan make? What is the actual distance from point *A* to point *B*?

_____

_____

15. Tia plotted a point *X* in Quadrant III. After she reflected the point across an axis, the reflected point was in Quadrant IV. Give a possible ordered pair for point *X* and its reflection. Describe how the point was reflected.

_____

16. A map is drawn on the coordinate plane. Each unit represents 12.5 miles. Thom has to drive from his office at point *G* to deliver some important papers to his boss at point *H*, following the indicated route. Thom drives steadily at 52 miles per hour. How long will it take him to get from point *G* to point *H*? Show your work.

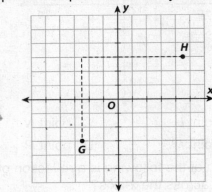

_____

_____

17. Use the coordinate grid below to draw a parallelogram that has one vertex in at least two quadrants, and has an area of 32 square units. Prove that your figure has the correct area using distance and area calculations.

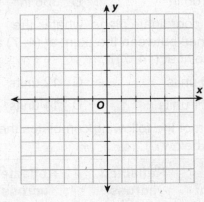

_____

_____

MODULE 14 **Distance and Area in the Coordinate Plane**

Module Quiz: D

1. Which point is the same distance from the y-axis as Point N?

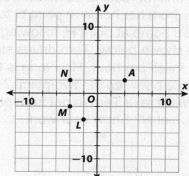

   A point L   C point A

   B point M

2. Which point is a reflection of (2, 5) across the x-axis?

   A (2, −5)   C (−2, −5)

   B (−2, 5)

3. What is the area of the triangle below?

Use $A = \dfrac{1}{2}bh$.

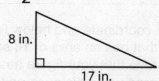

   A 35 in²   C 136 in²

   B 68 in²

4. On a coordinate plane, what is the distance between the point at (5, 3) and the point at (5, 9)? (Hint: Look at the y-coordinates.)

   A 14 units   C 6 units

   B 11 units

5. Which ordered pair completes the table below?

Point	Reflected across y-axis	Reflected across x-axis
(1, 5)		(1, −5)

   A (1, −5)   C (−1, 5)

   B (−1, −5)

6. On a coordinate plane, what is the distance between the point at (1, 9) and the point at (4, 9)? (Hint: Look at the x-coordinates.)

   A 3 units   C 0 units

   B 2 units

7. A polygon on a coordinate plane has 4 vertices. What is the shape of the polygon?

   A hexagon   C octagon

   B quadrilateral

8. What is the perimeter of the figure on the coordinate plane below?

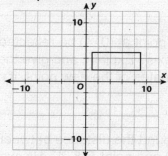

   A 32 units   C 22 units

   B 24 units

9. What is the area of the figure on the coordinate plane below?

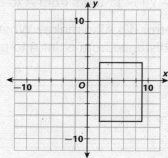

   A 30 square units

   B 70 square units

   C 140 square units

10. Which point is a reflection of (−3, −3) across the y-axis? (Hint: Look in Quadrant IV.)

   A (−3, 3)   C (3, −3)

   B (3, 3)

MODULE 14

Distance and Area in the Coordinate Plane

11. A point at (3, 5) is reflected across the *y*-axis. What is the distance of this new point from the *y*-axis? Explain how you know.

_____

_____

12. Can a point at (0, 4) be reflected across the *y*-axis? Explain, and give the coordinates of the new point, if possible.

_____

_____

13. Can a point at (0, 4) be reflected across the *x*-axis? Explain, and give the coordinates of the new point, if possible.

_____

_____

14. Alan found the distance between point *A*(3, 4) and point *B*(8, 4). His work is shown below.

    3 to the *y*-axis = 3 units

    8 to the *y*-axis = 8 units

    $|8| + |3| = 11$ units from *A* to *B*

What error did Alan make? What is the actual distance from point *A* to point *B*?

_____

_____

_____

15. Kate plotted a point *K* in Quadrant I. After she reflected the point across an axis, the reflected point was in Quadrant II. Give a possible ordered pair for point *K* and its reflection. Describe how the point was reflected.

_____

_____

16. A map is drawn on a coordinate plane. Each unit represents 10 miles. Terri drives from her home at point *G* to her friend's home at point *H*, following the route shown below. Terri drives steadily at 50 miles per hour. How long is the distance between the two points? How long will it take Terri to get from point *G* to point *H*? Show your work.

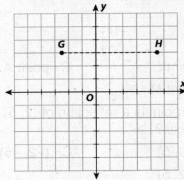

_____

_____

17. Use the coordinate grid below to draw a square that has an area of 16 square units. Prove that your figure has the correct area using distance and area calculations.

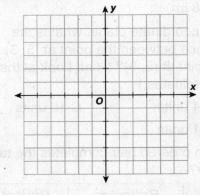

_____

_____

_____

MODULE 15

Surface Area and Volume of Solids
Module Quiz: B

1. Which correctly describes the net of a square pyramid?

    A two squares, three triangles

    B one square, three triangles

    C one square, four triangles

    D two squares, four triangles

2. Which net is **not** the net of a cube?

    A 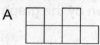   C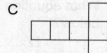

    B 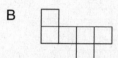   D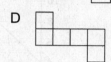

3. What is the surface area of the rectangular prism below?

    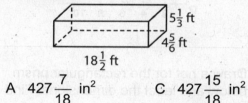

    A $427\frac{7}{18}$ in^2 C $427\frac{15}{18}$ in^2

    B $427\frac{13}{18}$ in^2 D $427\frac{17}{18}$ in^2

4. A point at (–4, 7) is reflected across the *x*-axis. What is the ordered pair of the reflected point?

    A (4, 7)   C (–4, –7)

    B (7, –4)   D (–7, –4)

5. A rectangular prism has a volume of 1374.28 cubic inches. The prism is 9.4 inches wide and 17.2 inches long. What is the height of the prism?

    A 7.6 in.   C 79.9 in.

    B 8.5 in.   D 146.2 in.

6. Which expression is equivalent to the expression below?

    $$3x + 5(x - 2)$$

    A $3x + 5x - 2$ C $8x - 2$

    B $8x - 10$ D $3x + x - 10$

7. What is the surface area of the square pyramid below?

    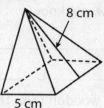

    A 45 cm^2 C 90 cm^2

    B 85 cm^2 D 105 cm^2

8. Which of these rectangular prisms has a surface area of 221.56 square feet?

    A a rectangular prism 5.6 inches wide, 8.2 inches long, and 4.7 inches tall

    B a rectangular prism 6.1 inches wide, 7.8 inches long, and 5.3 inches tall

    C a rectangular prism 5.9 feet wide, 8.5 feet long, and 4.4 feet tall

    D a rectangular prism 6.9 feet wide, 7.9 feet long, and 5.6 feet tall

9. A child's wading pool is 3.8 feet wide, 5.5 feet long, and 1.2 feet deep. How many gallons of water will the pool hold? (Use 1 ft^3 = 7.5 gal.)

    A 25.08 gal   C 188.1 gal

    B 64.12 gal   D 480.9 gal

10. One ring in the Stonehenge monument was originally made of 30 stones, each about $6\frac{1}{2}$ feet wide, 3 feet thick, and 13 feet tall. What is the approximate volume of the 17 stones that remain today?

    A 286 ft^3 C 3,862 ft^3

    B $286\frac{3}{5}$ ft^3 D $4,309\frac{1}{2}$ ft^3

11. A triangle has a height of 11.6 centimeters and an area of 54.52 square centimeters. What is its length?

    A 10.3 cm   C 8.4 cm

    B 9.4 cm   D 4.7 cm

MODULE 15 **Surface Area and Volume of Solids**

12. The volume of a cube is 216 cubic units. What is the length of each edge? Explain how you know.

_____

_____

13. Beth has a wooden box. The inside of the box is 5 inches wide, $8\frac{1}{4}$ inches long, and $4\frac{1}{2}$ inches deep. The box has no top. Beth wants to line the box with felt to protect the items she puts in the box. How many square inches of felt will she need?

_____

14. Explain why the net below will **not** make a cube.

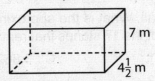

_____

_____

15. The rectangular prism below has a volume of $464\frac{3}{4}$ cubic meters.

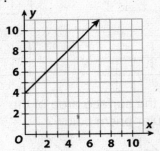

7 m

$4\frac{1}{2}$ m

a. Write an equation that could be used to find the length of the prism.

_____

b. Find the length. Show your work.

_____

16. Evaluate the expression below for $x = 2\frac{5}{8}$.

$$4x + 9(2x + 1)$$

_____

_____

17. What equation is shown by the graph below?

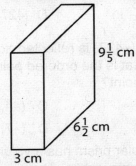

_____

18. Draw a net for the rectangular prism below and label the dimensions. Find the volume and surface area of the prism.

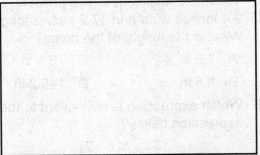

$9\frac{1}{5}$ cm

$6\frac{1}{2}$ cm

3 cm

MODULE
15

Surface Area and Volume of Solids
Module Quiz: D

1. Which correctly describes the net of a square?

   A six squares

   B one circle, four squares

   C two squares, three rectangles

2. Which net is the net of a cube?

   A 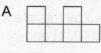   C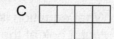

   B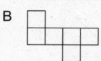

3. What is the surface area of this rectangular prism?

   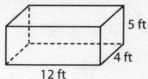

   A 128 ft²   C 256 ft²

   B 240 ft²

4. A point at (4, 6) is reflected across the x-axis. What is the y-coordinate of the reflected point?

   A 6   C –4

   B –6

5. A rectangular prism has a volume of 192 cubic inches. The prism is 4 inches wide and 8 inches long. What is the height of the prism?

   A 8 in.   C 4 in.

   B 6 in.

6. Which of the following expressions is equivalent to the expression below?

   $$3(2x + 4)$$

   A 3x + 4   C 6x + 4

   B 6x + 12

7. What is the surface area of this rectangular prism below?

   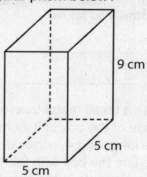

   A 210 cm²   C 240 cm²

   B 230 cm²

8. Which rectangular prism has a volume of 280 cubic inches?

   A a rectangular prism 4 inches wide, 8 inches long, and 9 inches tall

   B a rectangular prism 6 inches wide, 7 inches long, and 9 inches tall

   C a rectangular prism 5 inches wide, 7 inches long, and 8 inches tall

9. A child's wading pool is 4 feet wide, 6 feet long, and 1 foot deep. How many gallons of water will the pool hold?
   (Hint: Multiply the number of cubic feet by 7.5 gal.)

   A 180 gal   C 3.2 gal

   B 16.5 gal

10. Cement pillars for a porch are 2 feet wide, 2 feet thick, and 8 feet tall. There are 6 pillars in all. What is the total volume of the pillars?

    A 24 ft³   C 192 ft³

    B 32 ft³

11. A triangle has a height of 12 centimeters and an area of 48 square centimeters. Which equation could be used to find the length of the base, b?

    A 48 = (12 × b)   C 48 ÷ 12 = b

    B $48 = \frac{1}{2}(12 \times b)$

MODULE 15 **Surface Area and Volume of Solids**

12. The volume of a cube is 8 cubic units. What is the length of each edge? Explain how you know.

_____

_____

13. Erica has a small metal treasure box. The inside of the box is 3 inches wide, 6 inches long, and 4 inches deep. Erica wants to line the box with fabric to protect the items she puts in the box. How many square inches of fabric will she need? Show your work.

_____

_____

14. Explain why the net below will **not** make a cube.

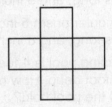

_____

_____

15. The rectangular prism below has a volume of 420 cubic meters.

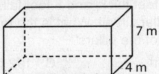

a. Complete the equation that could be used to find the length of the prism.
420 = _____ × _____ × length

b. Find the length. Show your work.

_____

16. Evaluate the expression below for x = 2.

$$3x + 5(x + 1)$$

_____

_____

17. What equation is shown by this graph? *Hint:* Look at the points (0, 1) and (1, 2).

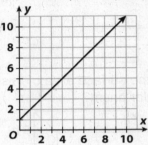

_____

18. Draw a net for the rectangular prism below and label the dimensions. Find the volume and surface area of the prism.

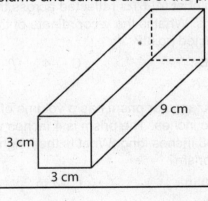

_____

_____

MODULE 16 Displaying, Analyzing, and Summarizing Data
Module Quiz: B

1. Anya read 20 pages on Monday, 30 pages on Tuesday, and 32 pages on Wednesday. Which is closest to the mean number of pages Anya read over the three-day period?

   A   20 pages   C   30 pages

   B   27 pages   D   32 pages

2. What is the interquartile range of the data represented in the box plot below?

   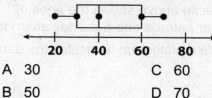

   A   30   C   60

   B   50   D   70

3. What is the median of the data represented in the line plot below?

   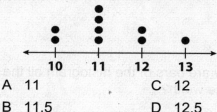

   A   11   C   12

   B   11.5   D   12.5

4. What is the solution to the equation below?

   $$4x = 36.8$$

   A $x = 9.2$ C $x = 40.8$

   B $x = 32.8$ D $x = 147.2$

5. A circle has a radius of 4 inches. What is the area of the circle?

   A 4π in^2

   B 8π in^2

   C $\frac{4}{3}\pi$ in^2

   D 16π in^2

Use the table for 6 and 7.

6. What is the mean for the data set below?

14	54	54	35
25	34	21	23

   A   25.1   C   32.5

   B   29.5   D   40.0

7. What is the mean absolute deviation for the data set?

   A   5.875   C   32.5

   B   11.75   D   94

8. For the data set below, which of the following measures is greatest?

   {20, 25, 30, 31, 32, 45, 45, 80}

   A   mean   C   range

   B   median   D   mode

Use the graph for 9 and 10.

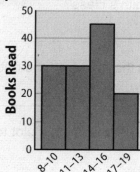

The histogram shows the number of books read by four different age groups over the summer.

9. What is the mode of the data?

   A   20 books   C   40 books

   B   30 books   D   45 books

10. How many more books did the 14–16-year-old group read than the 17–19-year old-group?

    A   5 books   C   15 books

    B   10 books   D   25 books

MODULE 16

Displaying, Analyzing, and Summarizing Data

Use the table for 11–16.

Student Heights (in.)

71	65	70	64	62
72	67	69	73	71
68	73	65	68	70
69	71	72	69	70

In the table above, Mr. Smith recorded the height of each student in his class.

11. What is the mean height of the students in Mr. Smith's class?

_____

12. What is the mean absolute deviation for the table?

_____

13. What is the median height of the students in Mr. Smith's class?

_____

14. What are the modes of the data?

_____

15. Draw a box-and-whisker plot to display the data.

16. What is the interquartile range for the data?

_____

Use the table for 17–19.

Ages	Number of Patrons
8–12	5
13–17	16
18–22	22
23–27	24
28–32	20

The table above shows the ages of theater patrons one Saturday afternoon.

17. Create a histogram to display the data.

18. Why are bars of the histogram all the same width?

_____

19. Can you tell how many 15-year olds attended the theater?

_____

_____

Name _____ Date _____ Class_____

Displaying, Analyzing, and Summarizing Data
Module Quiz: D

1. Ji rode her bicycle 8 miles on Tuesday and 10 miles on Wednesday. What is the mean number of miles she rode her bike in the two-day period?

   A 8 mi

   B 9 mi

   C 10 mi

2. What is the first quartile of the data represented in the box plot below?

   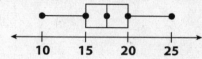

   A 10

   B 15

   C 20

3. What is the median of the data represented in the line plot below?

   A 2

   B 3

   C 4

4. What is the prime factorization of 45?

   A 5 • 3

   B 5 • 3 • 3

   C 5 • 9

Use the table for 5 and 6.

5. What is the mean for the data set below?

0	2	4	6
8	12	8	4

   A 5.0   C 6.0

   B 5.5

6. What is the mean absolute deviation for the data?

   A 2

   B 3

   C 5.5

7. Which value of x satisfies the equation below?

   $$5x = 45$$

   A $x = 9$ C $x = 225$

   B $x = 40$

Use the graph for 8 and 9.

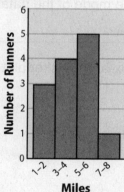

The histogram shows the number of runners who ran a given number of miles each week.

8. How many runners ran 5–6 miles a week?

   A 5   C 11

   B 6

9. How many more runners ran 5–6 miles a week than ran 7–8 miles a week?

   A 4   C 8

   B 5

MODULE 16 Displaying, Analyzing, and Summarizing Data

Use the table for 10–15.

Student Scores

82	86	90	94	88
76	74	74	92	96

In the table above, Ms. Brown recorded the score each student in her class earned on a math test.

10. What is the mean score for the students in Ms. Brown's class?

_____

11. What is the mean absolute deviation for the scores?

_____

12. What is the median score for the students in Ms. Brown's class?

_____

13. What is the mode of the data?

_____

14. Draw a box-and-whisker plot to show the data.

15. What is the first quartile for the data?

_____

Use the table for 16–19.

Allowance	Number of Students
$5–$10	1
$11–$16	5
$17–$22	3
$23–$28	1

16. Draw a histogram to show the data.

17. How many more students got $11–$16 than got $23–$28?

_____

18. Can you tell how many students got allowances of $15? Explain.

_____

_____

19. Why do the bars of a histogram touch?

_____

_____

_____

Name _____ Date _____ Class_____

UNIT
1

Numbers

Unit Test: A

1. Which situation would most likely be represented by a rational number that is **not** an integer?

   A number of students in a classroom

   B score on a math test

   C number of keys on a keyboard

   D price of a pencil

2. The temperature in Chicago was –5°C on Monday. Which of the following temperatures is lower than –5°C?

   A –6°C   C 1°C

   B –4°C   D 5°C

3. To which set or sets of numbers does the number 5 belong?

   A rational numbers only

   B integers only

   C integers and rational numbers only

   D integers, whole numbers, and rational numbers

4. Which number has the same absolute value as –2?

   A $-\dfrac{1}{2}$ C $\dfrac{1}{2}$

   B 0   D 2

5. What is the opposite of –5?

   A $-\dfrac{1}{5}$ C $\dfrac{1}{5}$

   B 0   D 5

6. Which number line shows –2 and its opposite?

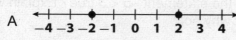

7. What is the greatest common factor (GCF) of 24 and 42?

   A 3   C 7

   B 6   D 12

8. Which of the following statements is **not** true?

   A –5 < –4   C 4 < 5

   B –2 < –3   D –2 < 5

9. Which of the following numbers is furthest from 0 on the number line?

   A –3   C 2

   B –2   D 4

10. Which of the following shows numbers ordered from least to greatest?

    A –2, –1, 0, 1

    B –2, 1, –1, 0

    C –2, –1, 1, 0

    D 1, 0, –1, –2

11. The temperature in Vancouver is –8°C, in Montreal it is –4°C, in Seattle it is –6°C, and in Buffalo it is –10°C. Which city is the coldest?

    A Vancouver

    B Montreal

    C Seattle

    D Buffalo

12. What is the least common multiple of 12 and 9?

    A 3   C 12

    B 9   D 36

UNIT
1
Numbers

13. What number has the same absolute value as –4?

_____

14. **Temperatures in Minneapolis**

Day	Temperature
Monday	–4.2°C
Tuesday	–4.1°C
Wednesday	–5.8°C
Thursday	–1.5°C

The table shows temperatures in Minneapolis on four weekdays. List the temperatures from least (coldest) to greatest (warmest).

_____

15. What is the value of |–8|?

_____

16. Thomasina wrote down a number that is both rational and a whole number. What is one possible number she could have written down?

_____

17. Find multiples of 4 and 5. Identify the least common multiple (LCM).

_____

18. Ali graphed the numbers –3 and 4 on the number line. Which number is further from 0? Explain.

_____

19. Write the common factors of 12 and 16. Identify the common factors and the greatest common factor.

_____

20. **Heights in Mr. Yu's Class**

Student	Height (ft)
Marilyn	5.1
Suki	$5\frac{1}{5}$
Brett	5.5
Amir	$5\frac{1}{4}$

The table shows the heights in feet for students in Mr. Yu's class.

List the heights in order from greatest to least.

_____

21. Write the number $3\frac{2}{5}$ in $\frac{a}{b}$ form.

_____

22. Kammi wrote the numbers –3, –3.5, 4, and –4.5 in order from least to greatest. How did she write the numbers?

_____

23. Is the statement –5 < 3 true? Explain why or why not.

_____

24. Phillip wrote an integer that is less than –2 and greater than –3.5. Which integer did he write?

_____

UNIT
1

Numbers
Unit Test: B

1.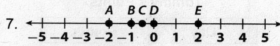

   Which of the lettered points is graphed at −3 on the number line above?

   A *A*

   B *B*

   C *C*

   D *D*

2. Ming prepared three chemical solutions with temperatures −5°C , −4°C, and −3°C. Which of the following correctly compares the three temperatures?

   A $-5 < -4 < -3$

   B $-5 < -3 < -4$

   C $-3 < -4 < -5$

   D $-3 < -5 < -4$

3. Which of the following shows an integer and its opposite?

   A $3, -3$

   B $3, \dfrac{1}{3}$

   C $-3, -\dfrac{1}{3}$

   D $-\dfrac{1}{3}, +\dfrac{1}{3}$

4. Which number has the same absolute value as −2?

   A $-\dfrac{1}{2}$

   B 0

   C $\dfrac{1}{2}$

   D 2

5. Jenni wrote a rational number that is positive. Which of the following is **not** a possible number that she wrote?

   A 0

   B 1

   C $\dfrac{7}{8}$

   D $5\dfrac{1}{4}$

6. Daria placed the numbers $-\dfrac{4}{7}$, 0.58, −0.6 and $\dfrac{5}{8}$ on the number line. Which of the numbers is furthest from zero?

   A −0.6

   B $-\dfrac{4}{7}$

   C 0.58

   D $\dfrac{5}{8}$

7.

   Which of the following points graphed above are opposites of each other?

   A *A* and *B*

   B *B* and *D*

   C *C* and *E*

   D *A* and *E*

8. Which of the following numbers is furthest from 0 on the number line?

   A −3

   B −2

   C 2

   D 4

9. Which number line shows the values of $|-2|$, $|3|$, $|4|$, and $|-5|$?

   A

   B

   C

   D

10. What is the LCM of 15 and 20?

    A 5

    B 30

    C 40

    D 60

11. What is the sum of any rational number and its opposite? Explain.

_____

_____

_____

12.   **Tommy's Points**

Day	Points
Monday	−7.21
Tuesday	7.22
Wednesday	$7\frac{1}{5}$
Thursday	$7\frac{3}{8}$

Tommy is playing a game in which he can score points each day. His scores for four days are shown in the table above. On which day did Tommy score the least points?

_____

13. If the numbers $2\frac{11}{12}$ and $3\frac{7}{9}$ are written in the form $\frac{a}{b}$, which will have the greater numerator?

_____

14. What is an example of a situation in which it is appropriate to use a rational number but **not** an integer?

_____

15. Carson claims that the opposite of any integer x is always a negative number. Is he correct? Explain why or why not.

_____

_____

16.   **Daily Temperatures in Calgary**

Day	Temperature
Monday	−8.1°C
Tuesday	−7.8°C
Wednesday	−8.05°C
Thursday	−8.18°C

The table shows the daily temperatures for a four-day period in Calgary.

List the temperatures in order from greatest to least.

_____

17. The absolute value of a number is added to the original number. Kayla says the sum is always equal to 0. Is she correct? Explain why or why not.

_____

_____

18. List the factors of 12 and 20. Identify the GCF.

_____

_____

UNIT
1

Numbers

Unit Test: C

1. Alessandra has a special deck of cards. Each card has a different integer on it. The cards are −1, −3, 5, 7, and −8. How many cards have a value that is less than −4?

   A none of these   C two

   B one   D three

2. Which set of rational numbers is correctly ordered from least to greatest?

   A −0.551, −0.550, −0.505, −0.555

   B −0.555, −0.550, −0.551, −0.505

   C −0.555, −0.551, −0.550, −0.505

   D −0.505, −0.550, −0.551, −0.555

3. Tamar wants to select an integer that is closer to zero than −3 on the number line. How many possible choices does she have?

   A one   C three

   B two   D four

4.

Point	Coordinate
A	−0.731
B	−0.730
C	−0.733
D	−0.735

Which number line shows the correct placement of the points listed in the table above?

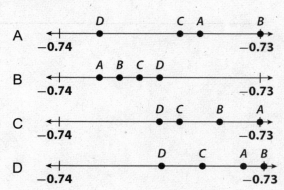

5. Which of the following lists of numbers is ordered from greatest to least?

   A $-\dfrac{5}{8}$, −0.61, −0.59, $-\dfrac{4}{7}$

   B $-\dfrac{5}{8}$, $-\dfrac{4}{7}$, −0.61, −0.59

   C $-\dfrac{4}{7}$, $-\dfrac{5}{8}$, −0.59, −0.61

   D $-\dfrac{4}{7}$, −0.59, −0.61, $-\dfrac{5}{8}$

6. **Martina's Inequalities**

−2 < 3	2 < 3	2 < −3	−4 < −5
−4 < 3	1 < 0	0 < −1	−3 < −2

Martina gets one point for each pair of integers she correctly compares. She wrote the statements above. How many points did Martina receive?

   A 2   C 4

   B 3   D 5

7. Kevin listed all of the integers with absolute value less than 2. Bria listed all of the integers with absolute value less than 4. How many more integers are on Bria's list than on Kevin's list?

   A two

   B four

   C seven

   D nine

8. What is the GCF of two prime numbers?

   A 0

   B 1

   C the first number

   D the second number

9. Tommy plotted the opposite of 6. Alicia plotted the opposite of 5. Which number is greater in value? Explain.

_____
_____
_____

10.   **Times for 200-meter Dash**

Runner	Time (s)
Allison	24.22
Carmelita	24.12
Shanay	23.98
Britney	23.95

Four runners ran the 200-meter dash. The times are shown in the table above. Which runner had the fastest time?

_____

11. Write the numbers -3.2, $-1\frac{7}{8}$, $-2\frac{5}{6}$ and $-3\frac{4}{5}$ in the form $\frac{a}{b}$, from greatest to least.

12. The opposite of x is y. What is the distance between x and y on the number line?

_____

13. If x and y are integers and $x < y$, how do the opposite of x and the opposite of y compare?

_____

14. **Daily Temperatures in Milwaukee**

Day	Temperature
Monday	−2.1°C
Tuesday	−2.0°C
Wednesday	−2.3°C
Thursday	−1.9°C

The table shows the daily temperatures for a four-day period in Milwaukee.

On which day or days was the temperature lower than −2.2°C?

_____

15. What is the LCM of 3, 4, and 5?

_____

16. A rational number is any number that can be written in the form $\frac{a}{b}$, where a and b are both integers and $b \neq 0$. Why is every integer a rational number?

_____
_____

UNIT 1

Numbers

Unit Test: D

1. What is the opposite of –6?

   A 0

   B $\frac{1}{6}$

   C 6

2. Which set of rational numbers is correctly ordered from least to greatest?

   A –0.3, –0.4, –0.5

   B –0.5, –0.4, –0.3

   C –0.5, –0.3, –0.4

3. Which number line shows –4, 1 and 3?

   A
   ```
   ←+—●—+—+—+—+—●—+—●—+—+→
    -5 -4 -3 -2 -1  0  1  2  3  4  5
   ```

   B
   ```
   ←+—●—●—+—+—+—+—+—●—+—+→
    -5 -4 -3 -2 -1  0  1  2  3  4  5
   ```

   C
   ```
   ←+—●—+—+—●—+—+—●—+—+—+→
    -5 -4 -3 -2 -1  0  1  2  3  4  5
   ```

4. Which number has the same absolute value as –21?

   A 0

   B $\frac{1}{21}$

   C 21

5. The elevation of New Orleans is on average 8 feet below sea level. Which correctly describes the opposite of New Orleans' elevation?

   A on average 8 feet below sea level

   B at sea level

   C on average 8 feet above sea level

6. Which shows the integers in order from greatest to least?

   A –2, 1, 5

   B 5, –2, 1

   C 5, 1, –2

7. Alecia placed the numbers 0.2, 0.4, –0.8 and 0.1 on the number line. Which of the numbers is furthest from zero?

   A –0.8

   B 0.1

   C 0.4

8. What is the GCF of 15 and 30?

   A 5

   B 15

   C 30

9. Which statement about rational numbers is correct?

   A All rational numbers are also integers.

   B Zero is **not** a rational number.

   C All integers are also rational numbers.

10. Anna wrote $4\frac{1}{2}$ in the form $\frac{a}{b}$. What number did she write?

    A $\frac{2}{9}$

    B $4\frac{1}{2}$

    C $\frac{9}{2}$

11. Which of the following is an example of a rational number that is **not** an integer?

    A $\frac{1}{5}$

    B 0

    C 4

UNIT
1

Numbers

12. Christopher claims that 4 is not a rational number because it is not written as a ratio of integers. Is he correct? Explain why or why not.

_____

_____

13. **Times in 400-meter Dash**

Runner	Time (s)
Kurt	59.6
Blaine	58.8
Rachel	60.4
Finn	59.5

Four runners ran the 400-meter dash. The times are shown in the table above. Which runner had the fastest time?

_____

14. Write the numbers $-\frac{2}{5}$, $-\frac{3}{5}$, $\frac{2}{5}$ and $\frac{4}{5}$ from greatest to least.

_____

15. How many integers have absolute value equal to 3? What are the integers?

_____

16.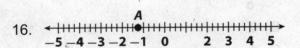

In the number line above, what is the coordinate of point A?

_____

17. What is an example of a rational number that is not an integer?

_____

18. **Daily Temperatures in New York**

Day	Temperature
Monday	1°C
Tuesday	2°C
Wednesday	5°C
Thursday	−1°C

The table shows the daily temperatures for a four-day period in New York.

On which day was the temperature warmest?

_____

19. What is the LCM of 3 and 5?

_____

20. Brian compared the absolute values of the numbers $-\frac{1}{2}$, $\frac{3}{4}$, and $-\frac{1}{4}$. Which of the numbers has the greatest absolute value?

_____

Numbers
Performance Task

Fifteen members of the math club each wore a T-shirt with a number printed on the front. The students' names and their numbers are listed below.

Abey	$3\frac{1}{2}$	Farha	$-\frac{2}{3}$	Kate	$\frac{7}{8}$
Brittany	-5	Greg	111	Lila	5
Cesar	2	Henri	3.14	Mirsada	-2.3
Davon	0.75	Iris	-9	Nikesha	1.5
Eric	17	Jorge	0	Oren	-12.6

Using the numbers on their T-shirts as a guide, the students divided themselves into the three teams below.

The Whole Numbers   Integers Without Wholes
Rationals But No Integers

1. On which team should Iris play? Explain.

   _____

   _____

2. Which two students have opposite numbers? On which team(s) should each play?

   _____

   _____

3. Players are going to stand in line by number from least to greatest. List the players on Rationals But No Integers from least to greatest.

   _____

   _____

4. Find the absolute values for all the numbers of the students on the Rationals But No Integers team, and then list the students from the least to greatest number. Explain why the list changes from Exercise 3.

   _____

   _____

   _____

5. The greatest common factor for Cesar (2) and Eric (17) is _____

   The least common multiple for Cesar (2) and a new player Pedro (4) is

   _____ .

   Two new players, Quentin (3) and Roya (8), have a least common

   multiple of _____ .

UNIT
2

Number Operations

Unit Test: A

1. A large bag of cashews weighs $8\frac{1}{3}$ pounds. One serving is $\frac{1}{3}$ pound. How many servings are in the bag?

   A $23\frac{13}{15}$ C 25

   B $24\frac{1}{15}$ D $25\frac{7}{15}$

2. What is the reciprocal of $\frac{5}{8}$?

   A $-\frac{8}{5}$ C -5

   B $-\frac{5}{8}$ D $\frac{8}{5}$

3. Mariel wrote these checks from her checking account: $10, $10, $31, and $10. Which number shows the change in the balance of her account?

   A $-$61$ C $1
   B $-$1$ D $61

4. Mr. Franklin paid $33.20 for 8 gallons of gas. What is the price of 1 gallon of gas?

   A $4.05   C $4.15
   B $4.13   D $4.25

5. The area of a library tabletop is $27\frac{1}{8}$ square feet. The table is $3\frac{1}{2}$ feet wide. What is the length of the table?

   A 7 ft   C $7\frac{7}{8}$ ft

   B $7\frac{3}{4}$ ft   D 8 ft

6. Which expression has the same value as $8 - (-4)$?

   A $-8 + 4$ C $8 + (-4)$
   B $-8 + (-4)$ D $4 - (-8)$

7. Deion has a $\frac{3}{4}$-pound bag of dog treats. He will give his dog $\frac{1}{8}$ pound of the treats after they play each day. How many days will the bag last?

   A 6 days   C 8 days
   B 7 days   D 9 days

8. A horseshoe weighs 8.2 ounces. The nails make up 0.2 of that weight. What is the weight of the horseshoe without the nails?

   A 1.64 oz   C 9.84 oz
   B 6.56 oz   D 16.4 oz

9. A trampoline has a rectangular jumping surface that is 10.3 feet long and 9.2 feet wide. What is the area of the jumping surface?

   A 9.476 ft^2 C 947.6 ft^2
   B 94.76 ft^2 D 9,476 ft^2

10. How does the product of two negative factors compare to the original factors?

    A The product is less than the factors.

    B The product will be equal to one factor.

    C The product will be greater than or equal to one factor.

    D The product will be greater than the factors.

11. Which expression has an answer that is negative?

    A $(-48) \div 6$ C $(-6)(-3)$
    B $(-48) \div (-6)$ D $(6)(3)$

12. In 4 hours, the temperature steadily fell from 0°F to −12°F. What was the average change in temperature per hour?

    A −8°F   C −2°F
    B −3°F   D 3°F

UNIT 2 **Number Operations**

13. Of the animals at the shelter, $\frac{5}{8}$ are cats. Of the cats, $\frac{2}{3}$ are kittens. What fraction of the animals at the shelter are kittens?

_____

14. Ian has a 12.2-ounce bottle of ketchup. He uses $\frac{1}{20}$ of the ketchup every time he has a buffalo burger. How many ounces of ketchup are left after Ian has eaten 4 buffalo burgers?

_____

15. a. Mr. Gordon weighs 205 pounds. Multiply his Earth weight by 0.91 to find how much he would weigh on the planet Venus.

_____

   b. What is the difference between Mr. Gordon's Earth weight and his weight on Venus?

_____

16. Write an integer expression that has the same value as $36 \div (-9) + (-5)$.

_____

17. The diameter of a U.S. penny is $\frac{3}{4}$ inch. How many pennies would it take to make a row 42 inches long?

_____

18. A football team lost 4 yards on each of 2 plays, gained 14 yards on the third play, and lost 5 yards on the fourth play. Write and find the value of an integer expression to find the change in their field position.

_____

19. Dwayne earns $11.45 per hour. Last week he worked $38\frac{1}{4}$ hours. How much did he earn last week?

_____

20. Explain how you can determine the sign of an integer quotient without dividing.

_____

_____

_____

21. Maya tried to play a new video game. On her first 4 tries, she lost 14 points, lost 8 points, won 2 points, and lost 8 points, and finally gave up. Write and find the value of an integer expression to show her final score.

_____

22. a. Brooke paid $45 for a course on candle-making. She spent $106 for wax and supplies, but later returned one $8 candle mold. Write and find the value of an integer expression to show the change in the amount of money she has.

_____

   b. If Brooke sells her candles for $9 each, how many will she have to sell before she makes a profit?

_____

Name _____ Date _____ Class_____

Number Operations

Unit Test: B

1. Marco paid $36.89 for 8.6 gallons of gas. What is the price of 1 gallon of gas?

   A $3.29   C $4.09

   B $3.89   D $4.29

2. The area of a rug is $36\frac{1}{4}$ square feet. The rug is $8\frac{3}{4}$ feet long. What is the length of the rug?

   A $4\frac{1}{7}$ C $4\frac{11}{12}$

   B $4\frac{2}{3}$ D $27\frac{1}{2}$

3. A caterer prepared a turkey that weighed $27\frac{1}{2}$ pounds. Each serving of turkey will be $\frac{1}{3}$ pound. How many whole servings will the turkey provide?

   A 70   C 82

   B 79   D 159

4. You have two fractions with denominators of 3 and 10. What number should you use as the least common denominator if you want to add them?

   A 3   C 15

   B 10   D 30

5. Erin has $1\frac{7}{8}$ pounds of trail mix. She wants to make $\frac{1}{12}$-pound bags of the mix for snacks. How many full bags can she make?

   A 20   C 22

   B 21   D 23

6. A bar of soap weighs 3.8 ounces. The ingredient glycerin makes up 0.4 of the weight of the soap. What is the weight of the glycerin in the bar of soap?

   A 1.52 oz   C 4.2 oz

   B 3.8 oz   D 15.2 oz

7. What is the reciprocal of $\frac{7}{12}$?

   A $-\frac{7}{12}$ C $\frac{12}{7}$

   B $-\frac{12}{7}$ D -7

8. Tyler wrote checks on his checking account for $20.53, $13.48, and $19.40. He also deposited $65.40 in the account. Which number describes the change in the balance of his account?

   A $ 11.99   C $ 44.87

   B $ 31.39   D $ 53.41

9. A swimming pool is 21.4 feet long and 12.75 feet wide. What area does the pool occupy?

   A 8.65 ft²   C 272.85 ft²

   B 34.15 ft²   D 2,728.50 ft²

10. How does finding the greatest common factor allow you to simplify $\frac{33}{55}$?

    A Multiply the numerator and denominator by 11.

    B Divide the numerator and denominator by 11.

    C Add 11 to the numerator and denominator.

    D Subtract 11 from the numerator and denominator.

11. What is the least common multiple you should use to find $\frac{4}{5} + \frac{5}{6}$?

    A 15   C 30

    B 20   D 60

12. In 12 hours, the temperature fell steadily from 17°F to 7°F. What was the average change in temperature per hour?

_____

13. Tomas bought a bottle of shampoo that held 10.5 fluid ounces. He uses $\frac{1}{16}$ of the shampoo every time he washes his hair. How many ounces of the shampoo are left after he washes his hair 6 times?

_____

14. Explain how to use the least common multiple to find $\frac{5}{9} - \frac{2}{15}$.

_____

15. Write some multiples of 5 and 8. Use the least common multiple to simplify $\frac{120}{160}$.

_____

16. Sanjay's dog weighs 46 pounds on Earth. Multiply the dog's Earth weight by 0.38 to find how much it would weigh on Mars, and by 2.36 to find how much it would weigh on Jupiter. How much less would the dog weigh on Mars than on Jupiter?

_____

17. A straw for a box drink is $4\frac{1}{8}$ inches long and costs $0.015 to make. The straws are laid end-to-end in a line until they extend $123\frac{3}{4}$ inches. How many straws are in the line and how much do they cost?

_____

18. A bag of potatoes weighs $7\frac{1}{2}$ pounds. Of the potatoes in the bag, $\frac{1}{6}$ are rotten. What is the weight of the good potatoes?

_____

19. Cereal costs $2.79 for 16.4 ounces. At this rate how much does 25 ounces of cereal cost?

_____

20. Describe the process of dividing a fraction by a fraction.

_____

21. Chuck earned $76 mowing lawns. The gas for the mower cost $12 and he bought a new string for the trimmer for $7. Write and find the value of an integer expression to find the amount of his profit.

_____

22. a. Marge has $14\frac{2}{5}$ feet of chain. She wants to make pieces $\frac{3}{8}$ foot long. How many can she make?

_____

   b. Solve the same problem using decimals. Show your work.

_____

UNIT 2	**Number Operations**

Unit Test: C

1. Mrs. Haines paid $43.94 for 12.7 gallons of gas. She used some credit card points to get 52¢ off per gallon. What is the original price of the gas per gallon?

   A $3.46

   B $3.52

   C $3.98

   D $4.08

2. The length of a living room rug is $12\frac{1}{2}$ feet, and the width is $10\frac{3}{4}$ feet. There is a loveseat that covers $12\frac{1}{2}$ square feet of the rug and an entertainment center that covers 6 square feet. What is the area of the rug that can be seen?

   A $115\frac{7}{8}$ ft^2

   B $117\frac{1}{2}$ ft^2

   C 122 ft^2

   D 124 ft^2

3. A caterer prepared a large ham that weighed $15\frac{1}{8}$ pounds. After cooking, the chef trimmed the ham and removed the bone, so the ham was $1\frac{3}{5}$ pound lighter. How many complete $\frac{5}{16}$-pound servings can she provide from this ham?

   A 43

   B $43\frac{7}{25}$

   C 44

   D 48

4. Do you use the greatest common factor or the least common multiple to add two fractions? In this example, what is it?
   $$\frac{4}{15}+\frac{5}{6}$$

   A greatest common factor, 3

   B greatest common factor, 30

   C least common multiple, 90

   D least common multiple, 30

5. Michele has a $1\frac{2}{3}$-pound box of cereal. She wants to make equal servings that completely use all the cereal. Which of these serving amounts would have no left-over cereal?

   A $\frac{1}{12}$ lb

   B $\frac{1}{10}$ lb

   C $\frac{1}{8}$ lb

   D $\frac{1}{5}$ lb

6. Juan bought a box of laundry soap that weighed 15.6 pounds. One 0.15-pound scoop of soap is enough to wash a regular load of laundry, but 2 scoops are needed to wash heavy work clothes. How many pounds of soap are left after Juan washes 8 regular loads and 5 heavy loads of laundry?

   A 1.95 lb

   B 12.45 lb

   C 12.9 lb

   D 13.65 lb

7. A swimming pool is 28.3 feet long and 18.6 feet wide. A section of the pool 10.1 feet by 4.7 feet is roped off for children only. What area of the pool is available for adults?

   A 47.47 ft^2

   B 47.89 ft^2

   C 478.91 ft^2

   D 526.38 ft^2

8. What number is best to use to simplify a fraction?

   A least common multiple

   B least common denominator

   C greatest common factor

   D greatest factor

9. On the track team, $\frac{3}{5}$ of the members are boys. Of these boys, $\frac{4}{7}$ are sixth-graders. Of the sixth-grade boys on the team, $\frac{1}{3}$ are runners. What fraction of the track team are sixth-grade boy runners?

_____

10. Explain how to determine the reciprocal of $4\frac{3}{8}$.

_____

_____

_____

11. Over a 12-hour period from 8 P.M. to 8 A.M., the temperature fell at a steady rate from 8°F to −16°F. If the temperature fell at the same rate every hour, what was the temperature at 4 A.M.?

_____

12. a. Shari used her savings to buy 15 pounds of flour at $0.42 per pound, 8 pounds of butter at $3.99 per pound, 1 pound of salt at $0.67, and 30 pounds of cherries at $1.49 per pound. What was the change in the amount of money in her savings?

_____

   b. Shari plans to bake cherry pies and sell them for $9.50 each. How many pies does she have to sell to make back her investment and make $100 profit?

_____

13. Cereal costs $2.79 for 16.4 ounces. At this rate, if you buy 25 ounces, how much change do you get from a $5 bill?

_____

14. a. A bag of apples weighs $7\frac{7}{8}$ pounds. By weight, $\frac{1}{18}$ of the apples are rotten. What is the weight of the good apples?

_____

   b. The full bag of apples cost $10.88. What should the bag cost when the rotten apples are removed?

_____

15. a. A standard brick is $3\frac{5}{8}$ inches wide and $7\frac{5}{8}$ inches long. Colton wants to edge his 16-foot-long sidewalk with brick on both sides. How many bricks does he need if he sets the bricks lengthwise along both sides? If he sets the bricks edgewise along both sides?

_____

   b. Each brick costs $0.63. What is the cost of the bricks for the lengthwise design? What is the cost of the bricks for the edgewise design?

_____

16. Why is it that when two positive fractions are multiplied, the product is less than the factors?

_____

_____

Number Operations

UNIT 2

Unit Test: D

1. A rug is 12 feet wide and $15\frac{1}{2}$ feet long. What is the area of the rug?

   A $37\frac{1}{2}$ ft²

   B 180 ft²

   C 186 ft²

2. Bruce bought $4\frac{3}{4}$ of ground turkey to make turkey burgers to grill at a barbecue. How many $\frac{1}{4}$-pound burgers can he make?

   A 19

   B 20

   C 21

3. Do you use the greatest common factor or the least common multiple to add two fractions? In this example, what is it?
   $$\frac{4}{15}+\frac{5}{6}$$

   A greatest common factor, 3

   B greatest common factor, 30

   C least common multiple, 30

4. A bottle holds 8.2 ounces of liquid soap. Jesse used 0.2 of the soap in the bottle to clean the kitchen floor. How many ounces of soap did she use?

   A 1.64 oz

   B 8.0 oz

   C 41 oz

5. What is the reciprocal of $\frac{1}{3}$?

   A $\frac{3}{1}$

   B $-\frac{1}{3}$

   C -3

6. Cooper deposited $63 into his checking account. He then wrote two checks, one for $20 and one for $35. How much of his original deposit does Cooper have left in his checking account?

   A $8

   B $12

   C $15

7. In Mrs. Wallace's science class, $\frac{1}{2}$ of the students are boys. Of the boys, $\frac{1}{8}$ are left-handed. What fraction of the students in Mrs. Wallace's science class are left-handed boys?

   A $\frac{1}{16}$

   B $\frac{1}{10}$

   C $\frac{1}{6}$

8. In 7 hours, the temperature on the slopes of a mountain ski resort fell from 9°F to 2°F. What was the average change per hour?

   A dropped 7°F

   B dropped 1°F

   C dropped 9°F

9. Which expression has a negative answer?

   A $-4 - (-7)$

   B $-5 - (-2)$

   C $-1 - (-8)$

UNIT 2

Number Operations

10. Trevor filled his car's gas tank with 17 gallons of gas. He paid $68.51. What was the price of 1 gallon of gas?

_____

11. What is the reciprocal of $3\frac{1}{8}$?

_____

12. Jamal used his savings to buy 15 pounds of flour at $0.42 per pound, 8 pounds of butter at $3.99 per pound, 1 pound of salt at $0.67 per pound, and 30 pounds of apples at $1.49 per pound. What was the change in the amount of money in his savings?

_____

13. Jamal plans to bake cherry pies and sell them for $9.50 each. How many pies does he have to sell to make back his investment and make $100 profit?

_____

14. A container that weighs $23\frac{2}{5}$ pounds holds sports equipment. Of the equipment in the container, $\frac{1}{3}$ of the weight is baseball equipment. What is the weight of the baseball equipment?

_____

15. Explain how to divide by a fraction.

_____

_____

16. Gabby earns $12.65 per hour. She worked 30.8 hours. What was her pay?

_____

17. Four runners formed a relay team at Jan's high school. The team completed the relay in 3.86 minutes. Each runner ran exactly the same time. What was each runner's time?

_____

18. Granola costs $2.79 for 16.4 ounces. At this rate how much does 25 ounces of granola cost?

_____

19. Two friends ordered a restaurant special in which they each received a meal and then shared a dessert. The final bill with tax and tip was $21.86. How much should each friend pay?

_____

20. a. A U.S. dime has a thickness of $1\frac{7}{20}$ millimeters. Gary has a stack of dimes $78\frac{3}{10}$ millimeters tall. How many dimes does he have?

_____

b. What is the value of the dimes?

_____

c. Each dime weighs 2.268 grams. What is the mass of the entire stack of dimes?

_____

UNIT 2

Number Operations
Performance Task

1. Min Jee is renovating a house. The living room is a rectangle $22\frac{2}{3}$ feet

    long and $17\frac{1}{4}$ feet wide. A closet in one corner takes up an area of

    $6\frac{2}{3}$ feet by 6 feet. Min Jee wants to put in new flooring in the living

    room but not the closet. Flooring is sold by the square yard for $13.59.
    How much flooring does she need and how much will it cost?

    _____

    _____

2. Jared is putting a new deck off the kitchen. The deck will be 94.95
   inches deep. He will use 16 boards that are each 5.7 inches wide. He
   has to leave a small space between the boards. If the 15 spaces
   between the boards are all equal, how wide will they be?

    _____

    _____

3. Min Jee wants to build a small patio using either brick or paver stones.
   It will be 70 inches long and 49 inches wide. Each brick covers an area

    of $3\frac{1}{2}$ inches by $7\frac{1}{2}$ inches, and costs $0.59. Each paver covers an

    area 8.4 inches by 8.4 inches and costs $1.88. Which would be less
    expensive to use, and by how much?

    _____

    _____

The following list shows the price of some building supplies.

Item	Price	Unit
paint	$13.99	quart
nails	$8.57	pound

4. Beth needs $5\frac{1}{4}$ quarts of paint to paint some walls. How much will it

    cost her? (Assume she can buy a fraction of a quart at the same rate.)

    _____

5. Carlos needs $2\frac{3}{4}$ pounds of nails. What will it cost him to the nearest

    cent? _____

UNIT 3

Proportionality: Ratios and Rates

Unit Test: A

1. Kelly ate 3 apples. This represents 50% of the bag of apples. How many apples were originally in the bag?

   A 3   C 5

   B 4   D 6

2. Approximately what percent of the rectangle below is shaded?

   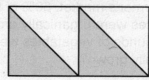

   A 25%   C 50%

   B 33%   D 67%

3. The ratio of blue marbles to white marbles in Simran's bag is equal to 1 to 2. If there are 20 blue marbles, how many white marbles are there?

   A 20   C 40

   B 30   D 50

4. Anthony cut a piece of metal that weighed 2,700 grams. Dionne cut a piece of metal that weighed 3,200 grams. How much heavier was Dionne's piece, in kilograms?

   A 0.5   C 50

   B 5   D 500

5. The ratio of green houses to white houses on Winthrop Street is equal to 2 to 3. There are 60 white houses on Winthrop Street. How many green houses are there?

   A 20   C 40

   B 30   D 60

6. What is 40% of 120?

   A 32   C 48

   B 40   D 60

7. The ratio of boys to girls in Mr. Baker's social studies class is 2 to 3. If there are 30 total students in the class, how many more girls are in the class than boys?

   A 6   C 10

   B 8   D 12

8. Kenton completed 30% of a 90-page reading assignment. How many pages did he read?

   A 24   C 30

   B 27   D 33

9. Nelly spends 25% of her free time surfing the Internet. If she spends approximately 1 hour per day surfing the Internet, how many hours of free time does she have each day?

   A 0.25   C 2

   B 1   D 4

10. Brent counted 10 red cards, 10 black cards, and 20 blue cards in a deck of cards. What is the ratio of red cards to other cards?

    A 1 : 1   C 2 : 1

    B 1 : 2   D 1 : 3

11. Winnie can walk 2 miles in 30 minutes. How many miles can she walk in 2 hours?

    A 2   C 6

    B 4   D 8

12. Cole has 12.4 meters of string. How many feet of string is this?

    A 1.24 ft   C 40.68

    B 24.8 ft   D 81.36

UNIT 3

Proportionality: Ratios and Rates

13. L'Shonda purchased a container of juice that contains 200 calories. The label says that 40% of the calories are from carbohydrates. How many calories are from carbohydrates?

_____

14. Cymra purchased a container of peanuts that weighs 4 kilograms. Luz purchased a container of peanuts that weighs 4,100 grams. How many more grams of peanuts did Luz purchase?

_____

15.   **Favorite Sport**

Football	45%
Baseball	15%
Basketball	20%
Tennis	20%

Remy recorded the favorite sport of students at his school. He surveyed 500 students. How many students chose Baseball?

_____

16. During the election for class president, 30% of the students voted for Lindsay, and 70% of the students voted for Sharif. 400 students voted in total. How many more students voted for Sharif than for Lindsay?

_____

17. The ratio of golf balls to tennis balls in the coach's bag is 20 to 5. If there are 100 golf balls in the bag, how many tennis balls are in the bag?

_____

18. Carlos bought 20 pounds of vegetables at the farmer's market. 60% of the vegetables were organically grown. How many pounds of vegetables were **not** organically grown?

_____

Use the table for 19 and 20.

19.   **Backpack Weight**

Student	Weight of Backpack
Amir	20,100 g
Betty	19.2 kg
Sandro	21,300 g
Lea	20,120 g
Maurizio	19.8 kg

Students in Ms. Victoria's class have backpacks of different weights, as shown in the table. Which student's backpack is the heaviest?

_____

20. How many pounds does Betty's backpack weigh?

_____

21. Lydia bought a package of pencils. There are 10 pink pencils and 5 blue pencils. What is the ratio of pink pencils to blue pencils?

_____

Name _____ Date _____ Class_____

1. Mitt ate 24 peanuts. This represents 75% of the bag of peanuts. How many peanuts were originally in the bag?

   A 24   C 48

   B 32   D 100

2. Approximately what percent of the rectangle below is shaded?

   A 25%   C 40%

   B 33%   D 67%

3. The ratio of pink marbles to white marbles in Samara's bag is equal to 1:5. What percent of the bag contains pink marbles?

   A $16\frac{2}{3}$%   C 25%

   B 20%   D $83\frac{1}{3}$%

4. Alissa cut a piece of string that was 17 feet long. Darnell cut a piece of string that was 5 yards long. Alissa wanted to cut her string so that it was the same length as Darnell's. How many feet did she need to cut off?

   A 1   C 4

   B 2   D 5

5. Antonia and Carla have the same percentage of green marbles in their bags of marbles. Antonia has 4 green marbles and 16 total marbles. Carla has 10 green marbles. How many of Carla's marbles are **not** green?

   A 10   C 30

   B 20   D 40

6. The ratio of boys to girls in Mr. Castillo's class is 2 to 3. Which of the following **cannot** be the total number of students in Mr. Castillo's class?

   A 20   C 25

   B 24   D 30

7. Alexandra completed 40% of a 50-question assignment. How many questions did she complete?

   A 10   C 25

   B 20   D 30

8. Andrew's sandwich consists of a 20-gram piece of cheese, a 60-gram piece of turkey, and two 30-gram slices of bread. What is the total weight of Andrew's sandwich, in kilograms?

   A 0.11 kg   C 110 kg

   B 0.14 kg   D 140 kg

9. Minxia counted 40 green cars and 20 silver cars in the parking lot. If the number of green cars stays the same, how many more silver cars would need to be added so the ratio of green cars to silver cars is 1 to 3?

   A 30   C 100

   B 80   D 120

10. Rajani can ride her skateboard 2 miles in 10 minutes. How many miles can she ride her skateboard in 1.5 hours?

    A 9 mi   C 15 mi

    B 12 mi   D 18 mi

11. In another country, a road sign reads "80 kilometers to the next gas station". How far is that distance to the nearest mile?

    A 40 mi   C 62 mi

    B 50 mi   D 98 mi

UNIT 3

Proportionality: Ratios and Rates

12. Tyrese purchased a container of juice that contains 220 calories. The label says that 60% of the calories are from carbohydrates. How many calories are **not** from carbohydrates?

_____

13. Ali purchased a container of mandarin oranges that weighs 3 kilograms. Mia purchased a container of mandarin oranges that weighs 3,250 grams. How many more grams of mandarin oranges did Mia purchase?

_____

14. **Favorite Sport**

Football	35%
Baseball	25%
Basketball	20%
Tennis	20%

Kassie recorded the favorite sport of students at her school. She surveyed 800 students. How many more students chose Baseball than Basketball?

_____

15. During the election for class president, 40% of the students voted for Jennifer, and 60% of the students voted for Kevin. 300 students voted in total. How many more students voted for Kevin than for Jennifer?

_____

16. The ratio of white marbles to blue marbles in Jai's bag is 2 to 5. If there are more than 50 marbles in the bag, what is the **minimum** number of marbles that can be in the bag?

_____

17. Shilpa bought 30 T-shirts at a clothing store. 20% of the T-shirts were blue and $\frac{1}{2}$ of the T-shirts were black. How many of the T-shirts were neither black nor blue?

_____

Use the table for 18 and 19.

18. **Bagged Lunch Weight**

Student	Weight of Lunch
Amery	545 g
Blaine	6.1 kg
Scott	491 g
Rosalinda	621 g
Zelda	6.25 kg

Students in Mr. Conway's class have bagged lunches of different weights, as shown in the table. Which student's lunch is the heaviest?

_____

19. What is the weight of Blaine's lunch to the nearest pound?

_____

UNIT 3

Proportionality: Ratios and Rates
Unit Test: C

1. Beatrix ate 21 raisins. This represents 30% of the box of raisins. How many raisins were originally in the box?

    A 7   C 51

    B 30   D 70

2. Approximately what percent of the large square below is shaded?

    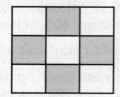

    A 33%   C 44%

    B 40%   D 55%

3. The ratio of green marbles to yellow marbles in Toby's bag is equal to 2:3. What percent of the marbles in the bag are green marbles?

    A 40%   C 60%

    B 50%   D $66\frac{2}{3}$%

4. Kendra bought a piece of fabric that was 14 feet long. Lisa bought a piece of fabric that was 3 yards long. Kendra wanted to cut her fabric so that it was the same length as Lisa's. How many feet did she need to cut off?

    A 1 ft   C 4 ft

    B 2 ft   D 5 ft

5. Tom and Jasper have the same percentage of blue marbles in their bags of marbles. Tom has 5 blue marbles and 20 total marbles. Jasper has 12 blue marbles. How many of Jasper's marbles are **not** blue?

    A 12   C 36

    B 24   D 48

6. The ratio of boys to girls in Mr. Chen's class is 4 to 5. Which of the following **cannot** be the total number of students in Mr. Chen's class?

    A 18   C 27

    B 20   D 36

7. Alexa and Brent are each working on a 30-question assignment. Alexa completed 20% of the questions. Brent completed 30% of the questions. How many more questions did Brent complete?

    A 1   C 6

    B 3   D 9

8. Martina filled a 100-mL container with water. Simone filled a 1.2-L container. How much more water did Simone have in her container?

    A 0.1 L   C 0.9 L

    B 0.2 L   D 1.1 L

9. Brian counted 15 red cars and 20 blue cars in the parking lot. If the number of red cars stays the same, how many more blue cars would need to be added so the ratio of red cars to blue cars is 1 to 2?

    A 10   C 20

    B 15   D 30

10. Wendy can ride her bike 0.8 miles in 6 minutes. How many miles can she ride bike in 1.5 hours?

    A 6 mi   C 12 mi

    B 7.5 mi   D 15 mi

11. How much longer is 3 meters than 3 yards?

    A 0.28 m   C 28 m

    B 2.8 m   D 280 m

Proportionality: Ratios and Rates

12. Tyrone purchased a container of juice that contains 150 calories. The label says that 70% of the calories are from carbohydrates. How many calories are **not** from carbohydrates?

_____

13. Wu purchased a container of peanuts that weighs 5 kilograms. Mindy purchased a container of peanuts that weighs 4,800 grams. How many more grams of peanuts did Wu purchase?

_____

14. **Favorite School Subject**

Math	15%
Science	20%
English	35%
History	30%

Jenn recorded the favorite school subject of students at her school. She surveyed 700 students. How many more students chose English than Science?

_____

15. During the election for class president, 40% of the students voted for Gerardo, 35% of the students voted for Leandro, and 25% of the students voted for Juju. 70 students voted for Leandro. How many more students voted for Gerardo than for Juju?

_____

16. The ratio of white pens to blue pens in Jake's drawer is 4 to 3. If Jake has more than 40 pens, what is the **minimum** number of pens that can be in Jake's drawer?

_____

17. Arik bought 20 calculators at the electronics store. 40% of the calculators were scientific calculators and $\frac{1}{2}$ of the calculators were graphing calculators. How many of the calculators were neither scientific calculators nor graphing calculators?

_____

Use the table for 18 and 19.

18.   **Juice Containers**

Student	Container Size
Darius	2.45 L
Jessie	299 mL
Kyle	3.5 L
Mark	1,493 mL
Faisal	4,391 mL

Students in Mr. Feld's class have juice containers of different sizes, as shown in the table. Which of the students has the largest container?

_____

19. What is the capacity of the smallest container in ounces?

_____

UNIT 3

Proportionality: Ratios and Rates
Unit Test: D

1. Effie ate 4 peaches. This represents 50% of the bag of peaches. How many peaches were originally in the bag?

   A 4

   B 6

   C 8

2. Approximately what percent of the rectangle below is shaded?

   A 25%

   B 50%

   C 75%

3. The ratio of red marbles to blue marbles in Simran's bag is equal to 1 to 1. If there are 20 red marbles, how many blue marbles are there?

   A 20

   B 30

   C 40

4. Jessie filled a container of water with 200 milliliters. Zaria filled a different container with 400 milliliters. How much more water did Zaria have, in **liters**?

   A 0.2 L

   B 20 L

   C 200 L

5. The distance on a map between Lake Village and Bay Cove is 2 inches. If 1 inch represents 15 miles, what is the actual distance between Lake Village and Bay Cove?

   A 2 mi

   B 15 mi

   C 30 mi

6. The ratio of boys to girls in Mr. Green's class is 4 to 5. There are 8 boys in the class. How many girls are in the class?

   A 5

   B 9

   C 10

7. Bethenny completed 20% of a 50-page reading assignment. How many pages did she read?

   A 10

   B 20

   C 50

8. Natasha spends 10% of her free time watching television. If she has approximately 300 minutes of free time each day, how many minutes does she spend watching TV?

   A 3 min

   B 10 min

   C 30 min

9. Allegra counted 10 red cards and 20 black cards in a deck of cards. What is the ratio of red cards to black cards?

   A 1 : 1

   B 1 : 2

   C 2 : 1

10. Arturo can walk 4 miles in 1 hour. How many miles can he walk 3 hours?

    A 12 mi

    B 16 mi

    C 20 mi

11. Since 1 inch is equal to 2.54 centimeters what does 1 centimeter equal in inches?

    A 0.25 in.

    B 0.39 in.

    C 1 in.

UNIT 3

Proportionality: Ratios and Rates

12. Devin purchased a container of sport drink that contains 300 calories. The label says that 80% of the calories are from carbohydrates. How many calories are from carbohydrates?

_____

13. Roberta purchased a container of cashews that weighs 5 kilograms. Lennie purchased a container of cashews that weighs 4,900 grams. How many more grams of cashews did Roberta purchase?

_____

14.

Favorite Sport

Football	35%
Baseball	25%
Basketball	30%
Tennis	10%

Luanne recorded the favorite sport of students at her school. She surveyed 200 students. How many students chose Tennis?

_____

15. During the election for class president, 40% of the students voted for Kellen, and 60% of the students voted for Robbie. 500 students voted in total. How many more students voted for Robbie than for Kellen?

_____

16. The ratio of wooden bats to metal bats in the baseball coach's bag is 2 to 1. If there are 20 wooden bats, how many metal bats are in the bag?

_____

17. Manny bought 12 pounds of vegetables at the supermarket. 75% of the vegetables were on sale. How many pounds of vegetables were **not** on sale?

_____

18.

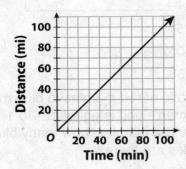

The graph above shows the distance traveled by Mr. Wentz as he drove on the freeway. According to the graph, how far did Mr. Wentz travel after driving for 40 minutes?

_____

19. How many kilometers are equal to 5 miles?

_____

20. Cora bought a package of erasers. There are 4 pink erasers and 12 blue erasers. What is the ratio of pink erasers to blue erasers?

_____

Proportionality: Ratios and Rates

UNIT 3

Performance Task

1. Jorge planted flowers in his garden. He planted one row of 12 tulips and one row of 36 daisies. What is the ratio of tulips to daisies that Jorge planted? Express the ratio as a fraction and as a decimal.

   _____

2. One of the plants in Jorge's garden grows at the rate of 2 inches in 3 months. A second plant grows at the rate of 3 inches in 2 months. Which plant grows at the faster rate? Explain.

   _____

   _____

3. Jorge's friend Anna planted a garden with the same ratio of tulips to daisies. Anna's garden has 48 tulips. How many total flowers are in Anna's garden?

   _____

4. Jorge's friend Kylie has a garden with 75 flowers in it. Kylie's garden only contains tulips and daisies. Is it possible for Kylie's garden to have the same ratio of tulips to daisies as Jorge's garden? Explain why or why not.

   _____

   _____

   _____

5. Jorge wants the ratio of tulips to daisies in his garden to be 2 to 5. He does not want to take any flowers out of his garden. How many of what type of flower should he plant in order to get the desired ratio?

   _____

   _____

6. Jorge wrote the following key for a scale drawing of his garden:
   1 cm = 2 ft

   Express this scale as inches to feet.

   _____

   _____

UNIT 4

Equivalent Expressions

Unit Test: A

1. Which expression has a value that is more than its base?

   A $\left(\dfrac{4}{5}\right)^3$ C 5^3

   B $\left(\dfrac{2}{3}\right)^4$ D $\left(\dfrac{1}{2}\right)^2$

2. Which expression is equivalent to $5.7 \times 5.7 \times 5.7$?

   A 5.7×3 C 5.7^3

   B $5^3 \times 7^3$ D 57^3

3. Which expression shows the prime factorization of 20?

   A $2^2 \times 5$ C 4×5

   B 2×10 D $4^2 \times 5$

4. Which number has only two factors?

   A 6   C 9

   B 8   D 11

5. Which operation should you do first when you simplify $85 + (25 \times 5)$?

   A addition

   B subtraction

   C multiplication

   D division

6. Simplify the expression below.

   $$12 \div (2 + 1)$$

   A 4   C 6

   B 5   D 7

7. Which expression is the same as 42 times x?

   A $\dfrac{42}{x}$

   B $42 + x$

   C $42 - x$

   D $42x$

8. Which phrase is the same as $5 + w$?

   A 5 times w

   B 5 divided by w

   C w plus 5

   D 5 take away w

9. Jenny folded 10 towels and divided them evenly into p piles. Which expression shows the number of towels in each pile?

   A $p - 10$ C $\dfrac{p}{10}$

   B $10 \times p$ D $\dfrac{10}{p}$

10. Evaluate $2n - 3$ for $n = 5$.

    A 2   C 5

    B 3   D 7

11. Tickets to the school play cost $9. The Wilson family bought 5 tickets. What was the total cost of the tickets?

    A $5   C $45

    B $9   D $90

12. Which property is used to write the equivalent expressions below?

    $$(2 \times 7) \times 3 = 2 \times (7 \times 3)$$

    A Associative Property of Multiplication

    B Commutative Property of Addition

    C Distributive Property

    D Identity Property of Addition

13. Which expression is equivalent to $5(a + b)$?

    A $5a + b$ C $5a + 5b$

    B $a + 5b$ D $(a + b)^5$

UNIT 4 Equivalent Expressions

14. Two students sit in the first row. In the second row, 2 students sit behind each of those students, and so on. How many students sit in the third row?

    _____

15. Write $5 \times 5 \times 5$ using exponents.

    _____

16. Find the prime factorization of 12.

    _____

17. A rectangle's length times its width is 18 square inches. What are the possible whole number lengths and widths of the rectangle?

    _____

18. Which operation should you do first when you simplify the expression below?

    $$(15 + 4) \times 3$$

    _____

19. Simplify the expression below using the order of operations.

    $$2 + 3^2 - 1$$

    _____

20. Write an algebraic expression that means the same as 50 take away b.

21. Write a phrase that means the same as $\dfrac{x}{4}$.

    _____

22. There are 20 students in a club. Next year, some new students will join. Write an expression to show how many students will be in the club next year. Use c for the number of new students who join.

    _____

23. What is $4y \times 2$ when is $y = 2$?

    _____

24. Evaluate $\dfrac{5}{9}(f - 32)$ when $f = 50$.

    _____

25. Simplify the expression below.

    $$2(3x + 8) = \text{_____}$$

26. Combine like terms to simplify $4y + 6x - 2y$.

UNIT 4 Equivalent Expressions

Unit Test: B

1. Which expression has a value that is more than the base of that expression?

   A $\left(\dfrac{4}{5}\right)^3$ C 5^3

   B $\left(\dfrac{2}{3}\right)^4$ D 4^0

2. Which expression is equivalent to $5.7 \times 5.7 \times 5.7 \times 5.7 \times 5.7 \times 5.7$?

   A 5.7×6 C 5.7^6

   B $5^6 \times 7^6$ D 57^6

3. Which expression shows the prime factorization of 90?

   A $2 \times 3^2 \times 5$ C $2 \times 5 \times 9$

   B $3^2 \times 10$ D $3^2 \times 5^2$

4. Which number has only two factors?

   A 12   C 15

   B 14   D 17

5. Which operation should you perform first when you simplify the expression below?
   $85 + (9 - 25 \times 5) \div 3$

   A addition

   B subtraction

   C multiplication

   D division

6. Simplify the expression below using the order of operations.

   $$12 + 9 \times 4^2 \div (2 + 1)$$

   A 43   C 335

   B 60   D 863

7. Which expression represents the product of 42 and x?

   A $\dfrac{42}{x}$

   B $42 + x$

   C $42 - x$

   D $42x$

8. Which phrase describes the algebraic expression $5 + w$?

   A the product of 5 and w

   B the quotient of 5 and w

   C w more than 5

   D 5 less than w

9. Jenny was doing laundry. She folded 10 towels and divided them evenly into p piles. Which expression represents the number of towels in each pile?

   A $p - 10$ C $\dfrac{p}{10}$

   B $10 \times p$ D $\dfrac{10}{p}$

10. Evaluate $9n - 15$ for $n = 5$.

    A 15   C 45

    B 30   D 60

11. Tickets to the school play cost $9 for adults and $5 for students. The Wilson family bought 3 adult tickets and 4 student tickets. What was the total cost of the tickets?

    A $47   C $63

    B $51   D $98

12. The expression $(2 \times 7) \times 3$ represents the number of times Brandon went to the beach each week during 3 months. Which property is applied to write the equivalent expression $2 \times (7 \times 3)$?

    A Distributive Property

    B Commutative Property of Addition

    C Associative Property of Multiplication

    D Identity Property of Multiplication

13. Which expression is equivalent to $2a + 5(b + 7a)$?

    A $37a + 5b$ C $9a + 5b$

    B $2a + 35b$ D $7a + 12b$

UNIT 4

Equivalent Expressions

14. Three students are sitting in the first row. In the second row, 3 students sit behind each of those students, and so on. How many students are sitting in the fifth row?

_____

15. Use exponents to write an equivalent expression for $2.9 \times 2.9 \times 2.9 \times 2.9$.

_____

16. Find the prime factorization of 456.

_____

17. Allison wants to cut out a rectangle with an area of 54 inches. What are the possible whole number lengths and widths of the rectangle?

_____

18. Which operation should you perform first when you simplify the expression below?

$$(15 \times 5 + 4) \times 3$$

_____

19. Simplify the expression below using the order of operations.

$$2 + 3(7 - 1) + 3^2$$

_____

20. Write an algebraic expression to represent b less than 50.

_____

21. Write a phrase to describe the algebraic expression $\dfrac{x}{24}$.

_____

22. There are 20 students in the drama club. Next year, 5 students will leave the drama club and some new students will join. If d is the number of students who will join the drama club, write an expression to represent the total number of students in the drama club next year.

_____

23. Evaluate $14y \div 2$ for $y = 6$.

_____

24. The expression $\dfrac{5}{9}(F - 32)$ gives the temperature in degrees Celsius for a given temperature in degrees Fahrenheit F. Find the temperature in degrees Celsius that is equivalent to 86°F.

_____

25. Use a property to write an equivalent expression for the expression below. Tell which property you used.

$$7(3x + 8) = \text{_____}$$

26. Combine like terms to write an equivalent expression for $4y^2 + 6x - 2y^2 + 12x$.

_____

Name _____ Date _____ Class_____

UNIT
4

Equivalent Expressions
Unit Test: C

1. Which expression has a value that is more than the base of that expression?

   A $\left(\dfrac{4}{5} + \dfrac{1}{8}\right)^3$ C $\left(\dfrac{5}{3} + \dfrac{2}{3}\right)^3$

   B $\left(\dfrac{2}{3} + \dfrac{1}{5}\right)^4$ D $\left(\dfrac{6}{7} + \dfrac{2}{3}\right)^0$

2. Which expression is NOT equivalent to 64?

   A 2^6 C 4^3

   B 3^4 D 8^2

3. Which expression shows the prime factorization of 1,250?

   A 2×5^4 C $2^6 \times 5$

   B $2^3 \times 3^2 \times 5$ D $3^2 \times 5^2$

4. Which number has only two factors?

   A 299   C 989

   B 749   D 1009

5. Which statement is true?

   A $15 + \left(7 - 5 \times 4^2\right) \div 2 = 34$

   B $7 + \left(13 - 81 \times 2^2\right) \div 5 = -48.8$

   C $86 + \left(9 - 5 \times 5^2\right) \div 3 = 47.3$

   D $10 + \left(4 - 9 \times 3^2\right) \div 4 = 11.25$

6. Simplify the expression below using the order of operations.

   $$12 + \dfrac{9 \times 4^2}{3} \div (2 + 8) - 5$$

   A $\dfrac{1}{2}$ C 45

   B 11.8   D 110

7. Which expression contains three terms and the product of a constant and a variable?

   A $3.7 \times b$ C $3.7 + b \div 5$

   B $3.7 - a$ D $3.7 \times 5b + a$

8. Which phrase describes the algebraic expression $5 + w^5$?

   A the product of 5 and w to the fifth power

   B the quotient of 5 to the fifth power and w

   C w to the fifth power plus 5

   D 5 minus w to the fifth power

9. Jenny took x number of items out of the dryer. She folded 10 items and put them in one pile. Then she folded the remaining items and divided them evenly into p piles. Which expression represents the number of items in each pile after the first one?

   A $p - 10 + x$ C $\dfrac{p}{10} + x$

   B $\dfrac{10 \times p}{x + 1}$ D $\dfrac{x - 10}{1 + p}$

10. Evaluate $9n^3 - 150$ for $n = 5$.

    A 150   C 1,455

    B 975   D 1,505

11. Tickets to the school play cost $9 for adults and $5 for students. The Wilson family bought 3 adult tickets and 4 student tickets. The Jackson family bought 2 adult tickets and 6 student tickets. What was the difference in the amount spent by the two families?

    A $1   C $36

    B $24   D $48

12. Which expression is NOT equivalent to $2a + 5(b + 7a)$?

    A $2a + 5b + 35a$

    B $2a + 12b$

    C $5(b) + 5(7a) + 2a$

    D $5b + 37a$

UNIT 4 Equivalent Expressions

13. Four students are sitting in the first row. In the second row, 4 students sit behind each of those students, and so on. After the fourth row is filled, one student leaves from each row. In the fifth row, 2 students sit behind each student in the fourth row. How many students are sitting in the fifth row?

_____

14. Write two expressions for 256 using exponents with different bases.

_____

15. Find the prime factorization of 2,181.

_____

16. Allison wants to cut out a rectangle with an area of 54 inches. She has one piece of paper measuring 9 by 12 inches. How many rectangles can she cut out from the piece of paper?

_____

17. Simplify the expression below using the order of operations.

$$2^8 + 3(7 \times 11 - 13) + \frac{3^2}{3}$$

_____

18. Describe a situation that can be modeled by the algebraic expression b divided by $\frac{1}{2}$.

_____

19. Write a phrase to describe the algebraic expression $\frac{x}{24} + 1 - 6.5$.

_____

20. There are 20 students in the drama club and 10 students in the photography club. Next year, 7 students will leave the club they are in and some new students will join one of the clubs. If d is the number of students who will join the drama club and p is the number of students who will join the photography club, write an expression to represent the total number of students in both clubs next year.

_____

21. Evaluate $14y^3 \div 2 + 901$ for $y = 6$.

_____

22. The expression $\frac{5}{9}(F - 32)$ gives the temperature in degrees Celsius for a given temperature in degrees Fahrenheit F. On Monday, it was 86°F. By Friday, the temperature had dropped to 61°F. What was the average temperature drop during each day in degrees Celsius? Round to the nearest tenth of a degree.

_____

23. Simplify the expression below. Then write a different expression equivalent to the simplified expression.

$$4y^2 + 6x - 2y^2 + 12x$$

_____

UNIT
4

Equivalent Expressions

Unit Test: D

1. Which number is the exponent in $\left(\frac{4}{5}\right)^3$?

   A 3

   B 4

   C 5

2. Which expression is the same as $7 \times 7 \times 7$?

   A 7×3

   B 2^7

   C 7^3

3. Which of the following shows the prime factorization of 20?

   A $2 \times 2 \times 5$

   B 2×10

   C 4×5

4. Which number has only two factors?

   A 6

   B 11

   C 15

5. What should you do first to simplify $8 + (2 \times 5)$?

   A add

   B subtract

   C multiply

6. Simplify the expression below.
   $$4 \times (2 + 1)$$

   A 2

   B 9

   C 12

7. Which of the following is the same as 4 plus x?

   A $\frac{4}{x}$

   B $4 + x$

   C $4 - x$

8. Which phrase means the same as $5 \times w$?

   A 5 times w

   B 5 divided by w

   C w plus 5

9. 10 towels are divided evenly into p piles. Which expression shows how many towels are in each pile?

   A $p - 10$

   B $10 \times p$

   C $\frac{10}{p}$

10. Evaluate $5n$ for $n = 2$.

    A 2

    B 5

    C 10

11. Tickets cost $9 each. How much are 5 tickets?

    A $5

    B $9

    C $45

12. Which expression is the same as $(2 \times 7) \times 3$?

    A $2 \times (7 \times 3)$

    B $2 - (7 + 3)$

    C $2 \div (7 - 3)$

13. Which expression is the same as $5a + b + 0$?

    A $5a + b$

    B $a + 0$

    C $(a + b)^0$

UNIT 4 **Equivalent Expressions**

14. Two students sit in the first row. In the second row, 2 students sit behind each of those students. How many students sit in the second row?

_____

15. Write 5×5 using exponents.

_____

16. Find the prime factorization of 13.

_____

17. List all the factors of 18.

_____

18. What should you do first when you simplify the expression below?

$$(5 + 4) \times 3$$

_____

19. Simplify $2 + 3^2$.

_____

20. Complete the expression so it means the same as 50 take away b.

$50 -$ _____

21. Complete the phrase so it means the same as $\dfrac{x}{4}$.

x divided by _____

22. There are 20 students in a club. Next year, x number of students will join. Complete the expression to show how many students will be in the club next year.

_____ $+ x$

23. What is $y \times 2$ when is $y = 4$?

_____

24. What is $\dfrac{1}{2}(f - 10)$ when $f = 16$?

_____

25. Write an equivalent expression for the one below.

$2 + (x + 8) =$ _____

26. Simplify $4y + 2y + 1$.

_____

Equivalent Expressions

Performance Task

Answer the questions.

1. Darla is creating a family tree. She starts by writing down the names of her two parents. For each of her parents, she writes down the names of their two parents, and so on. After six generations, how many names has she written down, not including herself? Write and evaluate an expression using an exponent to find out.

   _____

2. Darla wants to draw her family tree on a rectangular piece of paper. She has a large piece of paper that is 400 square inches.

   _____

   a. Write the prime factorization of 400.

      _____

   b. List all the possible whole-number lengths and widths of a piece of paper that has an area of 400 square inches.

      _____

      _____

   c. Which length and width would be best for Darla's project? Why?

      _____

      _____

3. Darla wants to get her family tree drawing framed. The perimeter of a rectangle is two times the length plus two times the width. Write an algebraic expression to represent the perimeter p of a rectangle.

   _____

4. A wood frame costs $1.50 per inch.

   a. Write an expression to find the cost of a wood frame. Use the algebraic expression you wrote in Exercise 3.

      _____

   b. Use a property to write an equivalent expression for the cost of a wood frame. Tell which property you used.

      _____

UNIT 5 — Equations and Inequalities
Unit Test: A

1. Jason worked 3 more hours than Keith. Jason worked 12 hours. Which equation represents this situation, if k is the number of hours Keith worked?

   A $12 + k = 3$

   B $12k = 3$

   C $k + 3 = 12$

   D $3k = 12$

2. For which equation is $x = 1$ a solution?

   A $4 - x = 1$

   B $4x = 1$

   C $x + 3 = 4$

   D $\dfrac{x}{4} = 1$

3. Bianca scored 12 goals. Together, Bianca and Diana scored 20 goals. How many goals did Diana score?

   A 4   C 12

   B 8   D 20

4. A wall has an area of 40 square feet. Its height is 8 feet. Which equation could you use to find its width?

   A $40 - w = 8$

   B $8w = 40$

   C $8 + w = 40$

   D $\dfrac{w}{8} = 40$

5. Which number line shows $x > 7$?

   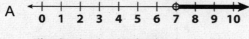

6. Where is point A located on the coordinate grid below?

   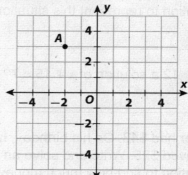

   A Quadrant I   C Quadrant III

   B Quadrant II   D Quadrant IV

7. Mike is renting a boat. The rental fee is $25 for each hour. He rented a boat for 3 hours. Which is the dependent variable in the situation?

   A the type of boat Mike rented

   B the hourly rental fee

   C the number of hours Mike boated

   D the amount Mike paid

8. Wendy is making lemonade. As shown below, Wendy mixes water and lemon juice. Which equation shows how much lemon juice is needed for 6 ounces of water?

Water in ounces	3	6	9	12
Lemon juice in ounces	1	2	3	4

   A $j = \dfrac{6}{3}$ C $j = 6(2)$

   B $6j = 3$ D $6 = \dfrac{j}{2}$

9. Paul graphed the equation $y = x$. Which point does the graph *not* pass through?

   A (0, 0)   C (9, 9)

   B (6, 6)   D (12, 14)

UNIT 5

Equations and Inequalities

10. Tamara has 12 pencils. There are 3 red pencils and p other pencils. Write an equation to represent this situation.

_____

11. Is $x = 12$ a solution of $x + 15 = 7$?

_____

12. Oliver had $43. On his birthday, he received $25. Write and solve an equation to find how much money Oliver has now.

equation: _____

solution: _____

13. Greta cut a ribbon into 12 pieces. Each piece was 6 inches long. Use the model below to write and solve an equation to find the length of the ribbon she started with.

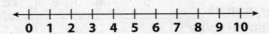

| length of ribbon | ÷ | 12 | = | 6 |

equation: _____

solution: _____

14. Graph an inequality to represent $t \leq 5$.

0 1 2 3 4 5 6 7 8 9 10

15. Graph and label points $A(2, 4)$ and $B(-1, -3)$ on the coordinate plane below.

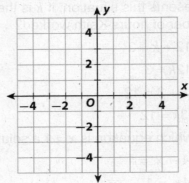

16. Tickets to a play cost $7 each. As the number of tickets increases, the total cost increases. What are the independent and dependent variables in this situation?

independent: _____

dependent: _____

17. The table shows how much Eric earns. Write an equation that relates h, the number of hours worked to p, his pay.

Hours Worked	1	2	3	4
Pay in Dollars	8	16	24	32

equation: _____

18. Graph the equation $y = x + 2$.

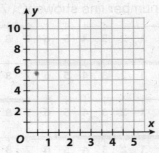

UNIT 5 · Equations and Inequalities

Unit Test: B

1. Jason has volunteered at the pet shelter 3 more times than Keith. Jason has volunteered 12 times. Which equation represents this situation?

   A $12 + k = 3$

   B $12k = 3$

   C $k + 3 = 12$

   D $3k = 12$

2. For which equation is $x = 5$ a solution?

   A $5x = 5$

   B $5 + x = 15$

   C $5 + 0 = x$

   D $\frac{x}{5} = 5$

3. Bianca scored 8 more goals than Diana. Bianca scored 12 goals. How many goals did Diana score?

   A 4   C 12

   B 8   D 20

4. Shawn is painting a wall with an area of 96 square feet. Its height is 8 feet. Which equation could you use to find its width?

   A $96 - w = 8$

   B $8w = 96$

   C $8 + w = 96$

   D $\frac{w}{8} = 96$

5. Marianne can say hello in more than 7 languages. Which number line could represent this situation?

   A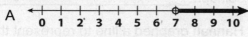

   B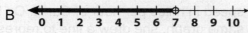

   C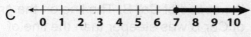

   D

6. What are the coordinates of point *A* on the coordinate grid below?

   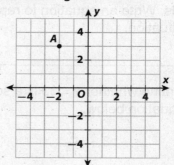

   A (2, 3)   C (2, −3)

   B (−2, 3)   D (−2, −3)

7. Mike is renting a boat. The hourly rental fee is the same per hour for any boat. Mike paid $50 to rent a canoe, and then $25 to rent a kayak. Which is the dependent variable in the situation?

   A the number of boats Mike rented

   B the hourly rental fee

   C the number of hours Mike boated

   D the amount Mike paid

8. Wendy is making lemonade. As shown below, Wendy mixes some water with some lemon juice to make lemonade. Which equation represents how much lemon juice is needed when Wendy uses 10 ounces of water?

Water in ounces	6	9	12	15
Lemon juice in ounces	2	3	4	5

   A $y = \frac{10}{3}$ C $y = 10(3)$

   B $10x = 3$ D $10 = \frac{x}{3}$

9. Paul graphed the equation $y = 6 + x$. Which point does the graph *not* pass through?

   A (0, 6)   C (9, 15)

   B (6, 12)   D (12, 20)

UNIT 5

Equations and Inequalities

10. Tamara has a box of 12 colored pencils. There are 3 red pencils and p other pencils. Write an equation to represent this situation.

_____

11. Determine whether $x = 33$ is a solution of the equation below.

$$3 = \frac{x}{11}$$

_____

12. Oliver had $43 on the day before his birthday. After he received some money for his birthday, he had $68. Write and solve an equation to find how much money Oliver received for his birthday.

equation:_____

solution:_____

13. Greta cut a length of ribbon into an equal number of pieces. She cut the length of ribbon into 12 pieces. Each piece was 6 inches long. Write and solve an equation to find the length of the ribbon she started with.

equation:_____

solution:_____

14. The temperature in the freezer must be 2°F or less. Write and graph an inequality to represent this situation.

inequality:_____

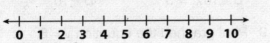

15. Graph and label points $A(2, 4)$, $B(-1, -3)$, $C(-4, 5)$ and $D(0, -3)$ on the coordinate plane below

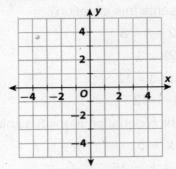

16. Students are selling tickets to a school fundraiser. For every 15 tickets a student sells, a student earns a T-shirt as a reward. What are the independent and dependent variables in this situation?

independent: _____

dependent:_____

17. The table shows how much Eric earns for pruning trees. Write an equation that relates t, the number of trees Eric prunes to p, the amount he earns. Solve your equation to find how much Eric earns if he prunes 7 trees.

Trees Pruned	2	4	6	8
Pay in Dollars	30	60	90	120

equation:_____

solution:_____

18. Hannah graphed a line to represent the speed in miles per hour of Car A. On the same graph, she drew a line to represent the speed of Car B. The line on the graph of Car B was steeper than the line of Car A. Which car is faster? Explain.

_____

_____

UNIT 5

Equations and Inequalities

Unit Test: C

1. Jason volunteered at the pet shelter twice as many times as Keith. Noah volunteered three times more often than Jason. Keith volunteered 4 times. Which equation represents the relationship between the number of times Noah and Keith volunteered?

   A $\dfrac{6}{n} = 4$ C $\dfrac{n}{6} = 4$

   B $n - 6 = 4$ D $n + 6 = 4$

2. For which equation is $x = 35$ a solution?

   A $55x = 925$

   B $15 + x = 75$

   C $\dfrac{105}{x} = 3$

   D $\dfrac{x}{5} = 9$

3. Angle *A* and angle *B* are complementary. Angle *A* measures 40°. What is the measure of angle *B*?

   A 40°   C 90°

   B 50°   D 140°

4. Shawn is painting a wall with an area of 168 square feet. Its height is 8 feet. Which equation could you use to find its width?

   A $168 - w = 8$

   B $8w = 168$

   C $8 + w = 168$

   D $\dfrac{w}{8} = 168$

5. Marianne speaks no fewer than 7 languages. Which number line could represent this situation?

   A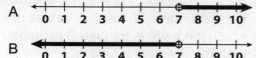

   B

   C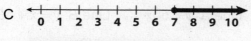

   D

6. A share of stock loses value in each week of a month. In which quadrant would the data points for this situation be graphed?

   A Quadrant I   C Quadrant III

   B Quadrant II   D Quadrant IV

7. Mike is renting a boat. The hourly rental fee is the same per hour for any boat. Mike paid $50 to rent a canoe, and then $25 to rent a kayak. If the number of hours is the independent variable, which could be the dependent variable?

   A the number of boats Mike rented

   B the hourly rental fee

   C the number of hours Mike boated

   D the amount Mike has to spend

8. Wendy is making lemonade. As shown below, Wendy mixes water with some lemon juice to make lemonade. Which equation represents how much lemon juice is needed when Wendy uses 13.35 ounces of water?

Water in ounces	6.75	9.75	12.75	15.75
Lemon juice in ounces	2.25	3.25	4.25	5.25

   A $y = \dfrac{13.35}{3}$ C $y = 13.35(3)$

   B $13.35x = 3$ D $13.35 = \dfrac{x}{3}$

9. Paul graphed the equation $y = 6.15 + x$. Which point does the graph *not* pass through?

   A (2.41, 8.56)   C (9.72, 15.87)

   B (6.09, 12.24)   D (12.42, 18.09)

UNIT 5	**Equations and Inequalities**

10. Tamara is 11 years old. Her sister Kelly is 2 years older than her. Tamara and Kelly have a sister, Jill, who is 3 years older than their ages combined. Write two equations that represent the relationship between the ages of the three sisters.

_____

11. Determine whether $x = 874$ is a solution of the equation below.

$$23 = \frac{x}{38}$$

_____

12. Oliver had $243 on the day before his birthday. After he received some money for his birthday, he had $568. He received $75 from his aunt and the rest from his parents. How much money did Oliver's parents give him for his birthday?

_____

13. Greta cut a length of ribbon into an equal number of pieces. She cut the length of ribbon into 12 pieces. Each piece was 6.25 inches long. Write and solve an equation to find the length of the ribbon she started with.

equation:_____

solution:_____

14. The temperature in the freezer must be no higher than 2°F. Write and graph an inequality to represent this situation.

inequality:_____

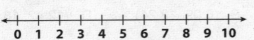

15. Graph and label points $A(2.5, 4)$, $B(-1.5, -3)$, $C(-4.5, 5)$ and $D(0, -3.5)$ on the coordinate plane below.

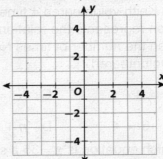

16. Students are selling tickets to a school fundraiser. Tickets cost $10. For every $100 in tickets a student sells, he or she earns 2% in cash as a bonus. Identify two different pairs of independent and dependent variables in this situation.

_____

_____

17. The table shows how much the Erickson Company earns for pruning trees. Write an equation that relates t, the number of trees the Erickson Company prunes to p, the amount the company is paid. Solve your equation to find how much the company earns if it prunes 70 trees.

Trees Pruned	2	4	6	8
Pay in Dollars	125	250	375	500

equation:_____

solution:_____

18. Hannah graphs Line A and B in Quadrant I of the same grid. List two values of x for which the y-value for Line B is greater than the y-value for Line A.

Line A: $y = 50x$ Line B: $y = x + 50$

_____

UNIT 5 Equations and Inequalities
Unit Test: D

1. Keith and Jason worked 12 hours. Jason worked 3 hours. Which equation shows this situation? Use the model below to help you.

   A $12 + k = 3$

   B $12k = 3$

   C $k + 3 = 12$

2. Which equation is true when is $x = 1$?

   A $3x = 3$

   B $3x = 2$

   C $3x = 1$

3. Bianca scored 2 goals. Together, Bianca and Diana scored 5 goals. How many goals did Diana score?

   A   2

   B   3

   C   5

4. A wall has an area of 40 square feet. Its height is 8 feet. Which equation could you use to find its width? Use the model below to help you.

   A $40 - w = 8$

   B $8w = 40$

   C $8 + w = 40$

5. Which number line shows $x > 7$?

   A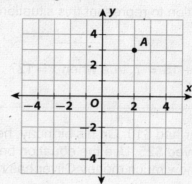

   B

   C

6. Where is point A located on the coordinate grid below?

   A   Quadrant I

   B   Quadrant II

   C   Quadrant III

7. Mike reads 5 pages an hour. The independent variable is time. What is the dependent variable?

   A   the number of books

   B   the number of hours

   C   the number of pages

8. Wendy is making lemonade. Which equation shows how much lemon juice is needed for 3 ounces of water?

Water in ounces	3	6	9
Lemon juice in ounces	1	2	3

   A $j = 1$

   B $3 + j = 1$

   C $j - 3 = 1$

9. Paul graphed the equation $y = x$. Which point does the graph *not* pass through?

   A   (0, 0)

   B   (5, 5)

   C   (10, 15)

UNIT 5

Equations and Inequalities

10. Tamara has 12 pencils. There are 3 red pencils and p other pencils. Complete the equation to represent this situation.

$$p + 3 = \underline{\hspace{1.5cm}}$$

11. Is $x + 15 = 7$ true when $x = 12$?

_____

12. Oliver had $10. On his birthday, he received $25. Use the equation below to find how much money Oliver has now.

equation: $10 + 25 = m$

solution:_____

13. Greta cut a ribbon into 12 pieces. Each piece was 6 inches long. Complete and solve the equation to find the length of the ribbon she started with.

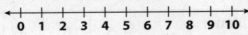

| length of ribbon | ÷ | 12 | = | 6 |

equation: $x \div 12 = 6$

solution:_____

14. Shade the number line to show $t \le 5$.

```
←—+——+——+——+——+——+——+——+——+——+——+—→
  0  1  2  3  4  5  6  7  8  9  10
```

15. Graph point (2, 4) on the coordinate plane below.

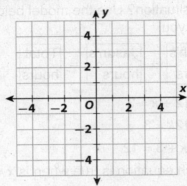

16. Tickets cost $7 each. As the number of tickets goes up, the total cost goes up. The independent variable is shown below. What is the dependent variable?

independent: number of tickets

dependent:_____

17. The table shows how much Eric earns. Complete the equation to show how the number of hours Eric works is related to his pay.

Hours Worked	1	2	3	4
Pay in Dollars	8	16	24	32

equation: $p = (\underline{\hspace{1cm}}) \times h$

18. Graph the equation $y = x$. The first point is done for you.

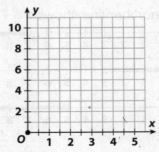

Equations and Inequalities
Performance Task

Answer the questions.

1. Waheeda wants to buy a skateboard. She has $15 in savings. A skateboard costs $75. How much more money does she need? Write and solve an equation to represent the situation.

   a. equation: _____   b. solution: _____

2. Suppose Waheeda wants to have some money left over after buying the skateboard. Write an inequality to show how much Waheeda needs to earn.

   _____

3. To earn money for the skateboard, Waheeda decides to run a lemonade stand. If she sells each glass of lemonade for $1.50, how many glasses of lemonade will she need to sell? Write and solve an equation to find the answer.

   a. equation: _____   b. solution: _____

4. Waheeda mixes water with some lemon juice to make lemonade. Write an equation to represent how much lemon juice is needed when Waheeda uses 10 ounces of water.

   _____

Water in ounces	6	9	12	15
Lemon juice in ounces	2	3	4	5

5. The amount Waheeda earns is related to the number of glasses of lemonade she sells.

   a. Identify the independent and dependent variables in the situation.

   _____

   b. Write an equation representing the amount Waheeda earns in relation to the number of glasses of lemonade she sells.

   _____

   c. In which Quadrant of a graph would her data appear? Explain.

   _____

   d. Graph the equation on a separate sheet of graph paper. Be sure to choose an appropriate scale for the *x* and *y* axes.

Name _____ Date _____ Class_____

1. The point (6, −5) is reflected across the y-axis. What are the coordinates of the reflected point?

   A (−6, −5)   C (−5, 6)

   B (6, 5)   D (−5, −6)

2. Which is a net for a cube?

   A 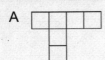   C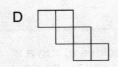

   B    D

3. What is the distance from point F at (2, −3) to point G at (9, −3)?

   A 7 units   C 4 units

   B 5 units   D 0 units

4. A polygon with 6 vertices is drawn on the coordinate plane. What do you know about the polygon?

   A It is an octagon.

   B It is a rhombus.

   C It is a hexagon.

   D It is a quadrilateral.

5. What is the surface area of a rectangular prism 8 inches wide, 14 inches long, and 2 inches deep?

   A 324 in^2 C 280 in^2

   B 312 in^2 D 56 in^2

6. What is the area of the parallelogram below?

   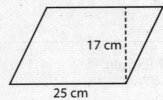

   A 37 cm^2 C 212.5 cm^2

   B 117 cm^2 D 425 cm^2

7. Which of the following equations will give you the area of the following figure?

   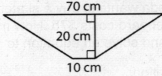

   A $A = \dfrac{70}{2} \times 20$

   B $A = \dfrac{70 + 20}{2} \times 10$

   C $A = \dfrac{70 + 10}{2} \times 20$

   D $A = (70 + 10) \times 10$

8. The two diagonals of a rhombus are 22 inches long and 5 inches long. What is the area of the rhombus?

   A 17 in^2 C 55 in^2

   B 27 in^2 D 110 in^2

9. A window is shaped like a parallelogram. The base is 16 inches long. The area is 608 square inches. What is the height of the window?

   A 19 in.   C 64 in.

   B 38 in.   D 76 in.

10. A drawer has a volume of 1,575 cubic inches. The drawer is 5 inches deep and 21 inches long. What is the width of the drawer?

    A 12 in.   C 15 in.

    B 14 in.   D 17 in.

11. Fahed wants to replace the windows in the front of his house. The front of his house has three windows shaped like parallelograms. Each window has a base of 3.25 feet and a height of 2 feet. What is the total area of all three windows?

    A 3.25 ft^2 C 9.75 ft^2

    B 6.5 ft^2 D 19.5 ft^2

Relationships in Geometry

12. Mark has a kite shaped like a rhombus. The two diagonals measure 15 inches and 6 inches. What is the area of Mark's kite?

_____

13. Brandon has a box 9.5 inches tall, 3.8 inches wide, and 4.2 inches long. How many square inches of wrapping paper does he need to wrap the box?

_____

14. The front face of Josh's roof is shaped like a triangle. It has a base of 100 feet and a height of 15 feet. What is the area of Josh's roof?

_____

15. Gabrielle has a decal shaped like a trapezoid. One base is 12 inches, and the other base is 7 inches. The area is 76 square inches. What is the height?

_____

16. A carpet remnant is shaped like a triangle. It has a height of 32 inches and a base of 8 inches. Write an equation to represent the area. Then find the area of the remnant.

_____

17. The floor of the school music room is being tiled. The room is shaped like a parallelogram. The parallelogram has a base of 25 feet and a height of 11 feet. Each package of tile will cover 5 square feet. How many packages of tile will be needed to tile the music room floor?

_____

18. The volume of a suitcase is 1,083 cubic inches. Its length is 19 inches, and its height is 9.5 inches. What is the width? Write an equation to represent the width. Then find the width of the suitcase.

_____

_____

19. A box of granola is 3 inches wide, 4 inches long, and 6 inches high. The box is half empty. What is the volume of granola left in the box?

_____

20. A fish tank is filled with water. The tank holds 150 gallons. Each cubic foot of water contains about 7.5 gallons. The tank is 5 feet long and 3 feet high. What is the width of the tank?

_____

21. Juan has a box that is filled with toys. The box is $3\frac{1}{2}$ feet long, 6 feet wide, and 3 feet high. What is the volume of the box?

_____

22. The owner of a smoothie company wants to rent a kiosk in the new mall. He is choosing between two spaces. Both have floor plans shaped like parallelograms. The first space is 12 feet wide and 16 feet long. The second space is 13 feet wide and 15 feet long. Which is the larger space? Explain.

_____

Name _____ Date _____ Class _____

UNIT 6

Relationships in Geometry
Unit Test: B

1. The point (6, –5) is reflected across the x-axis. What are the coordinates of the reflected point?

   A (–6, –5)   C (–5, –6)
   B (–5, 6)   D (6, 5)

2. Which is **not** a net for a cube?

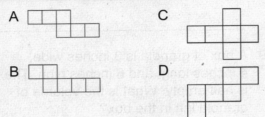

3. What is the distance from point H at (7, 6) to point J at (–5, 6) on the coordinate plane?

   A 1 unit   C 12 units
   B 2 units   D 14 units

4. A polygon with 3 vertices is drawn on the coordinate plane. What can you tell about the polygon?

   A It is a scalene triangle.
   B It is an isosceles triangle.
   C It is a triangle.
   D It is a right triangle.

5. A box is 12 centimeters wide, 12 centimeters long, and 15 centimeters tall. What is the total surface area of 4 such boxes?

   A 1,872 cm²   C 4,032 cm²
   B 3,744 cm²   D 14,976 cm²

6. A window is shaped like a parallelogram. The base of the window is 27 inches. Its area is 445.5 square inches. What is the height of the window?

   A 16.5 in.   C 33 in.
   B 8.25 in.   D 27 in.

7. What is the area of a right triangle 21 centimeters wide and 13 centimeters tall?

   A 136.5 cm²   C 139.5 cm²
   B 138.5 cm²   D 273 cm²

8. What is the perimeter of the rectangle?

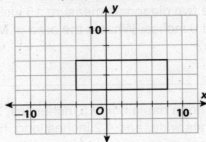

   A 48 units   C 16 units
   B 32 units   D 12 units

9. What is the area of the parallelogram below?

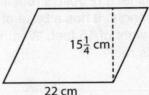

   A 167.75 cm²   C 341 cm²
   B 335.5 cm²   D 671 cm²

10. Which equation can be used to find the area of the figure below?

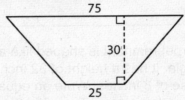

   A $A = \dfrac{75}{2} \times 30$

   B $A = \dfrac{75 - 25}{2} \times 30$

   C $A = \dfrac{75 + 25}{2} \times 30$

   D $A = (75 + 25) \times 30$

11. What is the area of the rhombus below?

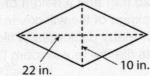

   A 32 in²   C 110 in²
   B 64 in²   D 220 in²

UNIT 6

Relationships in Geometry

12. Find the surface area of this rectangular prism. Write an equation and show your work.

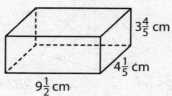

$3\frac{4}{5}$ cm
$4\frac{1}{5}$ cm
$9\frac{1}{2}$ cm

_____

_____

13. Mailena has a kite shaped like a rhombus. Its two diagonals measure 22 inches and 13 inches. What is the area of Mailena's kite?

_____

14. The front face of Jai's roof is shaped like a triangle. It has a base of 70 feet and a height of 16 feet. What is the area of Jai's roof?

_____

15. Janet has a decal shaped like a trapezoid. One base is 10.2 inches, and the other base is 5.3 inches. The area is 46.5 square inches. What is the height of the decal?

_____

16. The face of a triangular-shaped guitar has an area of 52 square inches and a height of 13 inches. Write an equation to find the length of the base. Then find the length of the base of the guitar's face.

_____

_____

17. The floor of the school art closet is being tiled. The closet is shaped like a parallelogram. The parallelogram has a base of 17.5 feet and a height of 6 feet. Each package of tile will cover 5 square feet. How many packages of tile will be needed to tile the music room floor?

_____

18. The volume of a suitcase is 4,331.25 cubic inches. The length of the suitcase is 22.5 inches and the width is 19.25 inches. What is the height? Show your work.

_____

_____

19. Eli has a box that is 2 inches wide, 4 inches long, and 10 inches high. Gary has a box whose volume is 3 times as great as Eli's. What is the volume of Gary's box?

_____

20. A trough is filled with water. The trough holds 315 gallons. Each cubic foot of water contains about 7.5 gallons. The trough is 7 feet long and 4 feet wide. What is the height of the trough?

_____

21. Marcus has a box that is $4\frac{1}{2}$ feet long, $\frac{1}{2}$ foot wide, and 2 feet high. What is the volume of the box?

_____

UNIT 6

Relationships in Geometry

Unit Test: C

1. The point (−3, −2) is reflected across the *x*-axis, and then reflected across the *y*-axis. What are the coordinates of the reflected point?

   A (3, 2)   C (−3, 2)

   B (3, −2)   D (−3, −2)

2. Which is **not** a net for a cube?

   A 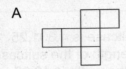   C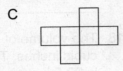

   B 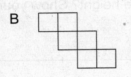   D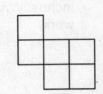

3. What is the distance from point *L* at (−8, 2) to point *J* at (6, 2) on the coordinate plane?

   A −14 units   C 14 units

   B 2 units   D 16 units

4. A polygon with 4 vertices is drawn on the coordinate plane. Two of the sides of the polygon are not parallel. Considering what you know, what is the best name for this polygon?

   A It is a rhombus.

   B It is a trapezoid.

   C It is a quadrilateral.

   D It is a parallelogram.

5. A box is $8\frac{1}{2}$ inches wide, $12\frac{3}{4}$ inches long and $5\frac{1}{2}$ inches tall. What is the total surface area of 3 such boxes?

   A $18,618\frac{1}{2}$ in^2 C $1,351\frac{1}{2}$ in^2

   B 6,206 in^2 D $450\frac{1}{2}$ in^2

6. What is the surface area of this square pyramid?

   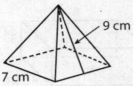

   A 126 m^2 C 252 m^2

   B 175 m^2 D 301 m^2

7. In his living room, Rashad has a window shaped like a parallelogram. It is 7.2 feet high and has a base of 8.7 feet. The area of the window in Rashad's bedroom is three times smaller. What is the area of the bedroom window?

   A 10.44 ft^2 C 62.64 ft^2

   B 20.88 ft^2 D 187.92 ft^2

8. A trapezoid is 14 centimeters high and has bases that measure 13.5 centimeters and 27.5 centimeters. What is the area of the trapezoid?

   A 143.5 cm^2 C 294 cm^2

   B 287 cm^2 D 574 cm^2

9. A rhombus has diagonals that measure 43.3 inches and 22.5 inches. What is the area of the rhombus?

   A 65.8 in^2 C 487.13 in^2

   B 131.6 in^2 D 974.25 in^2

10. A window is shaped like a parallelogram. The base of the window is 14.25 inches. The area is 356.25 square inches. What is the height of the window?

    A 12.5 in.   C 50 in.

    B 25 in.   D 250 in.

11. Ari has a kite shaped like a rhombus. The two diagonals measure 47 inches and 36 inches. What is the area of Ari's kite?

_____

12. What is the perimeter of this figure?

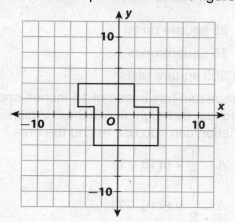

_____

13. The front face of Jamal's roof is shaped like a triangle. It has a base of 97.2 feet and a height of 17.25 feet. Jamal's neighbor's roof has an area of 942 square feet. What is the difference in area between Jamal's roof and his neighbor's?

_____

14. Shanté has a decal shaped like a trapezoid. One base is 16.4 inches, and the other base is 7.9 inches. The area is 157.95 square inches. What is the height of the decal?

_____

15. A triangular garden has a height of 14.20 meters and a base of 6.30 meters. A second garden is the same height as the first one but has a base twice as long. What is the total area of both gardens?

16. The floor of the school supply room is being tiled. The room is shaped like a parallelogram. The parallelogram has a base of 22.5 feet and a height of 11 feet. Each package of tile will cover 5 square feet. If the school buys 49 packages of tile, will that be enough to tile the supply room floor? Explain.

_____

_____

17. The volume of a suitcase is 8,556 cubic inches. It is 32 inches long and 15.5 inches high. Write an equation to represent the width. Then find the width of the suitcase.

_____

18. Janet has a box of granola 4 inches wide, 6 inches long, and 8 inches high. Gary's box is twice the volume of Janet's. Over the past week, Gary has eaten a third of his box. What is the volume of granola that Gary has left?

_____

19. A koi pond in an office lobby is filled with water. The pond is a rectangular prism and holds 1,305 gallons of water. Each cubic foot of water contains about 7.5 gallons. The pond is $14\frac{1}{2}$ feet long and 12 feet wide. What is the depth of the pond?

_____

20. Amy has a box that is $6\frac{1}{2}$ feet long, 3.25 feet wide, and 2 feet high. What is the volume of the box?

_____

UNIT 6

Relationships in Geometry

Unit Test: D

1. The point A is located at (2, 4) on the coordinate plane. If point A is reflected across the y-axis, what are the coordinates of the reflected point?

   A (2, –4)   B (–2, –4)

   C (–2, 4)

2. Which solid could be formed from this net?

   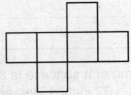

   A   rectangular prism

   B   square pyramid

   C   cube

3. What is the distance from point P at (2, 4) to point Q at (9, 4) on the coordinate plane?

   A 11 units   B 7 units

   C 5 units

4. A polygon with 4 vertices is drawn on the coordinate plane. What is the best name for this polygon?

   A   quadrilateral

   B   hexagon

   C   octagon

5. A box is 4 inches wide, 5 inches long, and 3 inches tall. Which equation could be used to find the surface area of the box?

   A $SA = 2(4 + 5) + 2(5 + 3) + 2(3 + 4)$

   B $SA = 2(4^2) + 2(5^2) + 2(3^2)$

   C $SA = 2(4 \times 5) + 2(5 \times 3) + 2(3 \times 4)$

6. A window is shaped like a parallelogram. The base of the window is 15 inches. The area is 450 square inches. What is the height?

   A 15 in.   B 30 in.

   C 45 in.

7. What is the area of the parallelogram below?

   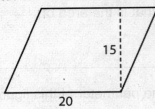

   A   35 square units

   B   75 square units

   C   300 square units

8. A trapezoid has bases of 15 inches and 7 inches. Its height is 6 inches. Which equation can you use to find the area?

   A $A = \dfrac{1}{2} \times 6(15 + 7)$

   B $A = \dfrac{1}{2} \times 6(15 - 7)$

   C $A = \dfrac{1}{2} \times 15(6 + 7)$

9. What is the area of the rhombus below?

   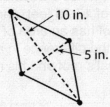

   A 15 in^2 B 25 in^2

   C 50 in^2

10. A kitchen drawer has a volume of 1,125 cubic inches. The drawer is 15 inches long and 5 inches deep. What is the width of the drawer?

    A 14 inches

    B 15 inches

    C 16 inches

UNIT 6 Relationships in Geometry

11. Miguel has a kite shaped like a rhombus. The two diagonals measure 10 inches and 3 inches. What is the area of the kite?

_____

12. What is the perimeter of this rectangle?

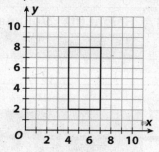

_____

13. The front face of Arpad's roof is shaped like a triangle. It has a base of 55 feet and a height of 10 feet. What is the area of Arpad's roof?

_____

14. Gina has a decal shaped like a trapezoid. The sum of the lengths of both bases is 30 inches. The area is 75 square inches. What is the height of the decal?

_____

15. The face of an electric guitar is shaped like a triangle. It has a height of 20 inches and a base of 7 inches. Write an equation you could use to find the area of the face of the guitar.

_____

16. The coach's equipment room is shaped like a parallelogram. The parallelogram has a base of 30 feet and height of 15 feet. What is the area of the equipment room?

_____

17. The volume of a suitcase is 1,200 cubic inches. Its length is 20 inches, and its height is 10 inches. What is the width? Write an equation to represent the width. Then find the width of the suitcase.

_____

18. A box of cereal bars is 3 inches wide, 4 inches long, and 5 inches high. What is the volume of the box of cereal bars?

_____

19. A bathtub is filled with water. It holds 60 cubic feet of water. The tub is 6 feet long and 5 feet wide. What is the height of the tub?

_____

20. Juan has a box that is 3 feet long, 2 feet wide, and 3 feet high. What is the volume of the box?

_____

21. The front of Priscilla's house has one large window shaped like a triangle. The window has a base of 7 feet and a height of 4 feet. What is the area of the window?

_____

22. The owner of a smoothie company wants to rent space in the new mall. He is choosing between two spaces. The floor plans are both shaped like parallelograms. The first parallelogram is 11 feet high with a base of 15 feet. The second space has an area of 160 square feet. How much larger is the first store than the second store?

_____

Relationships in Geometry
Performance Task

Sharing the Yard

A family's yard is 36 feet wide and 45 feet long. There is a patio in the yard that is 5 feet wide and 11.25 feet long.

Use the chart below to help you keep track of the items in the yard.

1. Fill in the information you already know.

Item	Length (ft)	Width (ft)	Area (ft²)	Height (ft)	Volume (ft³)
Patio					
Clubhouse					
Sandbox					
Garden					
Yard					

Write an equation for each and solve. As you read or find dimensions of items in the yard, add the dimensions to the table above.

2. The clubhouse is shaped like a rectangular prism. It is 12 feet long, 8 feet wide, and 6 feet high. What is the area and volume of the clubhouse?

_____

3. The base of the sandbox is shaped like a parallelogram. The parallelogram base has an area of 9 square feet and the sandbox has a volume of 13.5 cubic feet. What is the height of the sandbox?

_____

4. The garden is 25 feet long and 11.6 feet wide. What area does the garden cover?

_____

5. How many square feet of the yard are left for planting grass?

_____

6. Discus the best way to arrange the back yard for safety and convenience. Using grid paper, draw the backyard and all the items on a coordinate plane. Label all vertices of the items with an ordered pair to show each location. Compare your backyard to those drawn by other class members.

Name _____ Date _____ Class_____

Measurement and Data

Unit Test: A

1. Thomas hiked 6 miles on Monday, 10 miles on Tuesday, and 8 miles on Wednesday. Which value is closest to the mean number of miles he hiked over the three-day period?

   A 4 mi

   B 6 mi

   C 8 mi

   D 10 mi

2. What is the range of the data represented in the box plot below?

   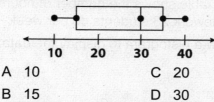

   A 10

   B 15

   C 20

   D 30

3. What is the median of the data represented in the line plot below?

   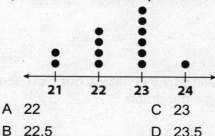

   A 22

   B 22.5

   C 23

   D 23.5

4. What is the median of the data set below?

   {0.5, 1.5, 2.5, 4.0}

   A 1.5

   B 2.0

   C 2.5

   D 3.0

Use the table for 5 and 6.

5. What is the mean for the data set below?

8	10	6	4
12	6	8	14

   A 8

   B 8.5

   C 10

   D 12

6. What is the mean absolute deviation for the data set?

   A 2.625

   B 3

   C 3.625

   D 21

7. For the data set below, which of the following measures is greatest?

   {2, 2, 2, 4, 6, 8, 12, 20}

   A mean

   B median

   C range

   D mode

Use the graph for 8 and 9.

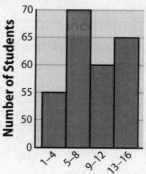

Grades

The histogram shows the number of students in each grade range at the county fair.

8. What grades were most students in?

   A 1–4

   B 5–8

   C 9–12

   D 13–16

9. How many more students were in grades 5–8 than 9–12?

   A 4

   B 5

   C 7

   D 10

UNIT
7

Measurement and Data

Use the table for 10–15.

Student Scores

90	80	95	90	84
72	66	88	98	100
86	90	92	94	80

In the table above, Mr. Brinkley recorded the score each student in his class earned on a recent math test.

10. What is the mean score for the students in Mr. Brinkley's class?

_____

11. What is the mean absolute deviation for the scores?

_____

12. What is the median score for the students in Mr. Brinkley's class?

_____

13. What is the mode of the data?

_____

14. Draw a box-and-whisker plot to display the data.

15. What is the interquartile range for the data?

_____

Use the table for 16–19.

Homework Hours	Number of Students
0–3	5
4–7	12
8–11	4
12–15	2

The table shows the number of hours of homework 23 students do per week.

16. Draw a histogram to display the data.

17. Explain why this data is **not** represented using a bar graph.

_____

_____

_____

18. How long do most students spend on homework per week?

_____

_____

19. Can you tell how many students spend 10 hours on homework each week?

_____

_____

UNIT 7	**Measurement and Data**
	Unit Test: B

1. Alexandra worked 5 hours on Monday, 4.5 hours on Tuesday, and 2.5 hours on Wednesday. Which is closest to the mean number of hours she worked over the three-day period?

   A 3 h   C 5 h

   B 4 h   D 6 h

2. What is the mean absolute deviation for Alexandra's hours?

   A 1   C 3

   B 2   D 4

3. What is the median of the data represented in the box plot below?

   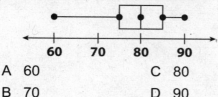

   A 60   C 80

   B 70   D 90

4. What is the median of the data represented in the line plot below?

   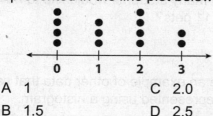

   A 1   C 2.0

   B 1.5   D 2.5

5. If *a* is a positive integer, what is the mean of the data below?

   {2*a*, 3*a*, 3*a*, 8*a*}

   A 2*a*   C 4*a*

   B 3*a*   D 16*a*

Use the table for 6–8.

6. What is the median for the data set below?

2	10	6.5	8.8
3	6	4	12.5

   A 6.0   C 6.6

   B 6.25   D 6.9

7. What is the mean of the data set?

   A 6   C 8

   B 6.6   D 52.8

8. What is the mean absolute deviation?

   A 2.875   C 6.6

   B 3   D 23

9. For the data set below, which of the following measures is greatest?

   {3, 3, 4, 5, 6, 8, 16, 20}

   A mean   C range

   B median   D mode

Use the graph for 10 and 11.

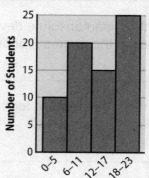

Games Played Weekly

The histogram shows the number of video games members of three classes play each week.

10. How many more students play 18–23 games than play 0–5 games?

   A 10   C 20

   B 15   D 25

11. Steven plays 10 video games each week. In which bar does he fall?

   A 0–5

   B 6–11

   C 12–17

   D 18–23

UNIT 7 Measurement and Data

Use the table for 12–17.

Student Scores

88	90	98	97	86
76	68	78	92	98
100	98	92	92	80
65	75	86	90	92

In the table above, Mr. Maramonte recorded the score each student in his class earned on a recent math test.

12. What is the mean score for the students in Mr. Maramonte's class?

_____

13. What is the mean absolute deviation for the scores to the nearest hundredth?

_____

14. What is the median score for the students in Mr. Maramonte's class?

_____

15. What is the mode of the data?

_____

16. Draw a box-and-whisker plot to display the data.

17. What is the interquartile range for the data?

_____

Use the table for 18–19.

Number of Pets	Number of Students
0–3	7
4–7	12
8–11	5
12–15	8

The table above shows the number of pets students in a class would like to have.

18. Draw a histogram to display the data.

19. How many students would like to have 4 to 11 pets?

_____

20. Give an example of other data that can be represented using a histogram.

_____

_____

UNIT 7

Measurement and Data
Unit Test: C

1. Gemma recorded the ages of students at an after-school club. The ages of the students are shown in the data set below.

   {11, 12, 12, 13, 15, 16}

   Another student joins the club. She is 17 years old. Which of the following does **not** change?

   A mean

   B median

   C range

   D mode

2. What is the median of the data represented in the box plot below?

   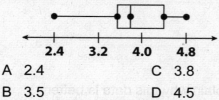

   A 2.4   C 3.8
   B 3.5   D 4.5

3. What is the median of the data represented in the line plot below?

   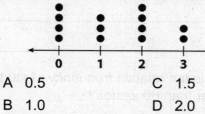

   A 0.5   C 1.5
   B 1.0   D 2.0

4. To find the mean absolute deviation, which of the following should you find first?

   A mode   C mean
   B range   D median

5. For which of the following data sets is the mean equal to the median?

   A {1, 4, 6, 7}   C {2, 4, 6, 9}
   B {2, 5, 6, 9}   D {1, 5, 9, 10}

Use the table for 6–8.

6. What is the median for the data set below?

   | 2.6 | 6.7 | 6.5 | 8.8 |
   | 3.8 | 7.3 | 4.0 | 12.5 |

   A 6.0   C 6.6
   B 6.25   D 6.9

7. What is the mean for the data to the nearest tenth?

   A 6.4   C 6.6
   B 6.5   D 52.2

8. What is the mean absolute deviation? Use the mean to the nearest tenth

   A 2.3   C 3.1
   B 2.4   D 18.4

9. For the data set below, which of the following measures is greatest?

   {2.5, 4.4, 4.4, 5.2, 6.3, 8.1, 9.9, 10.5}

   A mean   C range
   B median   D mode

Use the histogram for 10 and 11.

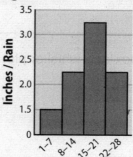

The histogram shows the amount of rain for 7-day periods in May.

10. Which 7-day period had the least rain?

    A 1–7   C 15–21
    B 8–14   D 22–28

11. On May 16 it rained 1.7 inches. How much did it rain for the rest of that week?

    A 0.75 in.   C 2.25 in.
    B 1.55 in.   D 3.25 in.

UNIT 7

Measurement and Data

Use the table for 12–17.

Student Scores

97	91	88	89	91
75	80	78	91	74
85	91	100	84	77
74	68	94	96	100

In the table above, Mr. Ramirez recorded the score each student in his class earned on a recent math test.

12. What is the mean score for the students in Mr. Ramirez's class?

_____

13. What is the mean absolute deviation? Use the mean to the nearest tenth.

_____

14. What is the median score for the students in Mr. Ramirez's class?

_____

15. What is the mode of the data?

_____

16. Draw a box-and-whisker plot to display the data.

17. What is the interquartile range for the data?

_____

Use the table for 18–21.

Student Heights (in.)

61	58	62	65	70
59	63	66	61	69
71	61	65	62	68
70	59	62	65	68

In the table above, Ms. Kalmansen recorded the height in inches of each student in her math class.

18. Draw a histogram to display the data.

19. Explain why this data is better represented by using a histogram rather than a bar graph.

_____

_____

20. What is the relative frequency of students shorter than 60 inches?

_____

21. Explain how you can use relative frequencies to create a circle graph of the data.

_____

_____

_____

UNIT 7

Measurement and Data

Unit Test: D

1. Alana rode her bicycle 10 miles on Tuesday and 20 miles on Wednesday. What is the mean number of miles she rode her bike in the two-day period?

   A 10 mi

   B 15 mi

   C 20 mi

2. What is the mean absolute deviation?

   A 5

   B 10

   C 20

3. What is the median of the data represented in the box plot below?

   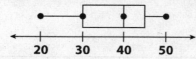

   A 20

   B 30

   C 40

4. What is the maximum value of the data represented in the line plot below?

   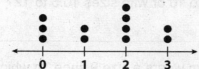

   A 2

   B 3

   C 4

5. What is the median of the set {4, 5, 6}?

   A 4

   B 5

   C 6

Use the table for 6–8.

6. What is the mean for the data set below?

1	2	4	4
5	6	6	8

   A 4.5

   B 5.0

   C 6.0

7. What is the mean absolute deviation?

   A 1.5

   B 1.75

   C 2

8. What is the median for the data below?

   {5, 10, 12, 20}

   A 11

   B 11.5

   C 12

Use the histogram for 9 and 10.

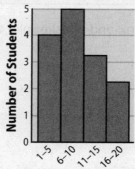

String Lengths (in.)

The histogram shows the lengths of kite strings held by students in a contest.

9. How long were most students' kite strings?

   A 1–5 in.   C 11–15 in.

   B 6–10 in.

10. Kai's kite string was 7.5 inches long. In which group was he?

   A 1–5 in.   C 16–20 in.

   B 6–10 in.

UNIT 7 Measurement and Data

Use the table for 11–16.

Student Scores

80	82	90	92	86
74	68	88	90	98

In the table above, Mr. Durkin recorded the score each student in his class earned on a math test.

11. What is the mean score for the students in Mr. Durkin's class?

_____

12. What is the mean absolute deviation?

_____

13. What is the median score for the students in Mr. Durkin's class?

_____

14. What is the mode of the data?

_____

15. Draw a box-and-whisker plot to show the data.

16. What is the first quartile for the data?

_____

Use the table for 17–20.

Shoe size	Number of boys
6.5–8	3
8.5–10	5
10.5–12	7

The table above shows the number of boys with common shoe sizes.

17. Draw a histogram to show the data.

_____

18. How many boys' shoe sizes are recorded?

_____

19. Are there more boys with shoe sizes 6.5 to 10 or with sizes 10.5 to 12?

_____

20. Thom wears a size 9 shoe. In which bar is his shoe size recorded?

_____

_____

UNIT 7	**Measurement and Data**

Performance Task

The table below shows student scores on a math test.

Student Test Scores

90	88	98	68	90	94	80
84	90	92	80	76	78	90
88	84	82	90	82	84	86
92	96	98	92	90	88	84

1. What was the mean test score? Show your work.

   _____

2. Explain how you would find the mean absolute deviation for these test scores.

   _____

   _____

   _____

3. What was the median test score? How do you know?

   _____

4. Create a box-and-whisker plot to display the data.

5. What is the interquartile range of the data?

   _____

6. Create a frequency histogram to display the data.

7. Explain why a bar graph would not be a good choice to represent the data.

   _____

   _____

Name _____ Date _____ Class_____

Benchmark Test Modules 1–5

1. Which of the following shows the integers in order from **least** to **greatest**?

    A 0, –3, 4, 8, –17, –20

    B –3, –17, –20, 0, 4, 8

    C –20, –17, –3, 0, 4, 8

    D 8, 4, 0, –3, –17, –20

2. What is the opposite of –6?

    A 6   C $\frac{1}{6}$

    B $\frac{6}{6}$ D $-\frac{1}{6}$

3. Which number line shows –5 and its opposite?

    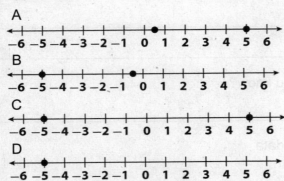

4. Which is **not** a true statement?

    A –8 < 7   C 7 > –8

    B –8 > –7   D 7 < 8

5. Which number has the same absolute value as 81?

    A 1   C –1

    B 0   D –81

6. To which set or sets does –20 belong?

    A whole number, integer and rational number

    B integer and rational number

    C negative integer

    D whole number and integer

7. What is the absolute value of –8.3?

    A 8.3   C 0

    B 3.8   D –8.3

8. Which shows the rational numbers in order from **least** to **greatest**?

    A 1.9, $5\frac{5}{8}$, –6, –8.2, 9, $-16\frac{1}{3}$

    B $-16\frac{1}{3}$, –8.2, –6, 1.9, $5\frac{5}{8}$, 9

    C –6, –8.2, $-16\frac{1}{3}$, 1.9, $5\frac{5}{8}$

    D 9, $5\frac{5}{8}$, 1.9, $-16\frac{1}{3}$, –8.2, –6

9. Which is the product of $\frac{5}{8} \times \frac{2}{3}$?

    A $\frac{5}{12}$ C $\frac{15}{16}$

    B $\frac{7}{11}$ D $8\frac{2}{3}$

10. Which is the quotient of $\frac{11}{12} \div \frac{5}{7}$?

    A $\frac{55}{84}$ C $\frac{77}{84}$

    B $\frac{16}{19}$ D $1\frac{17}{60}$

11. April has 3 pounds of trail mix. She puts equal amounts in each of 8 bags. How much trail mix is in each bag?

    A $\frac{8}{3}$ lb   C $\frac{1}{5}$ lb

    B $\frac{3}{8}$ lb   D $\frac{1}{24}$ lb

12. Which is the reciprocal of $2\frac{5}{8}$?

    A $-2\frac{8}{5}$ C $\frac{8}{21}$

    B $-2\frac{5}{8}$ D $2\frac{8}{5}$

13. Eli earns $12.50 per hour at his job. Last week he worked $34\frac{1}{2}$ hours. How much did he earn last week?

    A $425.00   C $431.25

    B $431   D $437.50

Benchmark Test Modules 1–5

14. Trayvon weighs 142 pounds. Multiply his weight on Earth by 0.92 to find his weight on the planet Saturn. What is the difference between Trayvon's weight on Earth and his weight on Saturn?

   A 11.36 lb   C 141.08 lb

   B 12.36 lb   D 142.92 lb

15. Of the dogs at the dog show, $\frac{1}{12}$ were classified as belonging to the Hound Group. Of the dogs in the Hound Group, $\frac{3}{10}$ were English Foxhounds. What fraction of the dogs at the show were English Foxhounds?

   A $\frac{4}{22}$ C $\frac{10}{12}$

   B $\frac{3}{12}$ D $\frac{1}{40}$

16. Which number line shows $|-3|$, $|-8|$, $|-2|$, and $|5|$?

   A
   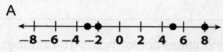
   B

   C

   D

17. Kendra is thinking of an integer greater than $-3\frac{2}{5}$ and less than -2.7. Which of the following numbers could Kendra be thinking of?

   A −2   C −3.5

   B −3   D −4

18. Mrs. Manning carries a very large purse. The purse and its contents weigh 5.18 pounds. If she takes her makeup out of the purse, it weighs only 3.76 pounds. How much makeup does Mrs. Manning carry in her purse?

   A 8.94 lb   C 1.42 lb

   B 1.52 lb   D 1.27 lb

19. A yoga mat is 74.8 inches long and 22.6 inches wide. What is the area of the mat?

   A 16.90 in²   C 1,690.48 in²

   B 169.04 in²   D 16,904.8 in²

20. A red candle is $11\frac{2}{5}$ inches tall. The label claims that the candle will melt $1\frac{1}{8}$ inch every hour it burns. If the label is correct, for how many hours will the candle burn?

   A $10\frac{2}{45}$ h   C 11.13 h

   B $10\frac{2}{15}$ h   D $11\frac{17}{40}$ h

21. The diameter of a U.S. quarter is 24.26 millimeters. How long is a line of 37 quarters laid edge to edge?

   A 8.97 mm

   B 89.76 mm

   C 897.62 mm

   D 8,976.2 mm

22. Mr. Curtis paid $48.51 for 12.6 gallons of gas. What is the price of one gallon of gas?

   A $3.86   C $3.84

   B $3.85   D $3.83

Benchmark Test Modules 1–5

23. A case of grapefruit weighs $35\frac{3}{4}$ pounds. Of this weight, $\frac{1}{8}$ is not ripe. What is the weight of the grapefruit that are ripe?

_____

24. Ed bought a bottle of fancy mustard that holds 8.5 ounces. Ed puts about $\frac{1}{25}$ of the mustard on each hot dog he eats. How much of the mustard is left in the bottle after he eats 7 hot dogs?

_____

25. The area of a rug is $4\frac{15}{32}$ square meters. The rug is $2\frac{3}{4}$ meters in length. How wide is the rug?

_____

26. What is the greatest common factor of 60 and 72?

_____

27. What is the least common multiple of 14 and 21?

_____

28. An art museum had 275,760 visitors last year. The museum was open every day of the year except for 5 holidays. How many visitors did the museum have each day, on average?

_____

29. Blair is making a granola recipe that calls for $2\frac{2}{3}$ cups of oats and $1\frac{1}{3}$ cups of cranberries. Blair mixes the oats and cranberries together. Each serving will contain $\frac{1}{2}$ cup of granola. How many servings of granola will Blair's recipe make?

_____

30. A box of powdered laundry detergent contains 5.2 ounces of detergent. It takes 0.7 ounce of detergent to clean a load of laundry. How many full loads can by cleaned with 3 boxes of this detergent?

_____

31. A painter mixed 98.7 gallons of blue paint with 67.05 gallons of red paint in a paint-mixing machine. How much total paint is in the machine?

_____

32. An insulated cooler holds 184 ounces of lemonade. How many full 12.4-ounce glasses of lemonade can be poured from the cooler?

_____

33. Bret has a fish tank that holds 320 fluid ounces of water. On average, the water evaporates from the tank at a rate of 3.84 ounces per day. Bret went on vacation for 2 weeks, and asked a friend to feed his fish. The fish tank was full of water when Bret left. To the nearest hundredth, how many fluid ounces of water were left in the tank when Bret returned from his vacation?

_____

Benchmark Test Modules 1–5

34. A rug has an area of 122.12 square feet. The rug is 8.7 feet wide. To the nearest hundredth, how many feet long is the rug?

_____

35. Tonya bought a bottle of body wash that contained 35.4 fluid ounces of soap. She uses about 1.25 ounces of body wash every time she showers. To the nearest hundredth, how many ounces of body wash are left in the bottle after Tonya has showered 15 times?

_____

36. Suki buys dog food in 13.4-pound bags. She feeds her dog 0.3 pound of food twice a day. How many full days will the bag of food last?

_____

37. A perfume manufacturer uses 0.875 pounds of rose petals to make each bottle of perfume. How many pounds of rose petals would be needed to make 86 bottles of perfume?

_____

38. Will bought a pedometer to measure how far he walks every day. According to the pedometer, he moves about $27\frac{5}{8}$ inches with each step he takes when he walks. How many feet did Will travel in 96 steps?

_____

39. Reuben jogs 2.25 miles every weekday. On weekends, he jogs 1.8 times as far. To the nearest hundredth, how many miles does Reuben jog in 2 full calendar weeks?

_____

40. Erik drove 439.92 miles on 15.6 gallons of gas. To the nearest hundredth, how many miles could he drive on 39.7 gallons of gas?

_____

41. A manufacturer buys bolts from a supplier. The bolts cost $0.17 each, but the manufacturer made a deal with the supplier and gets 4,000 bolts for $595.50. To the nearest cent, how much money does the manufacturer save on 4,000 bolts with this deal?

_____

42. The Indianapolis 500 gets its name because racecar drivers competing in the event drive 500 miles. In 1911, the winner of the Indianapolis 500 took 6.7 hours to complete the race. To the nearest hundredth, what was the average speed of the car in miles per hour?

_____

Mid-Year Test Modules 6–8

1. What is the ratio of squares to circles?

   ■ ● ◀ ■ ● ◀ ■ ●
   ◀ ■ ● ● ◀ ● ◀ ■ ●

   A 5 to 16   C 6 to 5

   B 5 to 6   D 16 to 5

2. On the class field trip, there were 4 teachers and 35 students. Which of the following is the ratio of students to teachers on this trip?

   A $\frac{4}{39}$ C $\frac{35}{4}$

   B $\frac{4}{35}$ D $\frac{39}{4}$

3. Which of the following ratios is **not** equivalent to the other three?

   A $\frac{2}{5}$ C 8 to 20

   B $\frac{4}{10}$ D 10 to 15

4. An 8-pound bag of apples costs $17.50. What is the unit price?

   A $0.22/lb   C $2.19/lb

   B $0.46/lb   D $4.57/lb

5. It took 20 minutes to print out a 250-page report. At this speed, how many pages could this printer produce in 30 minutes?

   A 260 pages   C 330 pages

   B 280 pages   D 375 pages

6. Dana measured the height of her bedroom wall to be 3 yards tall. Which of these is closest to the equivalent measurement?

   A 0.6 kilometers

   B 3.5 meters

   C 274.3 centimeters

   D 7834.7 millimeters

7. Mattias bought a package of 5 notebooks for $13.95. What is the unit price per notebook?

   A $0.36   C $3.58

   B $2.79   D $8.95

8. Which of the following ratios is equivalent to 8:3?

   A $\frac{3}{8}$ C $\frac{11}{8}$

   B $\frac{8}{11}$ D $\frac{16}{6}$

9. Trudy is making punch by mixing 1 can of concentrated juice with 3 cans of water. Which of the following combinations shows the same ratio of juice to water?

   A 2 cups of juice to 3 cups of water

   B 2 cups of juice to 6 cups of water

   C 2 cups of juice to 9 cups of water

   D 3 cups of juice to 6 cups of water

10. The table shows how much money three employees are paid per hour of work.

Employee	Hourly Rate ($)
Kyle	35
Sidney	40
Patricia	55

   Suppose each employee works for 30 hours next week. How much more than Sidney will Patricia be paid?

   A $45   C $900

   B $450   D $1,200

11. A carpenter worked for 4 days to finish a repair job. She charged $825 for 15 hours plus $278 for materials. What is the carpenter's rate per hour?

   A $55   C $74

   B $58   D $182

12. The graph below shows the rate of speed of a group of hikers.

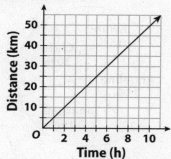

Which of the following is an ordered pair on the graph?

A (2, 10)

B (3, 20)

C (4, 25)

D (8, 50)

13. The table below shows the cost of renting a sailboat at a lake.

Cost of Renting a Sailboat

Cost ($)	300	450	900	1,200
Hours	2	3	6	8

Which of the following represents the cost?

A hours × 15

B hours × 150

C hours ÷ 150

D hours ÷ 300

14. The scale on a map shows that 1.5 centimeters represents 200 kilometers. On the map, two cities are 6 centimeters apart. What is the actual distance between theses two cities?

A 75 km   C 750 km

B 80 km   D 800 km

15. The numbers in the table below show a multiplicative relationship.

A	2	4	6	8	10
B	6	12	x	y	30

What are the two values for x and y?

A x = 14, y = 16

B x = 16, y = 18

C x = 18, y = 24

D x = 18, y = 28

16. The sixth grade is charging $9 per car to wash cars. The fifth grade is charging $8.50 per car. Suppose each grade washes 50 cars. How much more money will the sixth grade earn?

A $25   C $425

B $50   D $450

17. Hal can buy 6 yards of canvas at a total cost of $15. How much would it cost to buy 10 yards at the same price per yard?

A $16   C $25

B $17   D $40

18. The ratio of boys to girls at a day care center is 5 to 4. Which of the following **cannot** be the total number of children at the center?

A 27 children   C 60 children

B 54 children   D 72 children

19. The ratio of wins to losses for a basketball team is 2 : 3. Which of the following is a possible total number of games?

A 7 games   C 25 games

B 14 games   D 26 games

20. How many ounces of nuts are in a box that holds 3.2 pounds?

A 0.2 oz   C 20 oz

B 5.12 oz   D 51.2 oz

21. What percent of the circle below is shaded?

A 30%   C 60%

B 37.5%   D 62.5%

22. What percent of 18 is 27?

A 50%   C 133%

B 66.7%   D 150%

23. There are 65 students in a science club. 40% of them bought a club T-shirt with a picture of Albert Einstein. How many Einstein T-shirts were purchased?

A 20 T-shirts

B 24 T-shirts

C 25 T-shirts

D 26 T-shirts

24. Which of these is equivalent to 40%?

A $\frac{1}{4}$ C 0.04

B $\frac{2}{5}$ D 0.44

25. Marge has saved $350 toward the cost of her vacation. The vacation will cost $1,750. What percent of the cost of the vacation has Marge saved?

A 15%   C 25%

B 20%   D 30%

26. The committee to plant more trees has raised 40% of their goal. They want to raise $3,000. How much more money do they need to raise to meet their goal?

A $1,200   C $1,600

B $1,400   D $1,800

27. The results of a school election are shown in the circle graph below.

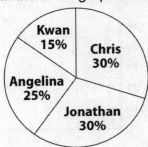

There were 2,500 votes cast in all. How many votes did Angelina receive?

A 375 votes   C 625 votes

B 500 votes   D 750 votes

28. Ms. Burger has graded 45 tests. This represents 60% of her 3 math classes. How many math students does Ms. Burger teach?

A 27 students   C 75 students

B 45 students   D 105 students

29. The costume committee has made 20 costumes. This is 80% of the total number of costumes needed for the school play. How many more costumes do they need to make?

A 5 costumes

B 8 costumes

C 16 costumes

D 25 costumes

30. One-fifth of the members of a senior citizen's club signed up for a computer workshop. What percent of the club did **not** sign up for the workshop?

A 15%   C 80%

B 20%   D 85%

31. A toy company wants to sell 1,600 toy airplanes this year. So far, they have sold 600. What percent of the sales goal have they reached?

A 20%   C 50%

B 37.5%   D 60%

Mid-Year Test Modules 6–8

32. The ratio of boys to girls in the checkers club at one school is 2:3. The number of club members is more than 20 and fewer than 30. How many club members are there?

_____

33. It took Elizabeth 10 days to read a 450-page biography. She read about the same number of pages of the book each day. How many pages did Elizabeth read each day?

_____

34. The ratio of cats to dogs at the city animal shelter today is 5:6. There are 35 cats at the shelter. How many dogs are at the shelter today?

_____

35. The staff of the Westport Public Library signed up 6 volunteers in the last 21 days. If the library staff continues to sign up volunteers at this rate, how many new volunteers will they get in the next 7-day week?

_____

36. A car driving cross-country traveled 180 miles in 4 hours. At this rate of speed, how many miles farther will the car travel in the next 3 hours?

_____

37. Jeremy measured the height of a basketball net to be 10 feet off the ground. What is the equivalent measurement in meters?

_____

38. The scale on a roadmap is listed as 1 inch: 80 miles. On the map, Belleville and San Jose are 1.5 inches apart. What is the actual distance in miles between the two cities?

_____

39. Belina bought $4\frac{1}{2}$ yards of red fabric. She also bought 6 yards of white fabric. How many more **inches** of white fabric than red fabric did Belina buy?

_____

40. Nels needs 15 gallons of lemonade for a company picnic. If he buys the lemonade in quart bottles, how many bottles does Nels need to buy?

_____

41. Travant is planning a garden that will cover 1,600 square yards. He wants the ratio of space planted with flowers to space planted with vegetables to be 3:5. How many square yards of flowers will Travant's garden have?

_____

42. What percent of the design below is shaded gray?

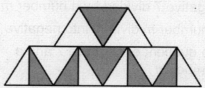

_____

Benchmark Test Modules 9–13

1. Which expression shows the prime factorization of 96?

   A $2^5 \times 3$ C 4×24

   B $2^3 \times 3^2$ D 48^2

2. Which power does **not** have a value of 1,024?

   A 2^{10} C 8^3

   B 4^5 D 32^2

3. Which step should be performed first when simplifying the expression below?

   $$47 - 3 - 23 \times 2 + 7$$

   A $-3 + 23$ C $47 - 3$

   B $2 + 7$ D 23×2

4. Mandy has 50 yards of fabric to make costumes for a play. She makes 12 skirts that take 3 yards each, and 9 hats that each take 1 yard. Which expression represents the number of yards of fabric that are left?

   A $50 - 12^3 - 9$

   B $50 - 3(12 + 9)$

   C $3 \times 12 + 9$

   D $50 - 3 \times 12 - 9$

5. Which phrase does **not** have the same meaning as $\dfrac{-7}{m}$?

   A negative 7 times a number m

   B negative 7 divided by a number m

   C a number m divided into negative 7

   D the quotient of negative 7 and a number m

6. Which property justifies the fact that $8(d - 5)$ is equivalent to $8d - 40$?

   A Commutative

   B Associative

   C Distributive

   D Identity

7. Which of the equations below represents the relationship shown in the table?

x	24	6	3	1
y	1	4	8	24

   A $y = 24x$ C $y = x - 2$

   B $y = x - 23$ D $y = \dfrac{24}{x}$

8. Which of the following equations represents the situation described below?

   Mike and his friends hiked 23 miles on Saturday. They hiked 7 miles less than that on Sunday. Their goal is to hike a total of 50 miles during their trip. How many miles did they hike on Sunday?

   A $m + 7 = 23$

   B $m + 7 = 50$

   C $23 + m = 7$

   D $50 - m = 23$

9. Which of the following is the solution to the equation below?

   $$12 = n + 5$$

   A 5   C 17

   B 7   D 60

10. Which of the following is the solution to the equation below?

    $$18 = \dfrac{y}{9}$$

    A 2   C 81

    B 20   D 162

11. Lana is 12 years old. Her sister is y years old. Lana is twice as old as her sister. How old is Lana's sister?

    A 2 years old

    B 3 years old

    C 6 years old

    D 24 years old

Benchmark Test Modules 9–13

12. Which number is **not** a solution to the inequality below?

$$x < 15$$

A −6   C 11

B −2   D 17

13. Which number is a possible solution to the inequality below?

$$x \le -3$$

A −4.75   C 1.25

B −2.25   D 3.75

14. Which number line represents the solution to the inequality $2.2 > x$?

A ![number line A]
   0   1   2   3

B ![number line B]
   0   1   2   3

C ![number line C]
   0   1   2   3

D ![number line D]
   0   1   2   3

15. The lowest temperature in January was 7°F. Which inequality represents all the temperatures x in January?

A $x \le 7$ C $x < 7$

B $x \ge 7$ D $x > 7$

16. A group of students is going on a field trip. Each bus can take up to 45 students. Which inequality represents the possible numbers x of students on the bus?

A $x \le 45$

B $x \ge 45$

C $x < 45$

D $x > 45$

17. Use the ordered pairs shown in the table below.

x	2	4	6	8
y	3	6	9	12

Which equation represents the data in the table?

A $x = 1.5y$ C $y = 1.5x$

B $x = \dfrac{1}{3}y$ D $y = \dfrac{2}{3}x$

Use the graph for 18–20.

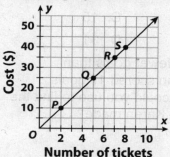

The graph shows the cost of buying raffle tickets.

18. What are the coordinates of point R?

A (7, 30)   C (35, 7)

B (7, 35)   D (40, 8)

19. Which equation shows the cost y in terms of the number of tickets x?

A $y = 2x$ C $y = 10x$

B $y = 5x$ D $y = 20x$

20. Ralph buys 35 raffle tickets. How much does he spend?

A $7   C $175

B $155   D $350

21. Which of the equations below represents the relationship shown in the table?

x	2	4	6	8
y	14	28	42	56

A $y = 7x$

B $y = x - 7$

C $y = x + 12$

D $y = \dfrac{2}{x}$

22. Which of the following is the solution to the equation below?

$$23 = w + 8$$

A 8

B 13

C 15

D 31

23. Karen scored 8 fewer goals than Siobhan. Siobhan scored 17 goals. Which equation could you use to find the number of goals Karen made?

A $g + 17 = 8$

B $g + 8 = 17$

C $17 - g = 8$

D $8 - g = 17$

24. Which of the following is the solution to the equation below?

$$16 = -\dfrac{32}{x}$$

A $-\dfrac{1}{2}$

B $\dfrac{1}{2}$

C -2

D 2

25. What is the area of the polygon shown below?

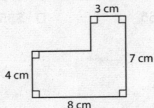

A 12 cm²

B 23 cm²

C 41 cm²

D 56 cm²

26. A parallelogram has a base of 14 centimeters and a height of 20 centimeters. What is the area of the parallelogram?

A 34 cm²

B 68 cm²

C 140 cm²

D 280 cm²

27. A right triangle has a height of 27 inches and a base of 30 inches. What is the area of the triangle?

A 57 in²

B 113 in²

C 405 in²

D 810 in²

28. Marsha used about 400 square 1-inch tiles to cover a tabletop that was shaped like a right triangle. The length of one leg of the right triangle was 16 inches. What was the length of the other leg of the triangle?

A 12.5 in.

B 25 in.

C 32 in.

D 50 in.

29. A box is 8 feet wide and 12 feet long. Vince uses 720 cubic feet of packing material to fill the box half full. What is the height of the box?

A 7.5 ft

B 15 ft

C 20 ft

D 30 ft

Use the prism for 30 and 31.

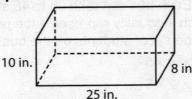

30. What is the area of the top surface?

A 43 in²

B 80 in²

C 200 in²

D 250 in²

31. What is the volume of the prism?

A 430 in³

B 800 in³

C 1,600 in³

D 2,000 in³

Benchmark Test Modules 9–13

32. What is the greatest prime factor of 78?

_____

33. Identical boxes are stacked on top of each other in a store display. The display uses 6 boxes across, 6 boxes deep, and 6 boxes tall. How many boxes are there in the display?

_____

34. What is the value of the expression below?

$$120 \div \frac{2^5}{8} + 50 \times (15 - 8)$$

_____

35. Evaluate the expression below for $g = 77$.

$$1.2g$$

_____

36. Solve the equation below.

$$k - 6.2 = 24.8$$

_____

37. Yesterday, Denny ran 2 fewer miles than Jill did. Jill ran 6.4 miles yesterday. How many miles did Denny run?

_____

38. Sam has to read a 144-page book for his literature class. He has 8 days to finish it. He wants to read about the same number of pages each day. How many pages per day must he read to finish the book in 8 days?

_____

39. Write an inequality to describe what is represented on the number line below.

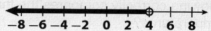

_____

Use the grid for 40 and 41.

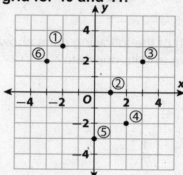

40. Write the number that labels the point that is located at (2, –2).

_____

41. Two of the numbered points shown on the grid are located on the same horizontal line. What is the y-coordinate of any point on this same line?

_____

End-of-Year Test

1. Which of the following points is graphed at the opposite of –2 on the number line below?

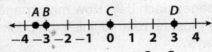

   A *A*

   B *B*

   C *C*

   D *D*

2. Candice recorded outdoor temperatures of –5°C, –1°C, and –2°C. Which of the following correctly compares the three temperatures?

   A $-5 < -1 < -2$

   B $-1 < -2 < -5$

   C $-2 < -1 < -5$

   D $-5 < -2 < -1$

3. Which of the following pairs shows an integer and its opposite?

   A $7, -7$

   B $7, \frac{1}{7}$

   C $-7, -\frac{1}{7}$

   D $-\frac{1}{7}, \frac{1}{7}$

4. Which number has the same absolute value as –5?

   A $-\frac{1}{5}$

   C 0

   B $\frac{1}{5}$

   D 5

5. What is the greatest common factor of 30 and 45?

   A 1

   C 15

   B 5

   D 30

6. What is the least common multiple of 16 and 24?

   A 4

   C 24

   B 16

   D 48

7. Jason plotted points on a number line at the four values below.

$$0.75, \ -\frac{2}{3}, \ -0.4, \ \frac{7}{8}$$

   Which of these values is farthest from zero?

   A 0.75

   C –0.4

   B $-\frac{2}{3}$

   D $\frac{7}{8}$

8. To which set or sets below does the number $-\frac{1}{2}$ belong?

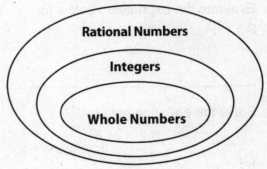

   A whole numbers only

   B rational numbers only

   C integers and rational numbers only

   D whole numbers, integers, and rational numbers

9. Which pair of points graphed below have values that are opposites?

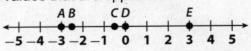

   A *A* and *B*

   C *C* and *E*

   B *B* and *D*

   D *A* and *E*

End-of-Year Test

10. Which number line shows the values of |1|, |−3|, |−4| and |5|?

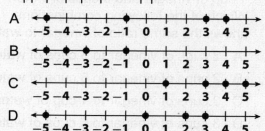

A ← ◆ + + ◆ + + + ◆ ◆ + →
   −5 −4 −3 −2 −1 0 1 2 3 4 5

B ← ◆ ◆ ◆ + + + + + + + + →
   −5 −4 −3 −2 −1 0 1 2 3 4 5

C ← + + + + + + ◆ + ◆ ◆ ◆ →
   −5 −4 −3 −2 −1 0 1 2 3 4 5

D ← ◆ + + + + ◆ + ◆ ◆ + + →
   −5 −4 −3 −2 −1 0 1 2 3 4 5

11. Susie divided a 9-pound bag of apples into 5 equal piles. How many pounds of apples are in each pile?

A $\frac{1}{5}$ lb   C $1\frac{4}{5}$ lb

B $\frac{5}{9}$ lb   D $1\frac{5}{4}$ lb

12. Stephen's glass holds 450 milliliters of milk. Farrah's glass holds $\frac{2}{5}$ as much milk. How much milk does Farrah's glass hold?

A 90 mL   C 225 mL

B 180 mL   D 360 mL

13. Which of the following expressions is equivalent to the expression below?

$$\frac{4}{7} \times \frac{5}{9}$$

A $\frac{5}{9} \div \frac{4}{7}$ C $\frac{4}{9} \div \frac{5}{7}$

B $\frac{4}{7} \div \frac{5}{9}$ D $\frac{4}{7} \div \frac{9}{5}$

14. Leah cut a $7\frac{1}{2}$-inch piece of ribbon into pieces that are each $\frac{3}{4}$ of an inch long. How many pieces of ribbon did she cut?

A 6 pieces   C 10 pieces

B 9 pieces   D 15 pieces

15. Jonas is making a trail mix recipe that calls for $3\frac{1}{2}$ cups of nuts and $1\frac{1}{2}$ cups of raisins. Jonas mixes the nuts and raisins together. He will then divide the mixture into plastic bags containing $\frac{1}{4}$ cup of trail mix in each bag. How many plastic bags does Jonas need?

A 1   C 20

B 5   D 50

16. Serena has 6,783 seeds to plant in her vegetable garden. She will plant 119 seeds per row. How many rows of vegetables will she have?

A 42   C 69

B 57   D 73

17. Jinwon hit a golf ball 145.7 yards. Kayla hit a golf ball 122.95 yards. How much farther did Jinwon hit a golf ball?

A 22.75 yards

B 30.25 yards

C 80.12 yards

D 108.36 yards

18. Gabriel drives 80 kilometers in one hour. If he drives at the same speed, how many kilometers can he drive in 3.75 hours?

A 24.75 km   C 80.75 km

B 30 km   D 300 km

End-of-Year Test

19. How many 0.4-liter glasses of water are contained in a 5.2-liter pitcher?

    A 1.3 glasses

    B 13 glasses

    C 13.4 glasses

    D 52 glasses

20. Alissa's budget is shown in the circle graph below. Her total monthly budget is $1,500. How much does Alissa spend on rent?

    A $250   C $450

    B $300   D $500

21. In Evan's math class, there are 17 boys and 21 girls. Which of the following is the ratio of boys to girls in the class?

    A $\frac{17}{38}$ C $\frac{17}{21}$

    B $\frac{21}{38}$ D $\frac{21}{17}$

22. Sara bought a 16-ounce jar of strawberry jam for $3.20. What is the unit price?

    A $0.02/oz

    B $0.50/oz

    C $0.20/oz

    D $5.00/oz

23. Zach is making a recipe that requires 1 cup of vinegar and 3 cups of water. Which of the following combinations shows the same ratio of vinegar to water?

    A 2 cups of vinegar to 3 cups of water

    B 2 cups of vinegar to 6 cups of water

    C 3 cups of vinegar to 1 cup of water

    D 3 cups of vinegar to 6 cups of water

24. Liam bought 8 quarts of juice at the grocery. How many gallons of juice did he buy?

    A 1 gal   C 3 gal

    B 2 gal   D 4 gal

25. Delia measured her bathtub to be 2 meters long. Which of these is an equivalent measurement?

    A 0.4 miles   C 8.2 ft

    B 3.5 yd   D 78.7 in.

26. Nora bikes 30 miles per hour. Jiro bikes 45 miles per hour. Nora and Jiro each bike for 5 hours. How many more miles does Jiro bike?

    A 15 mi   C 150 mi

    B 75 mi   D 225 mi

27. The table below shows the number of books on shelves at a library. Which of the following represents the number of books?

Books	42	63	105	147
Shelves	2	3	5	7

    A shelves × 3

    B shelves × 21

    C shelves + 28

    D shelves + 42

End-of-Year Test

28. On a certain map, 1.25 inches represents 20 miles. Longwood and Milltown are 5 inches apart on the map. What is the actual distance between Longwood and Milltown?

    A 20 mi   C 80 mi

    B 25 mi   D 100 mi

29. What percent of the rectangle below is shaded?

    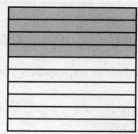

    A 20%   C 40%

    B 30%   D 80%

30. What is the value of the power below?

    $$(-4)^3$$

    A 12   C −64

    B −16   D 81

31. What are all the factors of 18?

    A 1, 2, 3, 6

    B 2, 3, 6, 9

    C 1, 2, 3, 6, 9

    D 1, 2, 3, 6, 9, 18

32. What is the value of the expression below?

    $$205 - (7 - 2)^3 \div 5$$

    A 16   C 40

    B 36   D 180

33. Which of the following expressions is equivalent to the expression below?

    $$2(7x + 3 - x)$$

    A $12x + 6$

    B $14x + 6$

    C $17x - 2$

    D $11x + 3$

34. Which is a solution of the equation below?

    $$m - 9 = 4$$

    A $m = -5$ C $m = 5$

    B $m = -13$ D $m = 13$

35. A 60° angle is complementary to an angle that measures $x°$. Which of the following equations represents this situation?

    A $60 + x = 90$

    B $60 = x + 90$

    C $60 + x = 180$

    D $60 = x + 180$

36. Which inequality is shown on the number line below?

    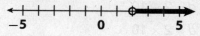

    A $p < 2$

    B $p \le 2$

    C $p > 2$

    D $p \ge 2$

37. Write an algebraic expression for the phrase below.

    12 less than twice a number n

    A $12 - n - n$ C $6 - 2n$

    B $2n - 12$ D $12n - 2$

38. Evaluate the expression below for $x = -4$.

$$6(x + 15)$$

A 5

B −5

C −66

D 66

39. Combine like terms to simplify the expression below.

$$14x - (2x - y) - y$$

A $12x$

B $14x - y$

C $12x - y$

D $14x$

40. A high-school band has d drummers and 10 violinists. There are 2 more violinists than drummers. Which of the following equations represents the situation?

A $d = 10 + 2$

B $d = 10 - 2$

C $d = 2 - 10$

D $d = 2 \times 10$

41. A student bought a book for $7.50 and a pen. The total cost was $9.50. Which of the following equations can be used to find the cost of the pen?

A $p = 7.5b$

B $p = 9.5b$

C $9.50 + p = 7.50$

D $7.50 + p = 9.50$

42. Which of the following is a solution to the equation below?

$$\frac{m}{2} = -5$$

A $m = -5$ C $m = -10$

B $m = -2$ D $m = 10$

Use the table for 43 and 44.

Auto Repair Charges

Hours, x	2	5	7
Charge, y ($)	180	450	630

43. Which equation expresses y in terms of x?

A $y = 90x$

B $y = 180x$

C $x = 90y$

D $x = 2y$

44. What is the charge for a repair that takes 1.5 hours?

A $360   C $150

B $270   D $135

End-of-Year Test

Use the graph for 45–47.

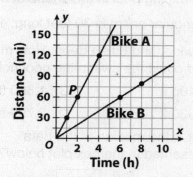

45. What are the coordinates of point *P*?

    A (2, 8)   C (60, 2)

    B (2, 60)   D (60, 8)

46. What is the dependent variable?

    A Bike A   C time

    B Bike B   D distance

47. Which equation represents Bike B?

    A $y = 6x$

    B $y = 10x$

    C $y = 60x$

    D $y = 80x$

48. A parallelogram has a base of 16 centimeters and a height of 4 centimeters. What is the area of the parallelogram?

    A 16 cm^2

    B 32 cm^2

    C 64 cm^2

    D 128 cm^2

49. A rectangular prism has a volume of 577.2 cubic feet. The prism is 5.2 feet long and 7.4 feet wide. What is the height of the prism?

    A 15 ft   C 78 ft

    B 39 ft   D 111 ft

50. What is the area of the trapezoid below?

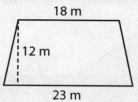

    A 216 m^2 C 2,484 m^2

    B 246 m^2 D 4,968 m^2

51. A right triangle has a height of 21 centimeters and a base of 11.6 centimeters. What is the area of the triangle?

    A 121.8 cm^2 C 487.2 cm^2

    B 243.6 cm^2 D 5,115.6 cm^2

52. What is the area of the rhombus shown below?

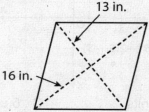

    A 3 in^2 C 208 in^2

    B 104 in^2 D 416 in^2

53. A triangle has an area of 221.16 square inches. The height of the triangle is 29.1 inches. What is the length of the base of the triangle?

    A 7.6 in.

    B 15.2 in.

    C 30.4 in.

    D 60.8 in.

54. A lawn in the shape of a trapezoid has an area of 1,833 square meters. The length of one base is 52 meters, and the length of the other base is 42 meters. What is the height of the trapezoid?

    A 35.25 m

    B 39 m

    C 43.6 m

    D 94 m

End-of-Year Test

55. What is the area of the polygon shown below?

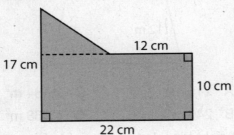

A 112 cm²   C 160 cm²

B 136 cm²   D 255 cm²

56. What is the distance between points *A* and *B* on the grid?

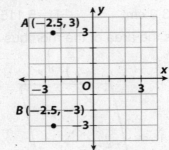

A 3 units   C 6 units

B 4.5 units   D 6.5 units

57. Charlene is wrapping the box below. How much wrapping paper will she need?

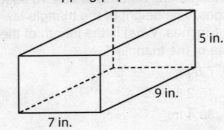

A 90 in²   C 178 in²

B 153 in²   D 286 in²

58. A swimming pool in the shape of a rectangular prism is 30 feet long, $15\frac{1}{2}$ feet wide, and 6 feet deep. How much water could the swimming pool hold?

A 465 ft³   C 1,860 ft³

B 930 ft³   D 2,790 ft³

59. What is the median of the data represented in the box plot below?

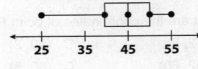

A 25   C 45

B 35   D 55

60. What is the range of the data represented in the dot plot below?

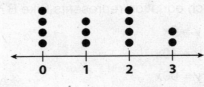

A 0   C 2

B 1   D 3

61. Sandra worked 6.2 hours on Wednesday, 5.5 hours on Thursday, and 3.5 hours on Friday. Which of the following is closest to the mean number of hours she worked over the three-day period?

A 3 h   C 5 h

B 4 h   D 6 h

End-of-Year Test

62. The histogram below shows the number of hours per month students in Mr. Carter's class watch television. How many students watch television between 11 and 20 hours per month?

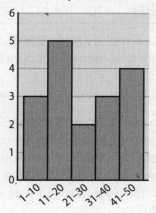

A 2

B 4

C 5

D 10

63. For 10 days in a row, Fiona and Gary timed how long they took to brush their teeth. Find the mean absolute deviation of each data set. Which person showed less variability in their teeth-brushing time?

Fiona's Time (seconds)
90, 85, 93, 97, 88, 91, 105, 98, 97, 96, 99, 98

Gary's Time (seconds)
75, 67, 115, 87, 46, 94, 65, 49, 87, 93, 55, 67

_____

_____

_____

64. Toni is designing a rug using a coordinate plane. She uses polygon *ABCD* with vertices *A*(6, 2), *B*(6, −2), *C*(−2, −2), and *D*(−2, 2). Each unit on the grid represents two feet. Plot the polygon on the grid below and find the area of the actual rug.

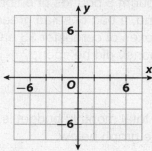

_____

65. Ava's dog weighs 56 kilograms. Marty's dog weighs $\frac{7}{8}$ as much. How much does Marty's dog weigh?

_____

66. Hayley cut a $10\frac{2}{3}$-foot rope into pieces that are each $\frac{8}{9}$ of a foot long. How many pieces of rope did she cut?

_____

67. A caterpillar crawls 25 inches in one minute. How far can it crawl in 4.5 minutes?

_____

End-of-Year Test

68. Jungwon has $41.25. Notepads cost $3.75 each. How many notepads can Jungwon buy?

_____

69. Noah bought 5 pounds of onions at $2 per pound, a bag of salad greens for $4, and 2 boxes of cereal for $3 each. How much money did he spend?

_____

70. Oliver's total monthly budget is shown in the circle graph below.

Oliver's monthly budget is $2,500. How much money does he save each month?

_____

71. Sara bought a 24-ounce can of tomato sauce for $8.40. What is the unit price per ounce?

_____

72. Conrad bought 2 gallons of bottled water at the supermarket. How many cups of water did he buy?

_____

73. The table below shows the fees David charges for yard work.

David's Yard Work Fees

Hours	2	4	6
Fee ($)	70	140	210

How much money does David charge for yard work that takes 4.5 hours?

_____

74. A falcon can fly at a speed of 87 kilometers per hour. A goose can fly at a speed of 78 kilometers per hour. Suppose a falcon and a goose each fly for 6 hours. How much farther will the falcon fly?

_____

75. On a city map, 2.5 inches represents 5 miles. The library and the bank are 3 inches apart on the map. What is the actual distance between the library and the bank?

_____

76. What is the value of the expression below?

$$(7)^3$$

_____

77. Use the order of operations to simplify the expression below.

$$975 \div 3 - (12 - 9)^3$$

_____

End-of-Year Test

78. Evaluate the expression below for $x = 15$.

    $5(x + 7)$

    _____

79. Last year, the tree in Pedro's front yard was 5.6 feet tall. This year, the tree is 2 feet less than the height of Pedro's house. Pedro's house is 17 feet tall. How tall is the tree?

    _____

80. A parallelogram has a base of 45 meters and a height of 11 meters. What is the area of the parallelogram?

    _____

81. A rectangular prism has a volume of 711.68 cubic inches. The prism is 4 inches long and 12.8 inches wide. What is the height of the prism?

    _____

82. What is the area of the triangle shown below?

    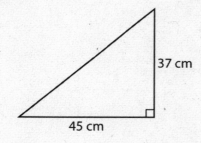

    _____

83. What is the area of the rhombus shown below?

    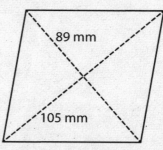

84. A triangle has an area of 227.04 square inches. The length of the base of the triangle is 47.3 inches. What is the height of the triangle?

    _____

85. A field in the shape of a trapezoid has an area of 13,687.5 square yards. The length of one base is 150 yards, and the length of the other base is 215 yards. What is the height of the trapezoid?

    _____

Answer Key

Placement Test

1. C
2. B
3. D
4. C
5. D
6. B
7. C
8. A
9. D
10. B
11. D
12. C
13. A
14. A
15. C
16. B
17. A
18. C
19. D
20. B
21. D
22. D
23. C
24. D
25. A
26. B
27. B
28. D
29. D
30. B
31. B
32. C
33. C
34. C
35. C
36. B

Answer Key

Beginning-of-Year Diagnostic Test

1. **A** Correct

   The opposite of 2 is –2. Locate the point where –2 is graphed on the number line. So, the opposite of 2 is graphed at point *A*.

   TEST PREP DOCTOR: Students who answered **B, C,** or **D** may not know what the opposite of a number is.

2. **A** Correct

   Graph –5, 2, and 1 on a number line. The numbers are ordered least to greatest from left to right. So, –5 < 1 < 2.

   TEST PREP DOCTOR: Students who answered **B** may have ignored the negative sign for –5°C. Students who answered **C** may have misunderstood the inequality symbol. Students who answered **D** may have understood that –5 is less than 2 or 1, but neglected to compare 2 and 1.

3. **A** Correct

   The number pair 7 and –7 are integers that are the same distance from 0 on opposite sides of the number line, so they are opposites.

   TEST PREP DOCTOR: Students who answered **B** chose the integer and its reciprocal. Students who answered **C** need to review the definition of opposite numbers. Students who answered **D** need to review the definition of integer.

4. **D** Correct

   Take away the negative sign to find the absolute value of –5. So, the absolute value of –5 is 5.

   TEST PREP DOCTOR: Students who answered **A** found the reciprocal of –5. Students who answered **B** or **C** need to review how to find absolute value.

5. **C** Correct

   List the factors of 4 and 8.
   Factors of 4: 1, 2, 4
   Factors of 8: 1, 2, 4, 8
   Then find the greatest factor that 4 and 8 have in common. So, 4 is the greatest common factor.

   TEST PREP DOCTOR: Students who answered **A, B** or **D** need to review how to find the greatest common factor of two numbers.

6. **D** Correct

   List the multiples of 10 and 20.
   Multiples of 10: 10, 20, 40, 50
   Multiples of 20: 20, 30, 40, 50
   Then find the least multiple that 10 and 20 have in common. So, 20 is the least common multiple.

   TEST PREP DOCTOR: Students who answered **A, B,** or **C** need to review how to find the least common multiple of two numbers.

7. **D** Correct

   Graph 0.75, $\frac{2}{3}$, 0.25 and $\frac{7}{8}$ on a number line. Locate the number that is the greatest distance away from 0. 0.25, 0.75 and $\frac{2}{3}$ are between 0 and $\frac{7}{8}$. So, $\frac{7}{8}$ is the furthest from 0.

   TEST PREP DOCTOR: Students who answered **A, B,** or **C** may have graphed the numbers incorrectly.

8. **B** Correct

   The number $\frac{1}{2}$ is a number that can be written in the form $\frac{a}{b}$, so it is a rational number. It is not an integer or a whole number because the denominator does not divide evenly into the numerator.

TEST PREP DOCTOR: Students who answered **A, C, or D** need to review the concepts of whole numbers, integers, and rational numbers.

9. **D** Correct

    Locate the points graphed at numbers that are the same distance from 0 on opposite sides of the number line. So, points *A* and *D* are opposites of each other.

    TEST PREP DOCTOR: Students who answered **A, B,** or **C** need to review the concept of opposites.

10. **C** Correct

    Find the absolute values of 1, –3, and 5. The absolute value of 1 is 1. The absolute value of –3 is 3. The absolute value of 5 is 5. Graph 1, 3, and 5 on the number line. So, the number line that shows 1, 3, and 5 graphed shows the values of $|1|$, $|-3|$ and $|5|$.

    TEST PREP DOCTOR: Students who answered **A** graphed the points without finding their absolute value. Students who answered **B** need to review the concept of absolute value. Students who answered **D** graphed the opposites of the numbers inside the absolute value signs.

11. **C** Correct

    Divide 3 by 2 and write as a mixed number: $\frac{3}{2} = 1\frac{1}{2}$. So, there are $1\frac{1}{2}$ pounds of apples in each pile.

    TEST PREP DOCTOR: Students who answered **A** or **D** may have made a computation error. Students who answered **B** misplaced the numbers in the numerator and denominator.

12. **B** Correct

    Multiply 40 by $\frac{2}{5}$, then simplify.

    $$40 \times \frac{2}{5} = \frac{40 \times 2}{5} = \frac{80}{5} = 16$$

    So, Farrah's glass holds 16 milliliters of milk.

    TEST PREP DOCTOR: Students who answered **A, C,** or **D** may have made a computation error.

13. **D** Correct

    Dividing by a fraction is the same as multiplying by its reciprocal. The reciprocal of $\frac{9}{5}$ is $\frac{5}{9}$, so $7 \div \frac{9}{5}$ is equal to $7 \times \frac{5}{9}$.

    TEST PREP DOCTOR: Students who answered **A, B** or **C** need to review how to divide a number by a fraction.

14. **C** Correct

    Divide 7 by $\frac{1}{2}$.

    $$7 \div \frac{1}{2} = 7 \times 2 = 14.$$

    So, Leah cut the ribbon into 14 pieces.

    TEST PREP DOCTOR: Students who answered **A** may have misunderstood the question. Students who answered **B** or **D** may have made a computational error.

15. **C** Correct

    Add 3 cups of nuts and 1 cups of raisins. Then, divide by $\frac{1}{2}$.

    $$(3 + 1) \div \frac{1}{2} = 4 \div \frac{1}{2}$$
    $$= 4 \times 2$$
    $$= 8$$

    So, Jonas will need 8 plastic bags.

    TEST PREP DOCTOR: Students who answered **A, B,** or **D** may have made a computation error.

16. B Correct

Divide 6,000 by 100.

$$\frac{6,000}{100} = 60$$

So, Serena will have 60 rows of vegetables.

TEST PREP DOCTOR: Students who answered **A, C,** or **D** may have made a computation error and need to review how to divide large numbers.

17. B Correct

Subtract 130.25 from 150.75.

$150.75 - 130.25 = 20.5$. So, Jessica hit a golf ball 20.5 yards farther than Kayla.

TEST PREP DOCTOR: Students who answered **A, C,** or **D** may have made a computation error.

18. C Correct

Multiply 80 by 1.5. $80 \times 1.5 = 120$. So, Gabriel drives 120 kilometers in 1.5 hours.

TEST PREP DOCTOR: Students who answered **A, B,** or **D** may have made a computation error.

19. C Correct

Divide 5.2 by 0.4. $5.2 \div 0.4 = 13$. So, 13 glasses of water can be poured from the pitcher.

TEST PREP DOCTOR: Students who answered **A** multiplied the numbers. Students who answered **B** or **D** may have made a computational error.

20. D Correct

Find the percent spent on rent in the circle graph. Write the percent as a decimal and multiply by 1,000.

$30\% = 0.3$

$1,000 \times 0.3 = 300$

So, Alissa spends $300 on rent each month.

TEST PREP DOCTOR: Students who answered **A** may have made a computation error. Students who answered **B** calculated the amount Alissa spends on other expenses. Students who answered **C** calculated the amount Alissa spends on groceries.

21. B Correct

Write the number of boys as the numerator and the number of girls as the denominator of a fraction. There are 7 boys and 10 girls, so, the ratio of boys to girls is $\frac{7}{10}$.

TEST PREP DOCTOR: Students who answered **A** may have transposed the numerator and denominator in writing the ratio. Students who answered **C** found the ratio of girls to the total number of students in Evan's math class. Students who answered **D** found the ratio of boys to the total number of students in Evan's math class.

22. A Correct

Divide $4 by 20 ounces.
$4 \div 20 = 0.2$. So, the unit price is $0.20/oz.

TEST PREP DOCTOR: Students who answered **B** or **C** may have made a computation error. Students who answered **D** divided 20 ounces by $4.

23. B Correct

Write the ratios of vinegar to water as fractions. Find the ratio that is an equivalent fraction. $\frac{1}{2} = \frac{2}{4}$, so 1 cup of vinegar and 2 cups of water has the same ratio as 2 cups of vinegar to 4 cups of water.

TEST PREP DOCTOR: Students who answered **A, C** or **D** need to review how to find equivalent ratios.

24. D Correct

1 gallon is equal to 4 quarts, so Liam bought 4 quarts of juice at the grocery.

TEST PREP DOCTOR: Students who answered **A**, **B** or **C** need to review how to convert gallons to quarts.

25. C Correct

1 meter is equal to about 3.3 feet.

TEST PREP DOCTOR: Students who answered **A**, **B** or **D** need to review how to convert metric measurements to customary measurements.

26. B Correct

Find the number of miles Nora bikes in 2 hours. Find the number of miles Jiro bikes in 2 hours. Subtract the number of miles Nora bikes in 2 hours from the number of miles Jiro bikes in 2 hours

Nora: $30 \times 2 = 60$

Jiro: $45 \times 2 = 90$

$90 - 60 = 30$

So, Jiro bikes 30 more miles than Nora in 2 hours.

TEST PREP DOCTOR: Students who answered **A** found how many more miles Jiro bikes than Nora in 1 hour. Students who answered **C** added the number of miles Nora and Jiro bike per hour. Students who answered **D** may have made a computation error.

27. B Correct

Look for the pattern in the table, then find the answer choice that represents the pattern. The pattern in the table is each shelf holds 21 books. For each shelf, you multiply by 21. So, shelves × 21 represents the number of books.

TEST PREP DOCTOR: Students who answered **A**, **C**, or **D** need to review how to look for a pattern in a table and how to represent information mathematically and verbally.

28. B Correct

Write a ratio and solve for the unknown quantity.

$$\frac{2 \text{ inches}}{20 \text{ miles}} = \frac{4 \text{ inches}}{\text{actual distance}}$$

$$\text{actual distance} = 4 \text{ inches} \left(\frac{20 \text{ miles}}{2 \text{ inches}} \right)$$

$$\text{actual distance} = 40 \text{ miles}$$

So, the actual distance between Longwood and Milltown is 40 miles.

TEST PREP DOCTOR: Students who answered **A**, **C**, or **D** may have made a computation error.

29. D Correct

Count the total number of strips in the rectangle. Count the number of shaded strips. Write the ratio of the number of shaded strips to the total number of strips. Write the ratio as a percent.

The total number of strips is 10 and the number of shaded strips is 5, so the ratio of the number of shaded strips to the total number of strips is $\frac{5}{10}$.

$$\frac{5}{10} = 0.5 = 50\%$$

So, 50% of the rectangle is shaded.

TEST PREP DOCTOR: Students who answered **A**, **B**, or **C** may have miscounted the number of strips or made a computation error.

30. D Correct

$4^2 = 4 \times 4 = 16$

TEST PREP DOCTOR: Students who answered **A**, **B** or **C** need to review how to evaluate an exponent.

31. C Correct

Find all the numbers that can be divided evenly into 9. So, 1, 3, and 9 are all the factors of 9.

TEST PREP DOCTOR: Students who answered **A** found an incomplete list of factors and incorrectly included 2. Students who answered **B** or **D** included the numbers 2 and 6, which are not a factor of 9. They need to review how to find all the factors of a number.

32. D Correct

Use the order of operations.

$$10 + (8 - 2)^2 \div 2 = 10 + (6)^2 \div 2$$
$$= 10 + 36 \div 2$$
$$= 10 + 18$$
$$= 28$$

So, $10 + (8 - 2)^2 \div 2 = 28$.

TEST PREP DOCTOR: Students who answered **A**, **B** or **C** may have made a computation error and need to review the order of operations.

33. B Correct

Simplify the expression.

$$2(7x + 3) = 14x + 6$$

So, $14x + 6$ is equivalent to $2(7x + 3)$.

TEST PREP DOCTOR: Students who answered **A**, **C** or **D** may have made computation errors and need to review the distributive property of multiplication.

34. D Correct

Solve for x:

$$x - 9 = 4$$
$$x = 4 + 9$$
$$x = 13$$

TEST PREP DOCTOR: Students who answered **A**, **B,** or **C** may have made computation errors.

35. A Correct

Two angles are complementary when the sum of their measures is 90°. So $45 + x = 90$ represents the situation in which a 45° angle is complementary to angle x.

TEST PREP DOCTOR: Students who answered **B** may have misrepresented the situation in the equation. Students who answered **C** or **D** need to review the definition of complementary angles.

36. C Correct

The arrow starts at 1, and the point is graphed with an open circle, so the graph represents all values greater than 1. So, the inequality shown is $p > 1$.

TEST PREP DOCTOR: Students who answered **A**, **B** or **D** need to review the meaning of inequality symbols.

37. D Correct

Write the phrase as an algebraic expression. "Twice a number n" can be written as $2n$. So, 2 less than twice a number n can be written as $2n - 2$.

TEST PREP DOCTOR: Students who answered **A**, **B** or **C** may need to review how to write phrases as algebraic expressions.

38. D Correct

Substitute 4 for x in the expression and evaluate.

$$6(x + 8) = 6(4 + 8) = 6(12) = 72$$

TEST PREP DOCTOR: Students who answered **A**, **B** or **C** may have made a computation error or need to review how to evaluate expressions for a variable.

39. B Correct

Use the order of operations and combine like terms to simplify the expression.

So, $14x - (2x + y) = 14x - 2x - y = 12x - y$.

TEST PREP DOCTOR: Students who answered **A**, **C** or **D** may have made a computation error.

40. B Correct

    Write the phrase as an algebraic expression. Number of drummers = number of violinists − 2, so $d = 5 − 2$.

    TEST PREP DOCTOR: Students who answered **A**, **C** or **D** need to review how to express situations as algebraic expressions.

41. D Correct

    Write the phrase as an algebraic expression and substitute known values. Cost of book + cost of pen = 9. Let p = the cost of the pen. So, $7 + p = 9$.

    TEST PREP DOCTOR: Students who answered **A**, **B** or **C** need to review how to express situations as algebraic expressions.

42. D Correct

    Solve the equation for m.

    $$\frac{m}{2} = 5$$

    $$m = 5 \times 2$$

    $$m = 10$$

    TEST PREP DOCTOR: Students who answered **A**, **B** or **C** may have made a computational error.

43. A Correct

    For each hour x of auto repair, the charge y is $90, so the equation that expresses y in terms of x is $y = 90x$.

    TEST PREP DOCTOR: Students who answered **B** or **D** may have misinterpreted the table data. Students who answered **C** transposed the x and y variables.

44. B Correct

    Use the equation $y = 90x$ and substitute 3 for x.

    $$y = 90x$$

    $$y = 90(3)$$

    $$y = 270$$

So, the charge for a repair that takes 3 hours is $270.

TEST PREP DOCTOR: Students who answered **A**, **C** or **D** may have made a computation error or used an incorrect equation based on misinterpreting the table data.

45. B Correct

    Locate point P on the graph. Write the location as a coordinate pair in the form (x, y). So, the coordinates of point P are (4, 80).

    TEST PREP DOCTOR: Students who answered **A** and **C** may have misread the graph. Students who answered **D** transposed the x and y coordinates.

46. D Correct

    The dependent variable is the variable that depends on another variable. In the graph, distance depends on time, so distance is the dependent variable.

    TEST PREP DOCTOR: Students who answered **A** or **B** need to review the concepts of dependent and independent variables. Students who answered **C** chose the independent variable and need to review the concepts of dependent and independent variables.

47. B Correct

    For the line representing Car B, write an equation that expresses y in terms of x. Since y is 5 times the value of x, $y = 5x$.

    TEST PREP DOCTOR: Students who answered **A**, **C,** or **D** need to review how to write an equation from information expressed in a graph.

48. C Correct

    Use the formula for the area of a parallelogram. Substitute known values for the base and height.

    $$A = b \times h$$

    $$A = 10 \times 4 = 40$$

    So, the area is 40 cm^2.

TEST PREP DOCTOR: Students who answered **A, B,** or **D** may have made computation errors or need to review the formula for area of a parallelogram.

49. **A** Correct

Use the formula for the volume of a rectangular prism. Substitute known values for the volume, length, and width.

$$V = l \times w \times h$$
$$210 = 5 \times 7 \times h$$
$$210 = 35 \times h$$
$$h = \frac{210}{35}$$
$$h = 6$$

So, the height of the prism is 6 feet.

TEST PREP DOCTOR: Students who answered **B, C,** or **D** may have made computation errors or need to review the formula for volume of a rectangular prism.

50. **A** Correct

Use the formula for area of a trapezoid.

$$A = \frac{1}{2}h(b_1 + b_2)$$
$$A = \frac{1}{2}(2)(4 + 5)$$
$$A = (1)(9)$$
$$A = 9$$

So, the area of the trapezoid is 9 m².

TEST PREP DOCTOR: Students who answered **B, C,** or **D** may have made computation errors or need to review the formula for area of a trapezoid.

51. **A** Correct

Use the formula for area of a triangle.

$$A = \frac{1}{2}bh$$
$$A = \frac{1}{2}(10)(20)$$
$$A = \frac{1}{2}(200)$$
$$A = 100$$

So, the area of the triangle is 100 cm².

TEST PREP DOCTOR: Students who answered **B, C,** or **D** may have made computation errors or need to review the formula for area of a triangle.

52. **B** Correct

Use the formula for the area of a rhombus.

$$A = \frac{d_1 d_2}{2}$$
$$A = \frac{(10)(15)}{2}$$
$$A = \frac{(150)}{2}$$
$$A = 75$$

So, the area of the rhombus is 75 in².

TEST PREP DOCTOR: Students who answered **A, C,** or **D** may have made computation errors or need to review the formula for area of a rhombus.

53. **C** Correct

Use the formula for area of a triangle and substitute known values for area and height.

$$A = \frac{1}{2}bh$$
$$240 = \frac{1}{2}b(15)$$
$$240 = 7.5b$$
$$b = 32$$

So, the length of the base of the triangle is 32 inches.

TEST PREP DOCTOR: Students who answered **A, B,** or **D** may have made computation errors or need to review the formula for area of a triangle.

54. **D** Correct

Use the formula for area of a trapezoid. Substitute known values.

$$A = \frac{1}{2}h(b_1 + b_2)$$

$$1,800 = \frac{1}{2}h(40 + 50)$$

$$1,800 = \frac{1}{2}h(90)$$

$$1,800 = 45h$$

$$h = 40$$

The "height" of the trapezoid shape is the width of the lawn, since it is flat on the ground. So, the width of the lawn is 40 m.

TEST PREP DOCTOR: Students who answered **A, B,** or **C** may have made computation errors or need to review the formula for area of a trapezoid.

55. **C** Correct

Separate the polygon into two rectangles. One measures 2 cm by 4 cm and the other measures 1 cm by 2 cm. Find the area of the two rectangles.

Rectangle 1: $2 \times 4 = 8$
Rectangle 2: $1 \times 2 = 2$

Find the sum of the areas.
$8 + 2 = 10$

So, the area of the polygon is 10 cm^2.

TEST PREP DOCTOR: Students who answered **A, B,** or **D** may have made computation errors or need to review how to find the area of a polygon.

56. **C** Correct

Count the number of squares between the points on the coordinate grid. There are 6 squares between point *A* and point *B*. One square equals 1 unit, so the distance between them is 6 units.

TEST PREP DOCTOR: Students who answered **A, B,** or **D** need to review how to find the distance between two points on a coordinate grid.

57. **D** Correct

Find the total surface area of the box:
$(2 \times 4) \times 2 = 16$
$(2 \times 6) \times 2 = 24$
$(4 \times 6) \times 2 = 48$

$16 + 24 + 48 = 88$

So, Charlene will need 88 in^2 of wrapping paper.

TEST PREP DOCTOR: Students who answered **A** or **B** may have made a computation error or need to review how to find the surface area of a rectangular prism. Students who answered **C** may have found the volume of the box.

58. **B** Correct

Use the formula for the volume of a rectangular prism.

$V = \text{length} \times \text{width} \times \text{depth}$
$V = 10 \times 20 \times 5 = 1,000$

So, the swimming pool could hold 1,000 ft^3 of water.

TEST PREP DOCTOR: Students who answered **A, C,** or **D** may have made a computation error or need to review how to find the volume of a rectangular prism.

59. **C** Correct

In a box plot, the vertical segment within the box represents the median of the data. So, the median of the data is 30.

TEST PREP DOCTOR: Students who answered **A, B,** or **D** may have misread the box plot and need to review how data is represented in a box plot.

60. **C** Correct

In a dot plot, the data value with the greatest frequency is the data value with the greatest number of dots above it. So, 2 has the greatest frequency.

TEST PREP DOCTOR: Students who answered **A, B,** or **D** may have misread the dot plot or need to review how data is represented in a dot plot.

61. **D** Correct

To calculate the mean of the data, find the sum of the data values and divide by the total number of data values.

$$\frac{6 + 5 + 4}{3} = \frac{15}{3} = 5$$

So, the mean of the data is 5.

TEST PREP DOCTOR: Students who answered **A, B,** or **C** may have made a computation error or need to review how to find the mean from a series of data values.

62. **A** Correct

Find the bar labeled "1-10" on the *x*-axis. Find the height of this bar: 3 units. One unit equals 1 student, so 3 students watch between 1 and 10 hours of television per month.

TEST PREP DOCTOR: Students who answered **B, C,** or **D** need to review how to read a histogram.

63. **B** Correct

Find the mean of each data set.

Fiona: $\frac{90 + 90 + 93}{3} = \frac{273}{3} = 91$

Gary: $\frac{70 + 67 + 115}{3} = \frac{252}{3} = 84$

Find the mean absolute deviation (MAD) of each data set. To find the MAD, find the absolute value of the difference between each data point and the mean, and calculate the mean of the absolute values.

Fiona:
$$|90 - 91| = |-1| = 1$$
$$|90 - 91| = |-1| = 1$$
$$|93 - 91| = |2| = 2$$

Fiona's MAD:

$$\frac{1 + 1 + 2}{3} = \frac{4}{3} = 1.\overline{3}$$

$$|70 - 84| = |-14| = 14$$

Gary: $|67 - 84| = |-17| = 17$

$$|115 - 84| = |31| = 31$$

Gary's MAD:

$$\frac{14 + 17 + 31}{3} = \frac{62}{3} = 20.\overline{6}$$

Gary's MAD is much higher than Fiona's, which indicates that Gary's teeth-brushing time is more variable than Fiona's.

TEST PREP DOCTOR: Students who answered **A, C,** or **D** need to review how to find and draw conclusions from the mean absolute deviation of a data set.

64. **D** Correct

Count the units to find the length and width of the polygon. The polygon is a square with side length 4 units, so multiply 4 by 4. $4 \times 4 = 16$. Each unit is 1 foot, so the area of the actual rug is 16 ft^2.

TEST PREP DOCTOR: Students who answered **A, B,** or **C** may have made a computation error.

65. **C** Correct

Multiply 52 by $\frac{3}{4}$. $52 \times \frac{3}{4} = 39$. So, Marty's dog weighs 39 kilograms.

TEST PREP DOCTOR: Students who answered **A, B,** or **D** may have made a computation error.

66. **C** Correct

Divide $10\frac{1}{2}$ by $\frac{1}{2}$.

$$\frac{10\frac{1}{2}}{\frac{1}{2}} = \frac{\frac{21}{2}}{\frac{1}{2}} = \frac{21}{2} \times \frac{2}{1} = 21$$

So, Hayley cut the rope into 21 pieces.

TEST PREP DOCTOR: Students who answered **A**, **B**, or **D** may have made a computation error.

67. **D** Correct

Multiply 25 by 5. $25 \times 5 = 125$. So, the caterpillar crawls 125 inches in 5 minutes.

TEST PREP DOCTOR: Students who answered **A** divided 25 by 5 instead of multiplying. Students who answered **B**, or **C** may have made a computation error.

68. **A** Correct

Divide 15 by 2.50.

$15 \div 2.50 = 6$

So, Jungwon can buy 6 notepads.

TEST PREP DOCTOR: Students who answered **B** added the cost of one notepad to the amount of money Jungwon has and rounded the answer. Students who answered **C** multiplied the amount of money that Jungwon has by the cost of a notepad and rounded the answer. Students who answered **D** made an error in placing the decimal.

69. **B** Correct

Multiply the number of pounds of onions Noah bought by the cost per pound, and add the cost of the salad greens.

$5(2) + 4 = 10 + 4 = 14$

So, Noah spent $14.

TEST PREP DOCTOR: Students who answered **A** forgot to include the salad greens. Students who answered **C** or **D** may have made a computation error.

70. **B** Correct

Find the percent budgeted to savings in the circle graph. Write the percent as a decimal and multiply by 2,000.

$25\% = 0.25$

$2{,}000 \times 0.25 = 500$

So, Oliver saves $500 each month.

TEST PREP DOCTOR: Students who answered **A** calculated the amount spent on other expenses. Students who answered **C** calculated the amount spent on groceries. Students who answered **D** calculated the amount spent on rent.

71. **A** Correct

Divide the price of the can of sauce by the number of ounces in the can.

$6 \div 24 = 0.25$

So, the unit price is $0.25 per ounce.

TEST PREP DOCTOR: Students who answered **B** may have made a computation error. Students who answered **C** made an error in placing the decimal. Students who answered **D** divided the number of ounces in a can by the cost of a can.

72. **C** Correct

There are 16 cups in 1 gallon, so Conrad bought 16 cups of water.

TEST PREP DOCTOR: Students who answered **A**, **B** or **D** need to review how to convert gallons to cups.

73. **C** Correct

Multiply the amount David charges per hour by 4. $\$35 \times 4 = \$140$. So, David charges $140 for yard work that takes 4 hours.

TEST PREP DOCTOR: Students who answered **A** found the amount David charges for only 1 hour of yard work. Students who answered **B** found the amount David charges for 2 hours of yard work. Students who answered **D** found the amount David charges for 5 hours of yard work.

74. **C** Correct

Multiply the falcon's speed by 2. Multiply the goose's speed by 2. Find the difference.

Falcon: $300 \times 2 = 600$

Goose: $140 \times 2 = 280$

$600 - 280 = 320$

So, a falcon will fly 320 more kilometers than a goose in 2 hours.

TEST PREP DOCTOR: Students who answered **A** found how many more kilometers a falcon will fly than a goose in only 1 hour. Students who answered **B** or **D** may have made a computation error.

75. **D** Correct

Write and solve a ratio comparing inches on the map to miles of actual distance.

$$\frac{2 \text{ inches}}{10 \text{ miles}} = \frac{5 \text{ inches}}{x \text{ miles}}$$

$$\frac{2}{10} = \frac{5}{x}$$

$$x = 5\left(\frac{10}{2}\right)$$

$$x = \frac{50}{2}$$

$$x = 25$$

So, the actual distance between the library and the bank is 25 miles.

TEST PREP DOCTOR: Students who answered **A** may have made an error setting up the ratios. Students who answered **B** or **C** may have made computation errors.

76. **D** Correct

Multiply $7 \times 7 \times 7 = 343$.
So, $(7)^3 = 343$.

TEST PREP DOCTOR: Students who answered **A**, **B** or **C** may have made computation errors and need to review how to find the value of exponents.

77. **B** Correct

Simplify the expression within the parentheses first, then compute the exponent and then divide.

$$990 \div (12 - 9)^2 = 990 \div (3)^2$$
$$= 990 \div 9$$
$$= 110$$

TEST PREP DOCTOR: Students who answered **A, C,** or **D** may have made computation errors or need to review the order of operations.

78. **D** Correct

Substitute 5 for x and evaluate the expression.

$5(x + 7) = 5(5 + 7) = 5(12) = 60$

TEST PREP DOCTOR: Students who answered **A, B,** or **C** may have made computation errors.

79. **B** Correct

Ignore extraneous information, e.g., the height of Pedro's tree last year. Subtract 2 feet from the height of Pedro's house. $17 - 2 = 15$. So, the tree is 15 feet tall.

TEST PREP DOCTOR: Students who answered **A** may have confused the height of the tree this year and last year. Students who answered **C** or **D** may have made computation errors.

80. **D** Correct

Use the formula for the area of a parallelogram. Substitute known values for the base and height.

$A = b \times h$

$A = 7 \times 10 = 70$

So, the area is 70 m^2.

TEST PREP DOCTOR: Students who answered **A, B,** or **C** may have made computation errors or need to review the formula for area of a parallelogram.

81. **C** Correct

Use the formula for area of a triangle.

$$A = \frac{1}{2}bh$$

$$A = \frac{1}{2}(30)(20)$$

$$A = \frac{1}{2}(600)$$

$$A = 300$$

So, the area of the triangle is 300 cm^2.

TEST PREP DOCTOR: Students who answered **A, B,** or **D** may have made computation errors or need to review the formula for area of a triangle.

82. **B** Correct

Use the formula for area of a rhombus.

$$A = \frac{d_1 d_2}{2}$$

$$A = \frac{(9)(12)}{2}$$

$$A = \frac{(108)}{2}$$

$$A = 54$$

So, the area of the rhombus is 54 mm^2.

TEST PREP DOCTOR: Students who answered **A, C,** or **D** may have made computation errors or need to review the formula for area of a rhombus.

83. **D** Correct

Use the formula for area of a triangle and substitute known values.

$$A = \frac{1}{2}bh$$

$$400 = \frac{1}{2}(10)h$$

$$400 = 5h$$

$$h = 80$$

So, the height of the triangle is 80 in.

TEST PREP DOCTOR: Students who answered **A, B,** or **C** may have made computation errors or need to review the formula for area of a triangle.

84. **A** Correct

Use the formula for area of a trapezoid. Substitute known values.

$$A = \frac{1}{2}h(b_1 + b_2)$$

$$342 = \frac{1}{2}h(17 + 21)$$

$$342 = \frac{1}{2}h(38)$$

$$342 = 19h$$

$$h = 18$$

So, the height of the trapezoid is 18 m.

TEST PREP DOCTOR: Students who answered **B, C,** or **D** may have made computation errors or need to review the formula for area of a trapezoid.

85. **B** Correct

Use the formula for the volume of a rectangular prism. Substitute known values for the volume, length, and width.

$$V = l \times w \times h$$

$$572 = 4 \times 13 \times h$$

$$572 = 52 \times h$$

$$h = \frac{572}{52}$$

$$h = 11$$

So, the height of the prism is 11 inches.

TEST PREP DOCTOR: Students who answered **A, C,** or **D** may have made computation errors or need to review the formula for volume of a rectangular prism.

Answer Key

Module Quizzes

MODULE 1 Integers

Module Quiz 1: B

1. C
2. B
3. C
4. D
5. B
6. D
7. C
8. D
9. C
10. D
11.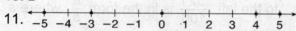
12. −7 > −11 or −11 < −7
13. distance; positive
14. negative; zero
15. > ; <
16. absolute value; 7
17. −8; The absolute value of 8 is 8, and its opposite is −8.
18. Beth
19. Earl
20. Dora
21. 756 ft

Module Quiz 1: D

1. B
2. C
3. B
4. A
5. C
6. B
7. A
8. A
9. B
10. C
11. A

12. ![number line from -5 to 5]
13. −7, −6, −3, −1, 1, 2, 5
14. distance
15. positive
16. <
17. 6
18. Student E
19. 89
20. Student C
21. Student B
22. −32
23. Fred and Jon; Hanna and Ilsa
24. Fred
25. Gina
26. −2, −1

MODULE 2 Factors and Multiples

Module Quiz 2: B

1. B
2. D
3. B
4. A
5. B
6. C
7. B
8. D
9. A
10. D
11. D
12. B
13. June
14. 3
15. 210
16. Find the LCM of 12 and 15.
17. 60th

18. 12 displays

19. 1 and 48; 3 and 16

20. Sample answers: 1 and 7; 7 and 14; 7 and 21

21. greatest common factor

22. 40 and 15

23. 5 areas

24. 8

Module Quiz 2: D

1. A
2. C
3. B
4. A
5. A
6. B
7. C
8. A
9. B
10. A
11. A
12. C
13. Ken
14. 4
15. 42
16. Find the LCM of 10 and 15.
17. 12th
18. 6 bracelets
19. Sample answer: 1 and 12 or 3 and 4
20. Sample answers: 5 and 10, 5 and 15
21. greatest common factor
22. 6 and 15
23. 3 groups
24. 2

MODULE 3 Rational Numbers

Module Quiz 3: B

1. C
2. A
3. A
4. D
5. D

6. A

7. D

8. She is not correct. $3.52 = \dfrac{352}{100}$. 352 and 100 are both integers, so $\dfrac{352}{100}$ is a ratio of integers.

9. Shelly

10. $-\dfrac{5}{3}, -\dfrac{11}{6}, -\dfrac{21}{10}, -\dfrac{11}{5}$

11. B, C, and D

12. They are both the same distance from zero on the number line.

13. Tuesday and Wednesday

14. 3.21 equals $\dfrac{321}{100}$ because dividing by 100 moves the decimal point two places to the left. $\dfrac{321}{100}$ is in the form $\dfrac{a}{b}$, where a and b are both integers.

15. $2\dfrac{3}{8}$

Module Quiz 3: D

1. C
2. C
3. C
4. B
5. A
6. C
7. C
8. C
9. B
10. C
11. 1.6
12. Mauricio
13. −1.8, −2.1, −2.5, −2.7
14. 65.6
15. $2\dfrac{1}{8}$
16. No. −3 can be written as $\dfrac{-3}{1}$.
17. Monday and Tuesday

18. $\dfrac{21}{2}$

19. −12.4

MODULE 4 Operations with Fractions

Module Quiz 4: B

1. C
2. D
3. D
4. C
5. C
6. B
7. B
8. A
9. B
10. 6 nights
11. 132.5625 ft^2
12. 12
13. 2
14. Yes. $14\dfrac{4}{5} \div 1\dfrac{1}{2} = 9\dfrac{13}{15} > 8$
15. $\dfrac{3}{56}$
16. Dustin
17. $\dfrac{32}{45}$
18. Yes. Dividing by $\dfrac{4}{5}$ is the same as multiplying by $\dfrac{5}{4}$, which can be thought of as multiplying by 5 then dividing by 4.
19. No. The width is $46\dfrac{7}{8} \div 7\dfrac{1}{2} = 6.25 > 6$. It will be too big.

Module Quiz 4: D

1. A
2. C
3. C
4. C
5. C
6. A

7. B
8. A
9. A
10. 3 nights
11. $62\dfrac{1}{2}$ ft^2
12. $\dfrac{5}{12}$
13. $\dfrac{2}{3}$
14. 32
15. 144
16. 3
17. $5 - \dfrac{2}{5} = \dfrac{25}{5} - \dfrac{2}{5} = \dfrac{23}{5} = 4\dfrac{3}{5}$
18. $\dfrac{5}{16}$
19. 3
20. $\dfrac{1}{2}$
21. Yes. Dividing by a fraction means multiplying by its reciprocal; the reciprocal of $\dfrac{1}{5}$ is 5.
22. 5
23. 6

MODULE 5 Operations with Decimals

Module Quiz 5: B

1. D
2. A
3. A
4. A
5. B
6. C
7. B
8. B
9. D
10. B
11. C
12. B

13. $36.90
14. $9.76
15. 15.0625 mi
16. 2 h
17. 9 weeks
18. $8/h
19. $0.15
20. $41.66
21. 15.6 oz

Module Quiz 5: D

1. C
2. B
3. B
4. C
5. C
6. A
7. B
8. C
9. C
10. A
11. B
12. A
13. $30
14. $5.41
15. 16.4
16. 21.1 s
17. 1
18. 10.1
19. 0.18
20. $8/h
21. $0.70
22. $11.49
23. 3 more glasses
24. 3

MODULE 6 Representing Ratios and Rates

Module Quiz 6: B

1. B
2. B
3. D

4. C
5. B
6. B
7. C
8. A
9. B
10. C
11. B
12. A
13. Sample answers: 10 white marbles and 15 blue marbles, 12 white marbles and 18 blue marbles
14. 22.5 cal
15. $\frac{7}{16}$ or 0.4375
16. 64 tigers
17. 60 sandwiches
18. 85 cards
19. 196 mi
20. 6.25 c
21. 20 knives
22. 5 h
23. 120 pages

Module Quiz 6: D

1. C
2. A
3. A
4. B
5. C
6. C
7. B
8. B
9. B
10. C
11. C
12. A
13. 600 trout
14. 20 cal
15. $\frac{2}{3}$
16. 30 cats
17. 30 blue tacks

18. 30 mi

19. $\frac{3}{4}$

20. $\frac{5}{6}$

21. $45

22. 80 pages

23. $0.22

MODULE 7 Applying Ratios and Rates

Module Quiz 7: B

1. A
2. C
3. A
4. C
5. D
6. C
7. A
8. D
9. B
10. A
11. 1 in. = 8 mi
12. 2,640 ft
13. Factory A produces 30 more machines.
14.

Time (h)	Distance (mi)
0	0
0.5	**1**
1	2
1.5	3
2	**4**
2.5	**5**
3	**6**

15. $6
16. 4
17. 8 qt
18. 50 rock songs
19. 1 gallon is about 3.79 liters, so multiply the number of gallons by 3.79.
20. similar: Both are lines through the origin. *y*-values increase as *x*-values increase; different: The 50-mph graph will be steeper.

21. Choice C

Module Quiz 7: D

1. B
2. A
3. B
4. C
5. C
6. A
7. B
8. A
9. C
10. 5 mi
11. 300 mL
12. 160 machines
13.

Time (h)	Distance (mi)
0	0
1	30
2	**60**
3	90

14. 1,500 m
15. 5
16. $35
17. 0.908 kg
18. Both students are correct; 10:20 and 1:2 are equivalent ratios.
19. 0.33 m
20. $\frac{3}{7}$
21. 2,500 g

MODULE 8 Percents

Module Quiz 8: B

1. A
2. D
3. B
4. D
5. A
6. D
7. C
8. B

9. C
10. A
11. 11%
12. 288
13. 30%
14. 20%
15. $168
16. 12% or 0.12
17. 20
18. 29
19. 6
20. 100
21. Kylie drank 140 mL, and Eugenia drank 157.5 mL; Eugenia drank more water.
22. 80

Module Quiz 8: D

1. C
2. A
3. B
4. B
5. C
6. C
7. C
8. A
9. A
10. 75%
11. 60
12. 25%
13. 5
14. $300
15. 80% or 0.8
16. 0.4
17. 75
18. 25%
19. $140
20. $33\frac{1}{3}$%
21. 7.5
22. 87.5%
23. $200

MODULE 9 Generating Equivalent Numerical Expressions

Module Quiz 9: B

1. A
2. D
3. D
4. C
5. D
6. D
7. B
8. C
9. A
10. B
11. C
12. C
13. D
14. $(-3)^2$
15. 27 blocks
16. $1 \times 28, 2 \times 14, 4 \times 7$
17. $15 \div (3 + 2) \times 11$
18. 5.3^4
19. $14.50
20. decreases
21. $2^3 \times 11$
22. 216
23. Sample answers: $16^1, 4^2, 2^4$
24. $89.35
25. 107
26. 6 ways

Module Quiz 9: D

1. A
2. C
3. B
4. A
5. B
6. B
7. C
8. A
9. A

10. C
11. C
12. C
13. $2 \times 3 \times 7$
14. 1
15. 17
16. multiplication
17. 120
18. 96
19. 6
20. Length = 91 ft; Width = 2 ft
21. 0
22. $(-17)^3$
23. $3(9) + 2(4)$
24. 5^2
25. 4^3

MODULE 10 Generating Equivalent Algebraic Expressions

Module Quiz 10: B

1. A
2. B
3. B
4. A
5. B
6. B
7. B
8. C
9. A
10. C
11. A
12. variable: t; constant: 18
13. $6k$
14. Sample answers: a number g minus 12; a number g decreased by 12; 12 less than a number g
15.

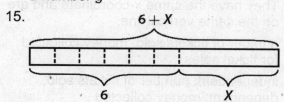

16. $v + 3$; $v - 2$
17. 1,225
18. $n + 6$; 66 in.; Chang is 66 in. tall.
19. Step 1: Substitute 3.7 for n; Step 2: Subtract 0.5 from 3.7; Step 3: Multiply by 6; Step 4: Add 12.8.
20. $5x^2 - 20x$
21. $4y + 4x$
22. 16 girls

Module Quiz 10: D

1. A
2. C
3. B
4. B
5. A
6. A
7. C
8. B
9. A
10. C
11. A
12. variable: n; constant: 3
13. $h \times 6$
14. a number g decreased by 12
15. $6 + x$; or $x + 6$
16. $v + 3$; $v - 2$
17. 35
18. $n + 6$; 66 in.; Chang is 66 in. tall.
19. $12.8 + 6(3.7 - 0.5)$; Subtract to find $3.7 - 0.5$.
20. $5x - 10$
21. $4y - 8$
22. 100

MODULE 11 Equations and Relationships

Module Quiz 11: B

1. B
2. C
3. D
4. B

5. B
6. A
7. C
8. B
9. D
10. D
11. B
12. D
13. B
14. no
15. Sample answer: $w + 12 = 38$
16. Sample answer: $s - 12 = 18$
17. no
18. $m = 16.8$
19. $p = 1.7$
20. Sample answer: $c - 3 = 18$; $c = 21$; Carter scored 21 points.
21. 7%
22. Sample answer: $m + 3 = 51$; $m = 48$; Mark is 48 in. tall.
23.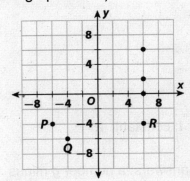
24. $d = 7.2$
25. Sample answer: $8c = 144$; $c = 18$; There are 18 members of the class.
26. Sample answer: $3s = 39$; $s = 13$; His sister found 13 seashells.

Module Quiz 11: D
1. C
2. B
3. A
4. B
5. A
6. A
7. B
8. C
9. A
10. C
11. no
12. $w + 2 = 8$
13. $b - 2 = 10$

14. yes
15. $m = 15$
16. $p = 9$
17. Sample answer: $c - 3 = 8$; $c = 11$; Carter scored 11 points.
18. 8%
19. Sample answer: $s + 3 = 56$; $s = 53$; Sue is 53 inches tall.
20.
21. $d = 12$
22. Sample answer: $6s = 24$; $s = 4$; There are 4 students.
23. Sample answer: $2s = 20$; $s = 10$; His sister found 10 seashells.

MODULE 12 Relationships in Two Variables

Module Quiz 12: B
1. C
2. B
3. D
4. D
5. C
6. B
7. C
8. C
9. (and graph for 11)

10. quadrant III
11. They have the same x-coordinate and are on the same vertical line.
12. number of tickets sold, money collected for ticket sales
13. independent: number of tickets sold; dependent: money collected

14. The money collected is 2 times the number of tickets.

15. $y = 10x$

16. $35

17.

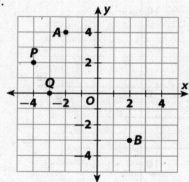

18. 40%

Module Quiz 12: D

1. C
2. C
3. B
4. B
5. B
6. B
7. C
8. A
9.

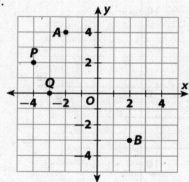

10. $P(-4, 2)$, $Q(-3, 0)$

11. first quadrant

12. number of tickets sold

13. amount of dollars collected

14. Multiply the number of tickets by 2.

15. $80

16. 6 h

17.

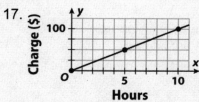

18. 20%

MODULE 13 Area and Polygons

Module Quiz 13: B

1. A
2. C
3. A
4. C
5. B
6. C
7. A
8. A
9. B
10. C

11. top and bottom: $2(5 \times 30) = 300$
side pieces: $2(5 \times 20) = 200$
center: $20 \times 30 = 600$
total area $= 1,100$ in².

12. Sample answer: You cannot tell the difference between the formulas for a rectangle and parallelogram because they are the same. The formula for the area of a rhombus uses the diagonals, so you could identify the rhombus. The formula for the area of a trapezoid includes adding the different bases, so you could identify the trapezoid.

13. A(trapezoid) $= \frac{1}{2}(21.4 + 30.5)(10.1) =$

262.095 ft²; A(rhombus) $= \frac{1}{2}(10.1)(8.6) =$

43.43 ft². $262.095 - 43.43 = 218.665$ ft².
The area of the unshaded part is 218.665 ft².

14. $y = x + 3$

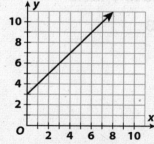

15. Both are correct. It doesn't matter which base is base 1 or base 2 because addition is commutative.

Module Quiz 13: D

1. A
2. B
3. B
4. A
5. B
6. A
7. B
8. C
9.

x	1	2	3	4	5
y	3	4	5	6	7

Ordered pairs: (1, 3), (2, 4), (3, 5), (4, 6), (5, 7)

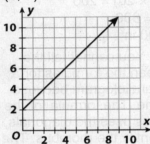

10. Divide the area by the length to find the height. 108 ÷ 18 = 6. The height is 6 in.

11. You could find the area of the triangle and the area of the rhombus, and then add to find the area of the whole figure.

12. The area is 5 × 7 = 35 in². The cutout piece on the left has an area of 2 × 3 = 6 in² as does the "bump" on the right.

MODULE 14 Distance and Area in the Coordinate Plane

Module Quiz 14: B

1. C
2. A
3. C
4. A
5. C
6. D
7. B
8. D
9. C

10. B

11. The distance would be the same, 7 units. When a point is reflected across an axis, the new point is always the same distance from the axis as the original point.

12. (5, −7); A reflection across the x-axis changes the sign of the second value in the ordered pair, and a reflection across the y-axis changes the sign of the first value in the ordered pair.

13. There would be no difference; it would be the same point, (5, −7).

14. He should have added the two distances instead of subtracting them because they are on opposite sides of the y-axis. The actual distance is |−8| + |3| = 11 units.

15. Sample answer: (−5, −3) to (5, −3). The point was reflected across the y-axis.

16. 13 × 12.5 = 162.5 ÷ 52 = 3.125; It would take him 3.125 hours to drive that distance.

17.

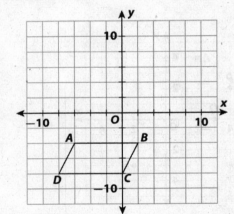

Sample answer: Distance from A to B = 8 units. Distance from line AB to line DC = 4 units. Area of parallelogram = bh; A = 8 × 4 = 32 square units

Module Quiz 14: D

1. C
2. A
3. B
4. C
5. C
6. A
7. B
8. C

9. B

10. C

11. The distance would be the same, 3 units. When a point is reflected across the y-axis, the new point is always the same distance from the y-axis as the original point.

12. No; The point lies on the y-axis, so it cannot be reflected across the y-axis.

13. Yes; The point is still on the y-axis but at (0, −4).

14. He should have subtracted the two distances instead of adding them because they are on the same side of the y-axis. The actual distance is $|8| - |3| = 5$ units.

15. Sample answer: (4, 7) to (−4, 7). The point is reflected across the y-axis.

16. $7 \times 10 = 70$; $70 \div 50 = 1.4$. It would take her 1.4 hours to drive that distance.

17.

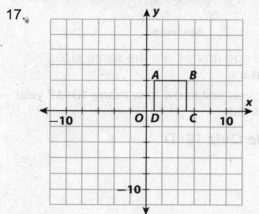

Sample answer: Length of each side = 4 units. Area of a square = s^2; $A = 4^2 = 16$ square units

MODULE 15 Surface Area and Volume of Solids

Module Quiz 15: B

1. C
2. A
3. B
4. C
5. B
6. B
7. D

8. A

9. C

10. D

11. B

12. An edge is 6 units long, because $6 \times 6 \times 6 = 216$.

13. $160\frac{1}{2}$ in^2

14. Sample answer: After you fold the row of four squares to form the four sides of the cube, the remaining two squares are both attached to the bottom edges, so neither of them can become the top face of the cube.

15. a. $464\frac{3}{4} = 7 \times 4\frac{1}{2} \times l$

    b. $l = 14\frac{95}{126}$ m

16. $66\frac{3}{4}$

17. $y = x + 4$

18. Check student's drawing.

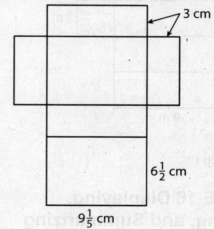

$V = 179\frac{2}{5}$ cm^3

$SA = 213\frac{4}{5}$ cm^2

Module Quiz 15: D

1. A
2. B
3. C
4. B
5. B

6. B

7. B

8. C

9. A

10. C

11. B

12. An edge is 2 units long because
$2 \times 2 \times 2 = 8$.

13. bottom: $2 \times 3 \times 6 = 36$ in^2; two long sides:
$2 \times 6 \times 4 = 48$ in^2; two short sides:
$2 \times 3 \times 4 = 24$ in^2; total: 108 in^2;

14. Sample answer: There are only 5
squares, and a cube has 6 square faces.

15. a. $420 = 7 \times 4 \times$ length

b. $\ell = 420 \div 28 = 15$; length = 15 m

16. 21

17. $y = x + 1$

18. Check student's drawing. Sample
drawing:

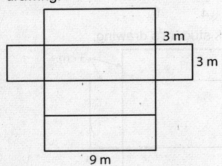

3 m

3 m

9 m

$V = 81$ m^3

$SA = 126$ m^2

MODULE 16 Displaying, Analyzing, and Summarizing Data

Module Quiz 16: B

1. B

2. A

3. A

4. A

5. D

6. C

7. B

8. C

9. B

10. D

11. 68.95 in.

12. 2.365

13. 69.5 in.

14. 69 in., 70 in., and 71 in.

15.

62   65   68   71   74

16. 3.5

17.

Number of Patrons

20

15

10

5

8-12 13-17 18-22 23-27 28-32

Age Group

18. The age groups are the same size,
4 years.

19. No, you just know how many 13–17 year
olds did.

Module Quiz 16: D

1. B

2. B

3. A

4. B

5. B

6. B

7. A

8. A

9. A

10. 85.2

11. 6.96

12. 87

13. 74

14.

74   80   86   92   98

15. 76

16.

17. 4
18. No, the histogram only shows the number who got between $11 and $16.
19. To include all numbers in the range; there are no gaps.

Answer Key

Unit Tests and Performance Tasks

UNIT 1 Numbers

Unit 1 Test: A

1. D
2. A
3. D
4. D
5. D
6. A
7. B
8. B
9. D
10. A
11. D
12. D
13. 4
14. −5.8, −4.2, −4.1, −1.5
15. 8
16. Answers will vary. Any whole number is correct.
17. 4: 4, 8, 12, 16, 20, 24 …

    5: 5, 10, 15, 20, 25, 30 …

    least common multiple: 20
18. 4. 4 is 4 units away from 0 on the number line; −3 is 3 units away.
19. 12: 1, 2, 3, 4, 6, 12

    16: 1, 2, 4, 8, 16

    common factors: 1, 2, 4

    greatest common factor: 4
20. 5.5, $5\frac{1}{4}$, $5\frac{1}{5}$, 5.1
21. $\frac{17}{5}$
22. −4.5, −3.5, −3, 4
23. Yes. 3 is to the right of −5 on the number line.
24. −3

Unit 1 Test: B

1. B
2. A
3. A
4. D
5. A
6. D
7. D
8. D
9. D
10. D
11. 0. The opposite of a number is the same distance from 0 on the number line, but in the opposite direction.
12. Monday
13. $2\frac{11}{12}$
14. Answers will vary. Sample answer: the price of items in a store
15. no; The opposite of −2 is +2.
16. −7.8, −8.05, −8.1, −8.18
17. no; counterexample: 2 + |2| = 4.
18. 12: 1, 2, 3, 4, 6, 12

    20: 1, 2, 4, 5, 10, 20

    greatest common factor: 4

Unit 1 Test: C

1. B
2. C
3. B
4. D
5. D
6. C
7. B
8. B
9. The opposite of 5. −5 is to the right of −6 on the number line.
10. Britney

11. $-\dfrac{15}{8}, -\dfrac{17}{6}, -\dfrac{16}{5}, -\dfrac{19}{5}$

12. $|x| + |y|$

13. $-y < -x$

14. Wednesday

15. 60

16. Every integer can be written as a fraction $\dfrac{a}{b}$, where a is the integer and $b = 1$.

Unit 1 Test: D

1. C
2. B
3. A
4. C
5. C
6. C
7. A
8. B
9. C
10. C
11. A

12. No. 4 can be written as $\dfrac{4}{1}$.

13. Blaine

14. $\dfrac{4}{5}, \dfrac{2}{5}, -\dfrac{2}{5}, -\dfrac{3}{5}$

15. Two. -3 and $+3$.

16. -1.25

17. Answers will vary. Sample answer: 0.5

18. Wednesday

19. 15

20. $\dfrac{3}{4}$

Unit 1 Performance Task

1. Integers Without Wholes; -9 is an integer but not a whole number because it its negative.

2. Brittany and Lila; Brittany: Integers Without Wholes; Lila: Whole Numbers

3. Oren, Mirsada, Farha, Davon, Kate, Nikesha, Henri, Abey

4. Farha, Davon, Kate, Nikesha, Mirsada, Henri, Abey, Oren. The three negative rational numbers $\left(-\dfrac{2}{3}, -2.3, \text{ and } -12.6\right)$ become positive, which changes the order.

5. 1; 4; 24

UNIT 2 Number Operations

Unit 2 Test: A

1. C
2. D
3. A
4. C
5. B
6. D
7. A
8. B
9. B
10. D
11. A
12. B

13. $\dfrac{5}{12}$

14. $9\dfrac{19}{25}$ oz or 9.76 oz

15. a. 186.55 lb

   b. 18.45 lb

16. Sample answer: $2(-4) - 1$

17. 56 pennies

18. $2(-4) + 14 + (-5) = 1$; The team gained 1 yd.

19. $437.96

20. If the integers have the same sign, the quotient will be positive. If the integers have different signs, the quotient will be negative.

21. $(-14) + 2(-8) + 2 = -28$; -28 points

22. a. $(-45) + (-106) + 8 = -143$

   b. She has to sell 16 candles before she makes a profit.

Unit 2 Test: B

1. D
2. A
3. C
4. D
5. C
6. A
7. C
8. A
9. C
10. B
11. C
12. $-\dfrac{5}{6}$
13. $6\dfrac{9}{16}$ fl oz, or 6.5625 fl oz
14. Use 45. $\dfrac{25}{45} - \dfrac{6}{45} = \dfrac{19}{45}$
15. multiples of 5: 5, 10, 15, 20, 25, 30, 35, 40, 45

    multiples of 8: 8, 16, 24, 32, 40, 48

    least common multiple: $40 \cdot \dfrac{120}{160} = \dfrac{3}{4}$
16. 91.08 lb
17. 30; $0.45
18. $6\dfrac{1}{4}$ lb
19. $4.25
20. Find the reciprocal of the divisor. Then multiply.
21. $76 + (-12) + (-7) = 57$; $57
22. a. 38

    b. $14.4 \div 0.375 = 38.4$ or 38 pieces

Unit 2 Test: C

1. C
2. A
3. A
4. D
5. A
6. C
7. C

8. C
9. $\dfrac{4}{35}$
10. Write the mixed number as an improper fraction, $\dfrac{35}{8}$, and then flip it: $\dfrac{8}{35}$.
11. $-8°F$
12. a. $-$83.59

    b. 20 pies
13. $0.75
14. a. $7\dfrac{7}{16}$ lb

    b. $10.28
15. a. 51 lengthwise bricks; 106 edgewise bricks

    b. $32.13; $66.78
16. Sample answer: When you multiply two fractions, you are taking a part of a part. The product (a part of a part) will be less than the parts.

Unit 2 Test: D

1. C
2. A
3. C
4. A
5. A
6. A
7. A
8. B
9. B
10. $4.03
11. $\dfrac{8}{25}$
12. $83.59
13. 19.3 or 20 whole pies
14. $7\dfrac{4}{5}$ lb
15. Find the reciprocal and multiply.
16. $389.62
17. 0.965 min
18. $4.25
19. $10.93

20. a. 58 dimes

    b. $5.80

    c. 131.544 g

Unit 2 Performance Task

1. They would need 39 yd^2 of flooring; $530.01

2. Spaces should be 0.25 in. [16 boards create 15 spaces.]

3. She needs 131 bricks or 49 pavers. The bricks cost $77.29, and the pavers cost $92.12. The bricks would cost $14.83 less.

4. $73.45

5. $23.57

UNIT 3 Proportionality: Ratios and Rates

Unit 3 Test: A

1. D
2. C
3. C
4. A
5. C
6. C
7. A
8. B
9. D
10. D
11. D
12. C
13. 80 cal
14. 100 g
15. 75 students
16. 160 more students
17. 25 tennis balls
18. 8 lb
19. Sandro's
20. 42.3 lb
21. 2 to 1

Unit 3 Test: B

1. B
2. B
3. A
4. B
5. C
6. B
7. B
8. B
9. C
10. D
11. B
12. 88 cal
13. 250 g
14. 40 students
15. 60 students
16. 56
17. 9
18. Zelda's
19. 13 lb

Unit 3 Test: C

1. D
2. C
3. A
4. D
5. C
6. B
7. B
8. D
9. A
10. C
11. A
12. 45 cal
13. 200 g
14. 105 students
15. 30 more students
16. 42
17. 2
18. Faisal
19. 10.11 oz

Unit 3 Test: D

1. C
2. B
3. A
4. A
5. C
6. C
7. A
8. C
9. B
10. A
11. B
12. 240 cal
13. 100 g
14. 20 students
15. 100 students
16. 10
17. 3 lb
18. 40 mi
19. 8 km
20. 1 to 3

Unit 3 Performance Task

1. 1 to 3; $\frac{1}{3}$, $0.3\overline{3}$

2. the second plant; the unit rate for plant 1 is 1 inch in $1\frac{1}{2}$ months. The unit rate for plant 2 is 1 inch in $\frac{2}{3}$ month.

3. Anna's garden has 4 times as many flowers. The total number of flowers in Jorge's garden is $12 + 36 = 48$. Anna's garden has $48 \times 4 = 192$ flowers.

4. No. To have the same ratio, the total number of flowers must be a multiple of 4. 75 is not a multiple of 4.

5. Answers may vary. Sample answer: One way he can do it is by adding 12 tulips and 24 daisies. This will give him $12 + 12 = 24$ tulips and $36 + 24 = 60$ daisies. The ratio of 24 : 60 is equivalent to 2 : 5.

6. 1 in. = 5.08 ft

UNIT 4 Equivalent Expressions

Unit 4 Test: A

1. C
2. C
3. A
4. D
5. C
6. A
7. D
8. C
9. D
10. D
11. C
12. A
13. C
14. 8 students
15. 5^3
16. $2^2 \times 3$
17. 1×18, 2×9, 3×6
18. add 15 and 4
19. 10
20. $50 - b$
21. x divided by 4, or the quotient of x and 4
22. $20 + c$
23. 16
24. 10
25. $6x + 16$
26. $2y + 6x$

Unit 4 Test: B

1. C
2. C
3. A
4. D
5. C
6. B
7. D
8. C
9. D
10. B
11. A

12. C

13. A

14. 243 students

15. 2.9^4

16. $2^3 \times 3 \times 19$

17. $1 \times 54, 2 \times 27, 3 \times 18, 6 \times 9$

18. multiply 15 by 5 inside the parentheses

19. 29

20. $50 - b$

21. x divided by 24, or the quotient of x and 24

22. $20 - 5 + d$ or $15 + d$

23. 42

24. $30°$

25. Sample answer: $7(3x) + 7(8)$, Distributive Property

26. $2y^2 + 18x$

Unit 4 Test: C

1. C

2. B

3. A

4. D

5. C

6. B

7. D

8. C

9. D

10. B

11. A

12. B

13. 510 students

14. $2^8, 4^4$

15. 3×727

16. two rectangles measuring 6×9 inches

17. 451

18. Sample answer: A length of rope measuring b inches is cut into half-inch pieces.

19. the quotient of x and 24 plus 1 minus 6.5

20. $30 - 7 + d + p$, or $23 + d + p$

21. 2,413

22. $3.5°$

23. $2y^2 + 18x$; Sample answer: $2(y^2 + 9x)$

Unit 4 Test: D

1. A

2. C

3. A

4. B

5. C

6. C

7. B

8. A

9. C

10. C

11. C

12. A

13. A

14. 4 students

15. 5^2

16. 1×13

17. 1, 2, 3, 6, 9, 18

18. add 5 and 4

19. 11

20. b

21. 4

22. 20

23. 8

24. 3

25. Sample answer: $(2 + x) + 8$

26. $6y + 1$

Unit 4 Performance Task

1. $2^6 = 64$

2. a. $2^4 \times 5^2$

   b. $1 \times 400, 2 \times 200, 4 \times 100, 5 \times 80,$ $8 \times 50, 10 \times 40, 16 \times 25, 20 \times 20$

   c. Answers will vary. Sample answer: 16 inches long $\times$ 25 inches wide, because the family tree will be wider than it is long.

3. $2l + 2w$

4. a. Sample answer: $1.5(2l + 2w)$

   b. Sample answer: $1.5(2l) + 1.5(2w)$, Distributive Property

UNIT 5 Equations and Inequalities

Unit 5 Test: A

1. C
2. C
3. B
4. B
5. A
6. B
7. D
8. A
9. D
10. Sample answer: $p + 3 = 12$
11. no
12. Sample answer: $43 + 25 = m$; $68
13. $x \div 12 = 6$; 72 in.
14.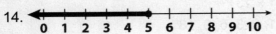
15.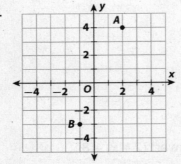
16. independent variable: the number of tickets; dependent variable: the cost
17. $p = 8h$
18.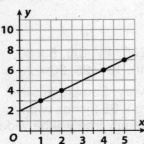

Unit 5 Test: B

1. C
2. C
3. A
4. B
5. A
6. B
7. D
8. A
9. D
10. Sample answer: $p + 3 = 12$
11. yes
12. Sample answer: $43 + m = 68$; $25
13. $6 = \dfrac{x}{12}$; 72 in.
14.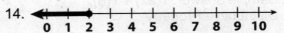
15.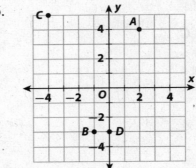
16. The independent variable is the number of tickets a student sells. The dependent variable is the number of t-shirts the student earns as a reward.
17. $p = 15t$; $105
18. Car B; it will have traveled farther in the same amount of time.

Unit 5 Test: C

1. C
2. C
3. B
4. B
5. C
6. D
7. D
8. A
9. D

10. Sample answer: $t + 2 = 13$; $j - 3 = t + k$

11. yes

12. $250

13. $6.25 = \dfrac{x}{12}$; 75 in.

14.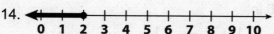

15.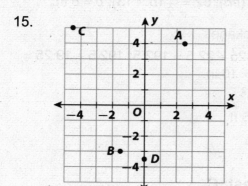

16. independent variable: the number of tickets a student sells, dependent variable: the number of dollars the student earns as a reward; independent variable: the dollar value of tickets a student sells, dependent variable: the amount the student receives as a cash bonus

17. $p = 62.5t$; $4,375

18. 0, 1

Unit 5 Test: D

1. C

2. A

3. B

4. B

5. A

6. A

7. C

8. A

9. C

10. 12

11. no

12. $35

13. 72 in.

14.

15.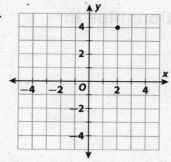

16. dependent variable: the cost

17. $p = 8h$

18.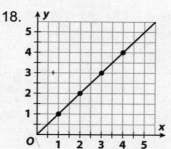

Unit 5 Performance Task

1. a. $x + 15 = 75$

   b. $60

2. $x > 60$

3. a. $1.50x = 60$

   b. 40 glasses of lemonade

4. $y = \dfrac{10}{3}$

5. a. independent: number of glasses of lemonade Waheeda sells; dependent: amount Waheeda earns

   b. $1.50g = e$

   c. Quadrant I; she can't sell a negative number of glasses of lemonade, and the cost of a glass of lemonade is a positive number, so all the data will be positive numbers.

   d. Answers will vary depending on scale chosen. Sample answer:

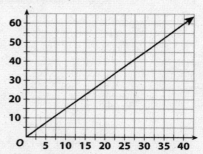

UNIT 6 Relationships in Geometry

Unit 6 Test: A

1. A
2. B
3. A
4. C
5. B
6. D
7. C
8. C
9. B
10. C
11. D
12. 45 in^2
13. 183.92 in^2
14. 750 ft^2
15. 8 in.
16. $A = \frac{1}{2}(32 \times 8) = 128$ in^2
17. 55 packages
18. $V = 19 \times 9.5 \times w$; $w = 6$ in.
19. 36 in^3
20. $1\frac{1}{3}$ ft wide
21. 63 ft^3
22. $12 \times 16 = 192$ ft^2; $13 \times 15 = 195$ ft^2; The second space is larger by 3 square feet.

Unit 6 Test: B

1. D
2. B
3. C
4. C
5. B
6. A
7. A
8. B
9. B
10. C
11. C

12. $SA = 2(lw + wh + hl)$; $183\frac{23}{25}$ or 183.92 cm^2
13. 143 in^2
14. 560 ft^2
15. 6 in.
16. $A = \frac{1}{2}(bh)$; $52 = \frac{1}{2}(b \times 13)$; $b = 8$ in.
17. 21 packages
18. $4{,}331.25 \div 22.5 = 192.5$; $192.5 \div 19.25 = 10$; $h = 10$ in.
19. 240 in^3
20. $h = 1.5$ ft
21. $4\frac{1}{2}$ ft^3

Unit 6 Test: C

1. A
2. D
3. C
4. B
5. D
6. B
7. B
8. B
9. C
10. B
11. 846 in^2
12. 36 units
13. 103.65 ft^2
14. 13 in.
15. 134.19 m^2
16. No, they need 49.5 boxes, so they have to buy 50 boxes.
17. $w = (8556 \div 32) \div 15.5$; $w = 17.25$ in.
18. 256 in^3
19. 1 ft
20. 42.25 ft^3 or $42\frac{1}{4}$ ft^3

Unit 6 Test: D

1. C
2. C
3. B

4. A
5. C
6. B
7. C
8. A
9. B
10. B
11. 15 in^2
12. 18 units
13. 275 ft^2
14. 5 in.
15. $A = \frac{1}{2}(20 \times 7)$
16. 450 ft^2
17. $1,200 = 20 \times 10 \times w$; $w = 6$ in.
18. 60 in^3
19. 2 ft
20. 18 ft^3
21. 14 ft^2
22. $11 \times 15 = 165$; $165 - 160 = 5$; The first store is 5 ft^2 larger than the second store.

Unit 6 Performance Task

1.

Item	L (ft)	W (ft)	A (ft^2)	H (ft)	V (ft^3)
Patio	11.25	5	56.25		
Clubhouse	12	8	96	6	576
Sandbox			9	1.5	13.5
Garden	25	11.6	290		
Yard	45	36	1,620		

2. $A = 12 \times 8 = 96$ ft^2; $V = 12 \times 8 \times 6$
   $= 576$ ft^3
3. $13.5 \div 9 = 1.5$ ft
4. $A = 25 \times 11.6 = 290$ ft^2
5. $A = 1,620 - (56.25 + 96 + 9 + 290)$
   $= 1,168.75$ ft^2
6. Drawings will vary. Check students' drawings for design and location of points on the grid.

UNIT 7 Measurement and Data

Unit 7 Test: A

1. C
2. D
3. C
4. B
5. B
6. A
7. C
8. B
9. D
10. 87
11. 7.0
12. 90
13. 90
14.

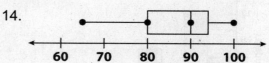

15. 14
16.

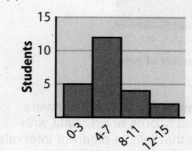

Hours of Homework

17. The bars on a histograph show a range of data. For example, 0–3 shows 1h, 1½h, 2h and so on. The data is continuous.
18. Between 4 and 7 hours
19. No, you just know that 4 students spend between 8 and 11 hours.

Unit 7 Test: B

1. B
2. A
3. C
4. A
5. C

6. B

7. B

8. A

9. C

10. B

11. B

12. 87.05

13. 8.24

14. 90

15. 92

16.
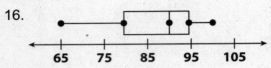

17. 15.5

18.
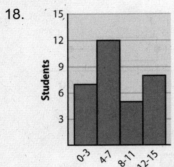

Number of Pets

19. 17

20. Answers will vary. Sample answers: student test scores or any data with frequency that falls in different intervals

Unit 7 Test: C

1. D

2. C

3. B

4. C

5. B

6. C

7. B

8. A

9. C

10. A

11. B

12. 86.15

13. 8.1

14. 88.5

15. 91

16.
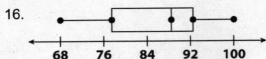

17. 15

18.
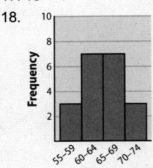

Interval

19. Answers will vary. Sample answer: The data is numerical and can be sorted into intervals.

20. $\frac{3}{20} = 15\%$

21. Answers will vary. Sample answer: Calculate the relative frequencies for each interval. The percent of the circle that represents each interval is equal to the relative frequency of that interval.

Unit 7 Test: D

1. B

2. A

3. C

4. B

5. B

6. A

7. B

8. A

9. B

10. B

11. 84.8

12. 7.04

13. 87

14. 90

15.
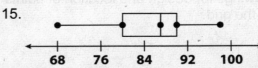

16. 80

17.
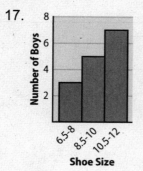

18. 15 boys

19. 6.5 to 10

20. 8.5 to 10, the second bar

Unit 7 Performance Task

1. The sum of the data points is 2,434. There are 28 data points. The mean is $\frac{2,434}{28} = 86.9$.

2. Find the difference from the mean test score for each of the 28 scores. Then find the mean of these differences.

3. The median, or middle number when the data points are arranged in order, is 88.

4.
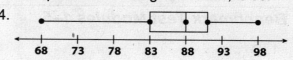

5. IQR = 91 − 83 = 8

6.
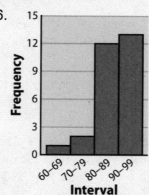

7. Answers will vary. Sample answer: The data is numerical and can be separated into intervals.

Answer Key

Benchmark Test Modules 1–5

1. C
2. A
3. C
4. B
5. D
6. B
7. A
8. B
9. A
10. D
11. B
12. C
13. C
14. A
15. D
16. C
17. B
18. C
19. C
20. B
21. C
22. B
23. $31\frac{9}{32}$ lb
24. 6.12 oz
25. $1\frac{5}{8}$ m

26. 12
27. 42
28. 766 visitors
29. 8 servings
30. 22 loads
31. 165.75 gal
32. 14 glasses
33. 266.24 oz
34. 14.04 ft
35. 16.65 oz
36. 22 full days
37. 75.25 lb
38. 221 ft
39. 38.7 mi
40. 1,119.54 mi
41. $84.50
42. 74.63 mph

Answer Key

Mid-Year Test Modules 6–8

1. B
2. C
3. D
4. C
5. D
6. C
7. B
8. D
9. B
10. B
11. A
12. A
13. B
14. D
15. C
16. A
17. C
18. C
19. C
20. D
21. B
22. C
23. D
24. B
25. B
26. D
27. C
28. C
29. A
30. C
31. B
32. 25 members
33. 45 pages
34. 42 dogs
35. 2 new volunteers
36. 135 mi
37. 3.048 m

38. 120 mi
39. 54 in.
40. 60 bottles
41. 600 yd^2
42. 40%

Answer Key

Benchmark Test Modules 9–13

1. A
2. C
3. D
4. D
5. A
6. C
7. D
8. A
9. B
10. D
11. C
12. D
13. A
14. D
15. B
16. A
17. C
18. B
19. B
20. C
21. A
22. C
23. B
24. C
25. C

26. D
27. C
28. D
29. B
30. C
31. D
32. 13
33. 216 boxes
34. 380
35. 92.4
36. 31
37. 4.4 mi
38. 18 pages
39. $x < 4$
40. 4
41. 2

Answer Key

End-of-Year Test

1. D	39. A
2. D	40. B
3. A	41. D
4. D	42. C
5. C	43. A
6. D	44. D
7. D	45. B
8. B	46. D
9. D	47. B
10. C	48. C
11. C	49. A
12. B	50. B
13. D	51. A
14. C	52. B
15. C	53. B
16. B	54. B
17. A	55. D
18. D	56. C
19. B	57. D
20. C	58. D
21. C	59. C
22. C	60. D
23. B	61. C
24. B	62. C

25. D

26. B

27. B

28. C

29. C

30. C

31. D

32. D

33. A

34. D

35. A

36. C

37. B

38. D

63. Fiona: 4.46; Gary: 16.83; Fiona showed less variability.

64.

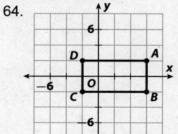

The area of the actual rug is 32 square feet.

65. 49 kg

66. 12 pieces

67. 112.5 in.

68. 11 notepads

69. $20

70. $625

71. $0.35 per oz

72. 32 cups

73. $157.50

74. 54 km

75. 6 mi

76. 343

77. 298

78. 110

79. 15 ft

80. 495 m^2

81. 13.9 in.

82. 832.5 cm^2

83. 4,672.5 mm^2

84. 9.6 in.

85. 75 yd